The Evaluation Society

THE EVALUATION SOCIETY

Peter Dahler-Larsen

STANFORD BUSINESS BOOKS
An Imprint of Stanford University Press
Stanford, California

Stanford University Press
Stanford, California

The Evaluation Society was originally published in Danish in
2001 under the title *Den Rituelle Reflektion* © 2001,
University Press of Southern Denmark.

Special discounts for bulk quantities of Stanford Business Books
are available to corporations, professional associations, and other
organizations. For details and discount information, contact the
special sales department of Stanford University Press.
Tel: (650) 736-1782, fax: (650) 736-1784

Printed in the United States of America on acid-free,
archival-quality paper

Library of Congress Cataloging-in-Publication Data

Dahler-Larsen, Peter, author.
  [Rituelle reflektion. English]
  The evaluation society / Peter Dahler-Larsen ; translated by
Steven Sampson.
    pages cm
  Translated from the Danish.
  Includes bibliographical references and index.
  ISBN 978-0-8047-7692-9 (cloth : alk. paper)
  ISBN 978-0-8047-8861-8 (pbk. : alk. paper)
  1. Organizational sociology.   2. Evaluation—Social aspects.
I. Title.
HM786.D35   2011
302'.13—dc22

                                              2011005828

Nothing that anyone had ever measured was still or could ever be the same as before.

—Daniel Kehlmann, *Measuring the World*

Contents

Foreword to the English Edition   *ix*

Introduction: The Evaluation Wave:
From Mystery to Analysis   I

PART 1: AN ORGANIZATIONAL ANALYSIS
OF EVALUATION

1   Organizational Understandings: Rational,
Learning, and Institutionalized Organization   33

2   Evaluation in the Institutionalized
Organization   65

PART 2: A SOCIOLOGICAL ANALYSIS
OF EVALUATION

3   Modernity and Its "Evaluation Imaginary"   99

4   Reflexive Modernity   120

5   Evaluation in Reflexive Modernity   144

6   Audit Society, Neorigorism, and Evaluation Machines   169

7   The Critique of Evaluation Machines   183

Epilogue: Perspectives for Evaluation   226

References   243

Index   261

Foreword to the English Edition

To analyze contemporary phenomena is always a Sisyphean challenge. The complexity of the unfolding social world is always greater than our attempts to understand it. The problem is not only complexity itself but our own embeddedness in it. As with all social science, it is like building a boat while being out on the open sea. This problem is especially applicable to our current wave of evaluation, which is comprehensive, uneven, complex, dynamic, and at the same time close to us as a part of the society in which we live.

In this English edition, the material has been revised so that it is internationally illustrative and does not require special knowledge of Danish conditions. The revision and updating of *Den Rituelle Reflektion* has in fact been the creation of a genuinely new book.

English-speaking readers are invited to consider the idea that not all books in the English language are written from an Anglo-Saxon perspective. Translation is more than a translation of words. For example, I would write that "environments demand" or "institutions think," whereas some would argue that only individuals can demand and think. The differences involved here are related not only to language but to differences in theoretical paradigms.

Books, like movies, are organized in different ways. Some movies have a very clear plot, and the camera focuses on a gun on the table for a long time to show that it plays a key role in the plot. By the end of the movie, we know who the killer was, we are relieved, and we stop thinking. Other movies are complex and winding and mysterious. Some figures have an unclear role in the plot. The idea is to engage the viewer and not be too conclusive. We think of the movie for a long time after we have seen it.

To be honest, I hope my book resembles the latter kind of movie rather than the first one. I hope you find the book enjoyable as it is.

Many people, too numerous to mention, deserve my gratitude for intellectual inspiration. I want to express my gratitude to Mira Rozalis for her constructive review and insightful remarks on earlier versions of the manuscript. One person, Thomas Schwandt, deserves special mention because his intellect and friendship have inspired me in so many ways.

The Evaluation Society

Introduction

The Evaluation Wave: From Mystery to Analysis

We live in the age of evaluation. In recent years, we have witnessed a boom in evaluation. Today, one can hardly enter a hospital, apply for a job, or seek information at city hall without having to evaluate or be evaluated. Many countries have established centers with full-time staff who do nothing else but evaluate—and these centers must themselves be evaluated. It is as if there is no limit to the feedback loops, as if one can look into a mirror that reflects itself in yet another mirror, as if the insatiable evaluation monster demands more and more food every day.

Lise and the Evaluation Wave

Lise is a "normal" person in a modern, Western country. She works as a school teacher. Here are the evaluations she has been involved in or affected by within a rather short period:

· She must provide evaluative input to a semiannual plan of action for each of her pupils.

· The grades she has given the pupils are part of a description on the Internet of the quality of her school.

· Her pupils are tested, and the results become part of a quality report drafted by the school administration.

· She participates in a pedagogical in-service training course and evaluates it.

- She is the mother of two children. One of them attends a day care center. Therefore Lise participates in a user-satisfaction survey concerning the quality of the center. She also takes part in a conversation between school and home concerning the child's development (based on grades, pupil's work plan, and the teacher's oral assessment).

- Her husband is a manager. Therefore she participates in a family survey intended to check whether managers under stress remember to take care of their work-life balance and attend to their family life appropriately.

- As a teenager, Lise participated in a summer camp. In connection with a fundraising project, this camp now wants to document the long-term effects of the camp's philosophy and activities on the individual participants.

- Lise is a member of a trade union. It wants to carry out a survey to check member satisfaction with the services they offer.

- By the way, Lise wants to quit smoking. The tools available to help her do so have been selected and evaluated by researchers and by the medical industry in ways that Lise does not know.

- Today's news is that because of budget cuts, some schools will be closed. Politicians say they will use the quality documentation from the schools in their decision making. Lise never thought the evaluative information she had helped produce would be used in that way.

The modern intuitive feeling that evaluation is spreading is supported by researchers' observations of how organizations and authorities operate.

We are well into the kind of process that Hellstern diagnosed back in 1986: evaluation is becoming integrated as administrative routine at many levels and in many types of institutions. Subsequent empirical studies report on intensive (Hansen 2003) and increasing evaluation activity, also internationally (Furubo, Rist, and Sandahl 2002), where evaluation is becoming a taken-for-granted aspect of public administration and organizational procedures for management and development. Individual evaluations are supplemented to an increasing degree by systems that regularly produce indicators and other ongoing evaluation information (Rist and Stame 2006).

Evaluation also fits in as a driving force or supplement to several fashionable formulas for modern organization and administration, among them "result-based management," "contract management," "outsourcing," and "benchmarking." Within New Public Management thinking generally, it is believed that "evaluation and efficiency measurements are the right ways of controlling public firms" (Lane 1993, 132).

Evaluation enters into a larger societal trend that also includes activities such as auditing, inspection, quality assurance, and accreditation—which together constitute "a huge and unavoidable social experiment which is conspicuously cross sectional and transnational" (Power 1997a, xv).

Evaluations are not something that the individual can reject. In our time, it is difficult to be against evaluation. One can only request that the evaluation be carried out at a later time (or with a different design). Evaluation has become an institution in our society. That there must be evaluation has gradually become what James March calls "protected discourse," something virtually sacred, about which the dominant forces in society do not pose questions.

The evaluation wave has to do with mentality and culture in many areas of our daily lives. If the evaluation mentality were not already so widespread in our society, evaluations in a strictly organizational and administrative sense would not be so widespread, either.

The World's First Evaluation?

In Christianity, God created the world: "God saw all that he had made, and it was very good." After that self-evaluation, He then introduced a day of rest (Vedung 1997; Gen. 1: 31, 2: 3, New English Bible).

Outside the Christian cultural area, Greek mythology has a fine story about Orpheus, who lost his beloved Eurydice. But after special negotiations with the gods, Orpheus is able to retrieve her from the Underworld, if he promises not to look back at her before they are both entirely out of that place. In the decisive moment, however, Orpheus looks back to evaluate the results of his hazardous journey and—just like that—Eurydice disappears forever. She is not

yet fully out of the realm of the dead, so he has broken his promise, with terrible consequences. In evaluation terminology, Orpheus
evaluated the results of his trip a bit too early.

The example shows that evaluation not only describes the reality
but to a great degree intervenes into it, tragically in this case. Evaluations *constitute* something. I will return to this issue later in the
book. It is also worth pondering whether what Orpheus undertook
was really an evaluation. Evaluation is hardly the same in all times
and eras. We shall return to the issue of how one can define evaluation and at the same time understand its social-historical differences
and significance.

A Swedish anthropologist (Rabo 1994) who examines Western society
from an anthropological perspective notes that evaluations are helping to
restructure our public life, nothing less. Others also point out that evaluations define the boundaries of our common affairs (Hellstern 1986, 306).
Evaluations have become part of our culture and are helping to structure
what it is we talk about, what we think are important problems, and what
we think we will do about these problems.

If the evaluation wave, as Power argues, is a gigantic and unavoidable
experiment, it is worth asking: What will be the results of this experiment? Evaluation researchers are beginning to observe that evaluation has
an "influence" reaching far beyond what has been intended, and beyond
how evaluation is officially "used" (Kirkhart 2000).

According to the self-understanding of the evaluation wave itself,
there is great reason for optimism. If evaluation requires a justification
(and this is not always the case), then according to its own statements
it can lead to learning, to social betterment (Mark, Henry, and Julnes
2000), increased efficiency, better management, more public information, and a lot of other good things. The task is only to discover the
correct evaluation tools, in the form of methods and processes. True
enough, there is variation in the degree of "messianism" among serious evaluation theorists, but among proponents of evaluation we often
find an inherent, optimistic betterment thinking by which evaluation is
viewed practically as a universal good. Resistance to evaluation is said to
be due to psychological factors or egotistical interests; it exists in order
to be surmounted.

A great deal of the evaluation field's self-legitimation is expressed in what Thomas Ziehe (2004) calls "smooth talk," a polished, and often management-based, optimistic jargon whereby the contradictions appear to dissolve, because it is practically impossible to be opposed to learning, documentation, effectiveness, and improvement.

Compared to the enormous cultural investments in evaluation in contemporary society, we know surprisingly little about how evaluation is formed and what its social consequences are. The theme of this book is how we can better understand evaluation as an organizational and social phenomenon.

But first, we must look at a definition of evaluation so we can identify the beast when we see it.

Definitions of Evaluation

It is always good scientific practice to delimit one's topic by means of a definition.

There are at least three good ways of understanding what is going on with definitions of evaluation. One is, of course, to focus on the conceptual content. How is the line drawn between evaluation and non-evaluation? What is the essence of evaluation? And what are the universal elements of all evaluations? The second form of understanding looks at the pragmatic side of a definition. What does the constructor of the definition want to accomplish by using the definition as a tool? Is it important to distinguish evaluation from commonsense judgments, from science, from politics, from practice, from consultancy? Is it important to establish evaluation as a distinct and separate activity in a way that was not obvious before the particular definition was made? Is it too tempting to purify, simplify, solidify, or glorify evaluation through the definition?

Third, one can understand definitions of evaluation in light of their sociohistorical significance. A definition of a societal phenomenon must respect the life that is in the phenomenon. We must avoid the trap of defining the concept of the phenomenon narrowly, which does not allow us to see the transformations that the phenomenon undergoes in sociohistorical terms. (If, in the 1950s, we had made narrow definitions of concepts such as "the family" or "the media," this would have led to serious shortcomings in analyses today.)

Similarly, a definition of evaluation must keep in mind that evaluation finds different forms depending on different contexts and on the basis of normative-ideological points of departure. A definition of evaluation is thus a product of a given sociopolitical reality. However, the relation between a concept and a society is complex, because a concept also embodies hopes and expectations of what ought to be—that is, of new potential realities in the making (Koselleck 2007).

I shall now look at several approaches to defining evaluation. I take the conceptual content as such as a starting point. After that, the whole book opens up toward an analysis of evaluation as a social phenomenon. So *definitions*, not a definition, of evaluation, are themselves part of the sociological story that this book tells.

A CONCEPTUAL-ANALYTICAL DEFINITION OF EVALUATION

Scriven (1991, 139) states that "evaluation refers to the process of determining the merit, worth, or value of something, or the product of that process. The evaluation process normally involves some identification of relevant standards of merit, worth, or value; some investigation of the performance of the evaluations on these standards; and some integration or synthesis of the results to achieve an overall evaluation or set of associated evaluations."

Scriven is one of the founding fathers of modern evaluation as a distinct field and one of the first to analytically distill what it means to do evaluation. His definition is interesting in many respects. The object of evaluation, the so-called evaluand, is described as "something." Perhaps it is the very generalization and abstraction of the evaluand, and its liberation from any specific and substantial human activity, that now makes it possible to conceive of evaluation as a distinct cognitive activity in and of itself. If you wanted to evaluate music, you might call a good musician. Now, if you want to evaluate that something, there is a need for an evaluation specialist. Scriven's definition inaugurates an era in which evaluation can be what Giddens (1990) would call a disembedded social practice, that is, a set of knowledges, methods, and ways of thinking that can travel across time and space and be applied to various other social practices. To do that, evaluation must be conceived as an abstract practice in its own right. This is exactly what Scriven does.

Scriven's definition is also interesting because it does not specify whether evaluation should be used for some particular purpose. He is trained as a philosopher but has not been forced to "adapt to the realities of social problem solving" (Shadish, Cook, and Leviton 1991, 117).

A METHODS-FOCUSED DEFINITION OF EVALUATION

Rossi and Freeman (1985, 19) define evaluation research as the "systematic application of social research procedures in assessing the conceptualization and design, implementation, and utility of social intervention programs . . . [It] involves the use of social research methodologies to judge and improve the planning, monitoring, effectiveness, and efficiency of health, education, welfare, and other human service programs."

Compared to Scriven's definition, Rossi and Freeman's mentions particular programs as objects of evaluation. It also describes particular purposes of evaluation: to judge and to improve the abovementioned programs. Yet the most clearly defining feature of this definition is its application of "social research methodologies." When social research methodology is applied to practical policy problems, then we have evaluation, or more precisely, evaluation research.

Given this aspect of the definition, evaluation can gain legitimacy through its basis in scientific methodology. On the other hand, it can be criticized if it is poorly conducted or if it runs into methodological controversies.

A PURPOSE-FOCUSED DEFINITION OF EVALUATION

Program evaluation is the systematic collection of information about the activities, characteristics, and outcomes of programs to make judgments about the program, improve program effectiveness, or inform decisions about future programming (Patton 1997, 23).

Although Patton of course might use methods to do evaluation, it seems as if any systematic method will do if it helps enhance the purpose. Patton is generally known for his utilization-focused approach to evaluation. In that light, his definition makes good sense. The verbs *judge, improve,* and *inform* describe the main purposes of evaluation.

Purpose-oriented definitions allow evaluation to take many forms. Depending on the specific purpose in a given situation, evaluation will unfold in a particular way. Evaluation has many faces, depending on circumstances. As a corollary, evaluation is likely to be contested, because stakeholders may hold their own views about how best to use evaluation.

A COMBINATORY APPROACH TO THE DEFINITION
OF EVALUATION AS A PRACTICE IN A CONTEXT

The consequence of such a contingency-oriented and contextual view is drawn in some contemporary definitions of evaluation that seek to combine key elements more or less flexibly.

For example, Rossi and Freeman, now together with Lipsey, talk about "the use of social research methods to systematically investigate the effectiveness in ways that are adapted to their political and organizational environments and are designed to inform social action to improve social conditions" (Rossi, Freeman, and Lipsey 2004, 16). Although social research methods are still mentioned explicitly, they are now not just applied but tailor-made for diverse political and organizational environments.

Evert Vedung (1997, 3) defines evaluation as "a careful retrospective assessment of the merit, worth, and value of administration, output, and outcome of government interventions, which is intended to play a role in future, practical action situations."

How Public Is the Object of Evaluation?

Vedung's definition is connected with his background in political science and his upbringing in Sweden, an archetypal example of a universalist Scandinavian welfare state. His linking together of evaluation and the public sector is perhaps generally easier to understand for a Scandinavian or a European than, for example, an American. Americans might find it unreasonable to limit evaluation to government interventions or public sector efforts. Certainly, we can find evaluation taking place in, for example, philanthropic organizations and foundations. Lindeberg (2007) shows how evaluation plays an important role in the private sector, as in connection with certification systems. Even though it is self-evident that evaluation is not limited to public sector organizations, it is nevertheless worth focusing on the theoretical significance of the word *public*. The *res publica* is the republic's common affairs, which involve all the domains where citizens must regulate their interaction in common, regardless of formal and legal distinctions between the public and private sectors. Evaluation is often of special interest to us because it touches on something of *public* interest. Even those evaluators and evaluation researchers who do not allow the word *public* in their definitions of evaluation subsequently bring norms and values into the discussion, which can reflect the importance of evaluations for public life. For precisely the same reasons, we might therefore discuss whether an evaluation is relevant, valid, fair, and democratic. Evaluation and the modern idea of democracy are closely linked. Evaluation is important in relation to how we handle *res publica*. Consequently, I am sympathetic to allowing the word *public* to enter into the determination of evaluation, even though evaluation certainly does not limit itself to government interventions or the public *sector* in a narrow sense.

Most integrative definitions of evaluation include four key factors with which any evaluation must deal: (1) an evaluand, (2) some assessment based on some criteria, (3) a systematic approach or methodology to collect information about how the evaluand performs on these criteria, and (4) a purpose or intended use. Many agree that evaluation is basically a systematic, methodological, and thus "assisted" way of investigating and assessing an activity of public interest in order to affect decisions or actions concerning this activity or similar activities.

Although there are many variations in exact definitions (see also Weiss 1998, 4; Cronbach et al. 1980, 14), the elements listed here are commonplace.

Good theory and well-executed evaluation have explicit and defensible assumptions about how each dimension justifies a specific type of evaluation practice (Shadish, Cook, and Leviton 1991). To an increasing extent, the resulting evaluation practice is variable, depending on organizational and political environments and social contexts. The link to social and political values is built directly into some definitions of evaluation. For example: "Systematic evaluation is conceptualized as a social and politicized practice that nonetheless aspires to some position of impartiality and fairness, so that evaluation can contribute meaningfully to the well-being of people in that specific context and beyond" (Shaw, Greene, and Mark 2006, 6).

Now the social and political embeddedness of evaluation as a practice is made more explicit than in any of the other definitions of evaluation. This is also the newest of the definitions that we have seen. This is no coincidence; the self-definition of evaluation has evolved considerably up to now.

In its early days, the field of evaluation was small and preoccupied with how it could define itself as a distinct field, analytically and conceptually. There was also a strong methodological emphasis. The common denominator for these early stages was the idea that evaluation could bring truth through clear thinking and analysis (Shadish, Cook, and Leviton 1991). In the second stage, the emphasis was on purpose, use, and pragmatism. To be useful, evaluation should be oriented toward making a difference. Finally, in the third stage evaluation becomes contingency-oriented. Thoughtful answers to the questions of the evaluand, the values and methods involved, and the intended use of the evaluation should be integrated in each evaluation, but evaluation itself is by definition contextual. It is a social practice.

Methodological or analytical isolationism does not work well in evaluation, at least not anymore. The field of evaluation has, to some extent, discovered that it is in interaction with its social context. Most evaluators know that, to be effective, they must attend to the social context in which they operate. This does not mean, however, that they are also conscious of the many organizational and social values and pre-understandings they bring into evaluation.

An analytical division of the history of evaluation into such differing stages does not necessarily assume an evolutionary approach to perfection. Instead, every era may inaugurate new controversies and difficulties. If evaluation is embedded in social practices, how is an aura of objectivity and impartiality maintained? How and to what extent is evaluation itself a continuation of norms and values in broader society that are not questioned in the same way that evaluation questions all sorts of evaluands?

To sum up, our work with the definitions of evaluation has shown two things underscoring the need for a sociological analysis of evaluation. The first is that the field of evaluation has not defined itself in the same way at all times. The second is that evaluators are beginning to see evaluation as embedded in social contexts. Again, however, this does not mean they are aware of all the organizational and societal norms and values on which they base their work.

Before we move on, it should be made clear how broad our view of evaluation is. Activities such as auditing, accreditation, quality assurance, benchmarking, etc., can to a great degree be considered within the same conceptual frame of reference as evaluation in general. They can thus be described, investigated, and discussed as forms of evaluation on the basis of their systematic procedures, values, utilization, and view of the evaluand.

My proposal, naturally, is not that all these processes be one and the same. They distinguish themselves from each other in essential ways. They are not carried out in the same contexts and not by the same people, and they do not have the same consequences. Several of the procedures mentioned (auditing, for example) operate with a much narrower range of values than is otherwise relevant for broad evaluation. And several of them are designed to influence quite specific decisions. To take an example, accreditation is used as a technique to approve and authorize institutions to provide education and issue education degrees.

However, from a sociohistorical perspective, it is also reasonable and analytically beneficial to consider auditing, accreditation, and certification under our common rubric. All of them have generalized themselves far beyond their original area. Auditing was originally a form of financial accounting, but it has now extended the field of inquiry to general assessment of whether an organization has properly functioning professional and management procedures (Power 2005). Accreditation originally functioned within insurance. For private hospitals to be insured, they had to meet several security prescriptions monitored on behalf of the insurance companies. Later on, accreditation expanded generally into a means of giving an institution formal authorization to carry out its operations. Quality assurance has had a specific history within engineering work with industrial production, but the concept gradually extended to include service provision, public sector, and organizational life more generally. In the several formulas, one can still trace their sectoral and institutional legacy because fundamental features in their thinking are retained, such as the idea of insurance in accreditation. It is decisive here, however, that each of these formulas has generalized itself, such that they now make numerous claims on a whole range of tasks falling generally within the field of evaluation. Furthermore, audit, accreditation, and several similar practices can be analyzed on the basis of the four fundamental dimensions in evaluation presented above: the evaluand, values or criteria, knowledge or methods, and use.

Up to a point, there is a functional overlap among audit, accreditation, quality assurance, and evaluation. Their division of labor is sometimes unclear. For example, many practitioners are uncertain whether the need for auditing is reduced if accreditation is obtained, and vice versa.

Put in more polemical terms, the only ones from whom one should not seek advice on these definitory questions are advocates for each of the practices mentioned above, such as auditing and accreditation. Proponents of each practice often emphasize its unique and specific character. As a rule, they would also underscore their own uniqueness and indispensability.

There are innumerable articles identifying similarities and differences between forms of evaluation, or between evaluation and audit. For example, comparison is often made between evaluation and performance monitoring in order to ascertain that each has its respective strengths and they can supplement one another. In these cases, however, evaluation is often depicted in a very reductionist way. To compare it with something else, it has to be confined within narrow categories.

I apply a different definitory strategy, namely viewing evaluation as an umbrella category covering a range of activities with varying forms. There are several analytical advantages to considering evaluation as a common area for all the aforementioned procedures. One can deduce something common about these forms of evaluation, such as social functions. One can also grasp possible social historical changes and variations in the configuration of the forms of evaluation within the field, which is essential for a sociological analysis of evaluation.

As a parallel, the sociology of food does not suggest that snails and hamburgers are the same thing. But the generic category of food is a precondition for a study of why some eat the former and some the latter, and for a study of how and why food is changing in form and social meanings. For a sociology of evaluation, we need a concept of evaluation that is sociohistorically broad, generic, open, and sensitive.

We ourselves are part of a society that is haunted by evaluation. We share many of this society's intuitive understandings. To pave the way for a sociological analysis of evaluation it is not sufficient to build on the self-definitions offered by the evaluation field. For our inherited, previous thinking about evaluation not to act as an obstacle, we must distance ourselves from evaluation a bit. We must make the familiar a little unfamiliar. To appreciate the dangers, difficulties, and controversies in evaluation, we must look at the processes of evaluation differently. We must proceed indirectly. In the next two sections, I apply anthropological, sociological, and interpretive questioning techniques to make us wonder, as much as we can, about the mysteries of evaluation. We can start by thinking of evaluation as a "liminal" and "assisted" form of "sense making."

Evaluation as Liminal and Assisted Sense Making

Evaluation is a situation where we stop and reflectively consider our experiences in the midst of a specific social practice. Here, evaluations resemble what human beings do in the broadest sense when they create meaning (Schutz 1973). The world does not dictate how it will be interpreted. If meaning is created, it is a result of active work in a given situation, where certain information and experiences are put together in certain ways (Weick 1995). Evaluation is ripe with meaning because in an evaluation one must identify a certain social practice (an evaluand) and give it some kind of value. An evaluation is therefore an occasion for reassessment and reinterpretation. It is also an occasion for disagreement. Meanings emerge or are renegotiated in evaluation.

Evaluation distinguishes itself, however, from other situations where sense making occurs, in that it is to a great degree "assisted" sense making (Mark, Henry, and Julnes 2000). Evaluation is an artificial or consciously constructed mechanism for creating meaning. There is no natural way to evaluate.

Evaluations are constructed for the occasion. They are formalized and are often based on laws, rules, assignments, or contracts; they embody systematic methods. In some respects, this reduces the freedom of discretion, at least for the people under evaluation, and to some extent also for others related to evaluation. Not all practices are legitimate evaluation practices. But in other respects, collectively in society, the freedom of choice is great, compared to, say, a religious or traditional society. When evaluation is assisted or "constructed" sense making, one must, at some place in the society, make a decision as to how this special, artificial, and somewhat disembedded apparatus must be organized and applied across a number of practical contexts. In doing so, society must decide how it will systematically consider (some of) its own affairs. Schwandt (2002) identifies this as a special modern undertaking: pursuing a form of assisted sense making as distinct as possible from what is believed to be the partisan, prejudicial, and unreflected viewpoints of everyday life. But no human point of view is entirely differentiated from the life of humans. No viewpoint is independent of everything else. In this sense, evaluation is trying to be something it cannot be.

It is difficult to hide the fact that assisted sense making is precisely constructed and not natural. We can expect a struggle, or argumentation in any case, about evaluation and how it is organized. This applies especially to the values on which the evaluation is based. Even though agreement can be achieved as to which methods are best suited for answering certain evaluation questions, no uncontroversial procedure exists, which leads to an unambiguous identification of the best values in any given evaluation. This is a fact that evaluation must endeavor to hold outside the debate, or at least somehow keep under control as an integrated part of the evaluation process, if it wants to reduce the risk of controversy about evaluation.

But evaluation is always potentially controversial. It is certainly artificially created, with the purpose, or in any case with the potential, to facilitate a *new* view of a customary practice that breaks with existing habits and convictions.

For these reasons, evaluation can be dangerous. It leads to what the Swedish anthropologist Annika Rabo calls "liminal states." The concept of liminal states, originally derived from the study of initiation rituals, connotes certain special forms of experience that arise, for example, when one leaves a culture and is on the way into a new culture. The concept can also refer to rituals within a culture, where one comes into contact with something other than everyday life. It connotes transition situations or special conditions where one is both inside and outside at the same time. A liminal state is the occasion for questions, reflections, disturbances, disappointments, emotions, and sometimes insights.

Evaluations are liminal because instead of simply being a part of normal practice, they create this extra space for the new and different interpretations. The assisted and artificial character of the evaluative makes it possible to choose a method or an unusual perspective to describe this practice from the outside. Even in cases of self-evaluation, the evaluation can be liminal because there is a difference between just being oneself, intuitively and practically, and evaluating oneself formally. Stated in a more radical way: one is perhaps not oneself in the same way after an evaluation. There occurs—or can occur—a transgression.

Liminal situations can generate insight into special values (Rabo 1994, 8) and can thus help reinforce identities or societal structures, or challenge these same identities or structures. Evaluation can support or threaten existing institutions, policies, programs, and personnel. It takes place in the interface between science and politics (Gordon, Lewis, and Young 1993, 5). Evaluation concerns both what is *true* about political initiatives and what one politically *desires* with these efforts. It thus distinguishes itself from other scientific or systematic studies that typically direct themselves toward the facts alone. One must also endeavor to ensure that the evaluation will be used in practice. That there can be a tension between the truth and the will, between knowledge and politics, is rather obvious. Not all of these issues are opened in all evaluations. But risk is enough to create the anxiety so characteristic of liminal situations.

In practice, evaluators and others experience the liminal aspects of evaluations in the form of protests and difficulties, and people's psychological tensions in assessing and being assessed, and on this occasion being socially inside or outside. There is anxiety and insecurity when we project potential dramatic consequences of evaluation, whether they are justified or not. One often has a feeling that there should have been a clear-cut plan for the purpose and process of an evaluation, but this is often not the case. On other occasions, people realize too late that they had very different notions of plans for evaluation in their head. The purpose of the evaluation constitutes on ongoing controversy rather than a common logical starting point. The evaluations are liminal because our practical experience with them often does not accord with the expectations promoted by the official rhetoric about evaluation. Controversy is in fact the rule rather than the exception.

At the societal level, evaluation can also be called liminal because it seeks to demarcate and illustrate the boundaries for important social ideas. This applies, for example, to rationalism, or modern society's notion that human beings, with the help of common sense, can bring themselves to control the natural world and the social world. Rationalism assumes a concrete form in the belief in progress, which lays out a particular pathway in the "social imaginary." Various forms of progress were unified under the general picture of rationalism. One could believe that technological progress was equal to political and social progress. Evaluations are the paradoxical children of rationalism (Vedung 1997). Evaluation constitutes attempts to use reasonable data collection to govern social formation, after it is recognized that collective human initiatives have not succeeded in automatically generating progress. But evaluation has also been through the range of experiences with the limits of rationalism: many good initiatives fail, there is limited knowledge about why this happens, the goals shift, there is disagreement about political goals, a simple distinction between means and ends cannot be maintained, etc. There are many worldviews, and they remain diverse and plural also after "Progress" has occurred.

It has been gradually recognized that the world is not so organized that it allows itself to be governed by such an arch-rationalist paradigm. We have gradually renounced trying to govern with the help of coherent, generalized plans. Faced with increasing societal complexity, the response must be decentralization, learning processes, and feedback loops. Yet, at the same time as evaluation constitutes a corrective to rationalism, it is still a child of rationalism. The evaluator continues to pursue a project of social betterment through reasonable use of data. Evaluation thus illustrates the boundaries for society's predominant ideas. It is an especially interesting boundary-drawing process because society must explicitly (1) declare its own evaluation questions; (2) design an artificial or assisted mechanism for addressing these questions; (3) deal with which of its areas it can tolerate having scrutinized; (4) observe the consequences of evaluation, and perhaps reflect upon a potential difference between intended consequences and actual consequences; (5) sometimes evaluate evaluation (meta-evaluate). All five of these points involve controversy.

There is no way to decide upon evaluation and not have potential social conflicts about how to design the evaluation, define its scope, and carry it out in practice. The rational instrument thus refuses to be purely rationally designed and implemented. Once we know that evaluation is artificial sense making, it is also social sense making, and thus limited in its rationality.

Nevertheless, contemporary society has what amounts to an obsession with evaluation. Society seems to think that more evaluation is better. According to Boltanski and Chiapello (2007, 32), "A society may be defined by the character of the tests it sets itself." What is it that society is trying to do with all this evaluation? Is it likely that transparency and effectiveness will result from all this evaluation, and then society will be happy? At the same time as evaluation is a child of society, we can also learn about society by closely following the emergence and development of the wave of evaluation. *The Evaluation Society* is thus both a topic in itself and a perspective on society.

What we learn from understanding evaluation as a liminal activity is that it is a wonderful object of sociological analysis. In evaluation, society seeks to reflect on itself while showing what it subliminally really thinks is important—important to maintain, important to believe, important to change, and important to avoid. No wonder evaluation is difficult. And mysterious.

The Mysteries Behind the Evaluation Wave

Why has the evaluation wave struck our type of modern society with such great force? I ask this question quite generally across social space, in that I recognize some countries have been struck by evaluation more rapidly than others (Albæk 1993; Furubo, Rist, and Sandahl 2002), just as there are variations between sectors, types of organization, and levels of administration. In a larger perspective, however, no societal type has previously evaluated so willingly and so frequently as our own.

One might raise the objection about the idea of a new wave of evaluation, and ask whether people have not always periodically looked back on their own activities. Haven't people always asked themselves what has gone well and what has gone wrong? Has the absolute monarch not hired a court bard to celebrate his accomplishments? Have small bands of hunters and gatherers not sat down around the fire, eating from the leg of cooked deer meat, and asked themselves whether it was a good hunt today? In other words, haven't we always been evaluating our activities?

My answer is that a tendency toward evaluation is possibly an anthropological constant, but it is not a *sociological* constant. In many societies, a range of fundamental social relationships are simply not put up for discussion. Only in our type of society is evaluation reified and institutionalized, such that we now possess a special set of methods known as "evaluation methods" and special people called "evaluators." Only in our type of society have we allocated to evaluation the resources, attention, and societal influence that it has today.

If one takes seriously the idea that the wave of evaluation denotes something typical of our time, it becomes difficult to believe in a simple universal and rational explanation of the evaluation wave. If evaluation consists of rational attempts to create general improvement, why have we not come upon them before? The purely rational types of explanations are often without nuance and sociohistorically insensitive (Jepperson and Meyer 1991, 204).

Every society forms itself on the background of a horizon of questions and answers, declared to be decisive within its own culture (Langer 1979). Thus one can ask: If the evaluation wave is typical of our time for our society, what kind of social imaginary meanings (Castoriadis 1987a) is the evaluation wave riding on and referring to? Our first question, therefore, is "In what way is the evaluation wave typical of our time?"

As a corollary, we can ask: "How, in our time, can one know that evaluations should be carried out in situations where one knows neither why nor for what they are to be used?" It is often politically, institutionally, or organizationally determined that evaluation must take place. The decision is frequently taken before one thinks over whether evaluation must be primarily summative or formative, or what benefit should be derived at all. It can be that the focus is placed on one or several of the oft-presented standard purposes of evaluation—accountability, learning, enlightenment, or information for the public (Chelimsky 2006)—but it can also be that there is no such focus. Evaluation is set in motion, and the struggle about utilization is taken up later, if at all. Why is there an interest in evaluation before there is an interest in its use?

Perhaps because from a political or managerial perspective, decision makers want to see the evaluation results before they commit themselves to a given course of action. However, in situations where the decision maker and the decision situation are far ahead in the future and unknown, approval is also given for evaluations to be carried out. It is a mystery that there is so much current talk of evaluations as a management tool, while the precise contribution of evaluation to a specific form of actual management is often not specified, except that "decision making will be more informed" or it will lead to better "steering" or better management or something like that. What kind of *faith in evaluation* lies behind this?

Why are evaluations often carried out using criteria that can be criticized as imprecise or misleading in relation to the quality of the products being investigated? Sometimes, quality is difficult to measure. However, the measurability of quality in the efforts in a given area varies with the characteristics of the area, effort, program, intervention, etc. For example, Abma and Noordegraf (2003) have set up a typology where two-sided, dynamic, and complex interventions are viewed as most difficult to evaluate. But the measurement optimism is great among proponents of evaluation; the attitude is that first we must have an evaluation and then we can eventually refine the measurements. As Holzer notes:

In the common absence of any yardstick of productivity, even crude information is of value, at least as a means of introducing systematic quantitative
analysis into the decision-making process. Once the precedent is established,
incremental refinements will undoubtedly lead to more sophisticated measures (M. Holzer, quoted by Lipsky 1980, 233).

The assumption, apparently, is that if evaluation is introduced, potential
measurement problems will be automatically resolved. But where is the
evidence for such an assumption? *If we have only imprecise or invalid indicators available, how can one be so sure that it is better to evaluate than not
to evaluate?*

Where do the values come from that guide evaluation in a particular
situation? Although we can often set up algorithms to guide an evaluator
as far as method is concerned, it is difficult to imagine a similar set of algorithms that help in the choice of values. Values relate not only to evaluation criteria but also to the evaluation process itself. What is a legitimate
evaluation process? Even in cases where the evaluation criteria and the
evaluation process are prescribed by given terms of reference, one can
certainly ask when such terms are legitimate and when they are not. In
evaluation, one must thus figure out how, in the absence of algorithms for
the value basis of evaluations, we can acquire *acceptable* values on which
to base our evaluation work.

Philosophically, we may never stop to discuss value conflicts, but practically we have to choose some criteria, at least while a particular evaluation is carried out in practice. How are endless value conflicts avoided
in practice? What kind of social and institutional support is necessary to
make a particular set of values in evaluation acceptable for the time being?

Additionally, how do organizations avoid listening too much to evaluations? On the one hand, evaluation is depicted as a way in which organizations are made responsive to their users (clients, patients, etc.) as well as
eventual cooperating partners or other stakeholders. On the other hand,
we know, both theoretically and practically, that organizations, especially
bureaucratic ones, usually allow themselves to change only slowly and
gradually. Large firms speak more than they listen, whether they are private or public.

Jørgensen and Melander (1992, 75) present "the responsive state" as one
among several models for the state. The concept reflects the view that
public organizations—based on the ideal of the market-controlled orga-

nization—must be organized according to the needs and preferences of the individual user. This view has had a certain popularity in recent years. But as Melander and Jørgensen, like Fountain (2001), correctly point out, this model contains significant contradictions. If everyone poses demands as individualized and atomized consumers without the model being balanced with other concerns, it becomes difficult to maintain the idea of a political community based on both democratic rights and citizen obligations. More than one public organization has also promised greater responsiveness in the beginning of evaluation but hesitated to draw the consequences when the results show what the users really want from the public organization. In practice, the public sector walks a difficult tightrope between being responsive to consumer demands and a whole range of other democratic, political, moral, economic, juridical, and organizational principles. Despite much talk of responsiveness, public organizations that use evaluations must as a consequence have some ways whereby they—perhaps subtly—*avoid* listening too much to evaluations. How do they do that?

This mystery is related to a larger, general one: If evaluation is an unusual situation where we must bring ourselves to see ordinary practice from a new perspective, is there not a limit as to how often the situation can be repeated and how deep it can penetrate? If the ideal is that one must be responsive, reflexive, and adaptable to change, what should one be *after* having been all these things? Even more responsive, reflexive, adaptable, and learning-oriented? If evaluations are to be institutionalized, do we not encounter an unavoidable paradox by trying to *routinize* the unusual? If what is unusual becomes routinized, should we then not also be evaluating evaluations? How often? Does this lead to an infinite regression or a dead end? If nothing else, the purely practical question becomes one of how to avoid the continuing nightmare of accelerating eternal evaluation and subsequent social restructuring.

We obtain a hint of a solution to this problem in a very disturbing research finding: many evaluation researchers agree that for some years the most important observation within the field has been that, considering the large number of evaluations carried out, there are very few cases of intentional, instrumental use of them (Albæk 1988, 43; de Leon 1988, 107; Greene 1994; Patton 1986; Premfors 1989, 138; Rist 1994, 545; Vedung 1997, 265; Weiss 1972, 11; Weiss and Bucuvalas 1980).

"Instrumental use" refers to evaluations being directly applied in accordance with their official purposes to change, fine-tune, terminate, or maintain an activity. Frequently, however, one finds no demonstrable signs that evaluation has had any influence on the actual decisions or practice. This observation, of course, has incited much debate, many viewpoints, and considerable development of methods within the field of evaluation. As early as 1986, lack of use was pointed out as "the main drive and deeper cause of all controversies about selection of appropriate methods, concepts, and theories in evaluation" (Hellstern 1986, 281). Why has the *problem of utilization* been so extensive and long-lasting, and how has it been possible to maintain faith in evaluation during the many years when evaluation was in a utilization crisis? This does not, in any case, accord well with a strictly rationalist view of evaluation. Would it not be sensible to ameliorate the utilization problem first and then promote dissemination of evaluation?

If evaluation is not driven by instrumental utilization, what other driving forces are there behind the evaluation wave? I ask this question from an idea common to cultural analysis: no social phenomenon is unimportant. If a phenomenon is there, and if it attracts attention and social energy, it is probably not without significance. So what kind of meaningful *consequences are produced besides the formal results* of evaluation?

These are the mysteries attached to the wave of evaluation. To see the connection between these mysteries and resolve them en bloc, we must consider evaluation not as an isolated instrumental affair but as a social, cultural, institutional, and (at times) ritual affair.

To do so, we must seek theoretical inspiration.

Theoretical Sources of Inspiration

Our first theoretical move is to break with conventional assumptions of individualism, rationality, and linearity in the evaluation process. Most textbooks on evaluation talk about the choices an individual evaluator can make to enhance particularly good use of evaluation. Others view evaluation as a social, political, and organizational practice that is, even though constructed by human beings, often not formed, shaped, and decided by individuals. Instead, evaluation is a symptom of cultural and political patterns. Advocates of the latter perspective cannot talk about the "decision" to evaluate without thinking of the collective and institutional frameworks in which evaluation is mandated.

Next, researchers, evaluators, practitioners, and students of evaluation hold varying assumptions about the degree of rationality in the production of knowledge. Under strict assumptions of rationality, evaluation is an instrument human beings design deliberately in order to produce knowledge that helps solve specific problems in specific situations. Without these assumptions, evaluation can be understood as fad, a fashion, or an institutional ritual; or the result of a negotiated institutional order, and the outcomes are thus uncertain.

Last but not least, people hold varying assumptions about the degree of linearity in evaluation processes. Some assume that once a particular purpose of an evaluation has been decided, then the consequences are known. Without assumptions of some linearity in an evaluation process, the stipulated purpose does not help us predict the actual use. Instead, the use of the evaluation may be less than, more than, or qualitatively different from the official purpose.

In what follows in this section, I shall present theoretical contributions I have found helpful in breaking with assumptions of individualism, rationality, and linearity. What they have in common is their inherent sociological approach to production and use of (evaluative) knowledge.

In Berger and Luckmann's perspective, knowledge is whatever counts as taken-for-granted reality within a given social context (1966, 3). In this social constructivist view, each social context provides a socially available stock of knowledge that helps predefine reality. Institutions furnish us with templates for roles, norms, behaviors, and legitimations, only a few of which we have the capacity and motivation to question. In fact, institutions apply normative, cognitive, and regulatory mechanisms to maintain a particular social order. However, Berger and Luckmann emphasize that the normative order—the world of norms taken for granted—constitutes perhaps the most foundational and constitutive layer of reality.

In contrast to scientific and rationalistic conceptions of knowledge, the sociological view of knowledge does not seek to be based on given principles of truth or validity; instead it demonstrates that whatever is taken to be true, or valid, or useful, or effective in a given context depends on how social acceptability, legitimation, and a taken-for-granted institutional order are fabricated through social construction.

What We Can Learn from Drekkingarhylur

Many ask questions of evaluation as if questions about validity and method were the most important; but can we really evaluate X using method Y? (As one example, can we really measure school quality by means of children's scores on performance tests?) From a sociological perspective, a society can in fact decide to let any test meaningfully stand for practically any topic. If in doubt, look into Drekkingarhylur (the "Drowning Hole") in the Icelandic national park at Thingvellir. Drekkingarhylur is a small and deep pond of water. Herein, women were thrown who were accused of being unfaithful, of killing their own children, etc. Different historical accounts mention a number of types of crime. As we shall see, it is not the type that matters. With their hands tied, the victims had only a slight chance of survival. If they reappeared on the surface of the pool, it was taken as an indication that they had supernatural powers; witches could be punished (again). Is this procedure fair and valid? Not at all, by our contemporary standards. But the sociologically relevant observation is that in medieval Iceland this worked in practice as a test for witchcraft. To insist that the method was unfair and invalid does not help our sociological analysis. What we must understand is how this testing was organized, how it fit into a cultural and political regime that depended on witchcraft in fighting against it, and what real consequences all this had. What we can learn from Drekkingarhylur is the cultural relativity of the tests— or evaluations, if you will—that societies carry out related to what they see as important problems. For each society, the test is very real and has undeniably real consequences. But each test or evaluation is constructed within a given historical, cultural, and societal context. The last drowning in Drekkingarhylur took place in 1749.

Contemporary studies in the sociology of knowledge underscore the dynamic and indeterminate nature of knowledge production processes. Knorr-Cetina (1981) and Latour (1987) have shown that advances in knowledge are delicate achievements which owe their specific form to a large number of socially contingent factors. Necessary factors are not only infrastructure, finance, and the like but also crucial support, on the part of key actors in decisive moments, for relatively loosely structured ideas that only later turn out to become winning ideas. Sometimes a breakthrough is in the pipeline for years because an important factor is missing. Along the way, finances, organizations, relations of trust, commitments, equipment, and key ideas are negotiated and renegotiated. Various stakeholders and institutions may stay on board for their own reasons. Others are excluded or leave voluntarily. Social support is a key factor, and it cannot be taken for granted.

This "sociologization" of knowledge is understood as if it assumes an irrational and ideological basis for all knowledge. Longino (2002) suggests that the fact that all knowledge is produced in social contexts does not mean all rationality must be abandoned in models explaining how this takes place. Under particular circumstances, introducing a particular social regime of knowledge production is a fairly rational response to a problem. For example, in a given scientific community scientists may work fairly rationally toward results that will be socially acceptable to other scientists. Evaluators may also behave fairly rationally in a given evaluation situation. However, this is no guarantee for rationality in the larger societal perspective.

A knowledge regime may have a number of unforeseen consequences; the road to evaluative hell may be paved with good intentions. In a similar vein, evaluation may be introduced for good reasons but still have unpredictable and paradoxical consequences.

Stehr (1994) emphasizes the socially productive role of knowledge in contemporary society. However, the social world is not smoothed out and neatly packaged such that knowledge can be applied with well-known consequences. The typical result is *an increasingly fragile social order.* New knowledge leads to social change, but quite nonlinearly.

A number of factors help explain why transmission of knowledge into changing social relations is far from linear and straightforward, among them power differentials, value conflicts, and unintended consequences of earlier applications of knowledge. Streams of knowledge are therefore, in their effects, confronted with value changes with which they are never fully synchronized. Finally, as a sort of synthesizing point, the reflexivity of modern social relations is itself a nonlinear and thus destabilizing factor (Giddens 1990, 44). In other words, it is the very nature of knowledge in modern society not to have linear consequences.

> Knowledge is not an insight into the essence of things, but a social accomplishment with uncertain consequences. Knowledge is "open-ended" in the sense that its "use" is not an inherent property, but depends on the articulation, representation and appropriation of knowledge in particular contexts (Woolgar 2004, 6).

Even though systematically produced knowledge could earlier play a social role similar to that of traditional religion with respect to certainty and authority, uncertainties in knowledge are becoming clearer today. In today's knowledge society, it also becomes obvious that each new piece of knowledge does not always reduce ignorance and exclude alternative views. Some pieces of knowledge are partly contradictory, suggesting or recommending different social pathways. Some knowledge-producing systems on the societal or institutional level (such as governments and schools) interact in spiraling regulatory logics that paradoxically produce more risk and more need for control at the same time as others seek to avoid being enrolled in further control regimes (Rothstein, Huber, and Gaskell 2006).

Instead, there are complex social forces seeking control over different knowledge productions, and there are many motives other than to approximate truth. Most of the social forces that regulate evaluation processes unfold in the context of modern organizations. It is conventional thinking that organizations are based on goals (some would believe: even shared goals).

Of Course There Are Clear Goals!

A consultant was once asked to evaluate some organizational changes that had been in operation in a municipality for a few years. He began to ask whether there were any clear goals behind these changes. The staff members for the municipality began a vehement discussion about what the goals were, with some believing there were no clear goals. Finally, the chief administrative officer had had enough. He went into the archive room and found a dusty document with a description of objectives. He threw it onto the table, remarking, "Here, you can see for yourselves! So now there shouldn't be any doubt about what kinds of goals we have!"

A standard definition of *organization*, for example, is "coordination of many people's different actions with the intention of fulfillment of common goals." It is correct that modern organizations (in contrast to other social units such as churches, families, and movements) are specifically directed toward narrowly defined goals (Etzioni 1964; Scott 1992). In recent years, however, organizational theory has been preoccupied with one long problematization of assumptions about rational, uniform, clear, unambiguous, and consistent goals. Instead, organizations are now depicted as learning organizations, in which lessons are learned only stepwise and retrospectively, as loosely linked systems (Weick 1979) where each actor brings his or her own goals and understanding of goals (Silverman 1970), where preferences and means-ends connections are problematic (March and Olsen 1976), and where "most attempts at social control are clumsy and unpredictable" (Perrow 1977, 103). Under such conditions, the "goals" are usually first determined by retrospective interpretation of the actions that should rationally lead to the goals (Weick 1979). Evaluation thus defines goals as much as the other way around.

To highlight how this renewed understanding of organizational life unfolds, I will look at organizations as rational systems, as learning systems, and as institutionalized systems in turn.

I devote a particular attention to the latter perspective because it suggests that what modern organizations can do to achieve trust and confidence is to act so as to appear rational, and attempt to live up to the environment's otherwise contradictory demands (Meyer and Rowan 1977). Ambiguity arises when an organization adopts a formula such as evaluation primarily because it is socially and normatively expected. Ambiguity emerges when evaluations begin to work (for example, by beginning to define goals). Ambiguity appears when evaluation shows itself to have several unintended consequences.

The essence of neo-institutional theory—that ambiguities, loose couplings, and paradoxes flow from organizational attempts to live up to social norms and values—in fact demonstrates the necessity of sociological analysis along with the organizational one. In a sociological perspective, any phenomenon is always understood in the context of how the entire society is organized. The unity of the social imaginary makes every society precisely the society it is (Castoriadis 1987a). A meaning of a specific social phenomenon is defined within this larger horizon demarcated by the social imaginary. We must thus understand the sociohistorical meaning of evaluation, if one uses Castoriadis' terms. To do so, I have found a tripartite frame of reference—"modernity," "reflexive modernity" (Beck 1992; Beck, Giddens, and Lash 1994), and "the audit society" (Power 1997a)—especially beneficial.

About This Book

The central question in this book is, Which ideas and values characterize the kind of society that can be called an "evaluation society"? What is the "evaluation imaginary" (Schwandt 2009) in a given epoch, that is to say, the views and assumptions undergirding evaluation, but at the same time themselves undergirded by broader views, norms, and values in society?

To consider a phenomenon sociologically means there are forces at work that are greater than what any individual member of the society can see. Something becomes an institution when one can no longer see what it is. In a sociological perspective, a phenomenon is always something other than what it says about itself. Our analysis is thus likely to reveal that evaluators bring to their work many ideals, values, norms, and understandings that are taken for granted as they are embedded in the larger organizational and societal frameworks around evaluation.

In each of the three moments above—modernity, reflexive modernity, and the audit society—evaluation represents particular forms, values, and purposes. But it is also contested and full of tension. As we analyze evaluation sociologically, we will see that it does not always do what it says it does.

In the broad evaluation field, there is often great interest in marking, constructing, and consolidating evaluation as an entirely unique field. Many evaluators are so preoccupied with applying evaluation to bettering the world, or at least with promoting the field of evaluation, that they develop a blind spot in seeing other consequences of evaluation than those they themselves believe are good and proper (Mark and Henry 2002).

If we reveal these understandings and their social and organizational underpinnings, perhaps our understanding of evaluation will be more realistic and more complex than the optimistic self-understanding that evaluation tends to present of itself.

Other good books attempt something resembling this task (Power 1997a; Schwandt 2002). But Power's *The Audit Society* focuses explicitly on auditing and not evaluation as such. And Power does not specifically link his work to organizational theory, even though I am indebted to many of his insights as well as for the inspiration for this book's title. Schwandt's professional platform is philosophy rather than sociology, but I also stand in great debt to him, more than it is possible to express through sporadic references. It is hardly a coincidence that two of these keen observers have professional standpoints on the margins of the evaluation field or outside it. They do not see themselves as advocates of evaluation or a particular type of evaluation.

Intelligent and serious evaluation researchers, however, are elucidating key evaluation questions, and they are interested in researching how evaluation is in fact executed and how it actually works in our type of society. Good evaluators ask for research on evaluation (Mark 2008).

Part of this research can certainly be conceptually, philosophically, or sociologically oriented, among which my perspective is primarily the last one. Some will find it too critical, others not critical enough.

It is, however, unreasonable to demand that an analysis should reach very specific conclusions in order to be categorized as "critical." As Schwandt (2006) shows, a self-acclaimed critical position can easily come to overlook insightful contributions from other positions. Ultimately, the criticism can prove innocuous if it promises not to criticize the positions that have declared themselves to be critical.

Sometimes critique is taken seriously in practice. Boltanski and Chiapello expertly show how powerful organizations in modern society have reformed themselves as a result of critique. The critique is polyvalent because it is aimed at a certain social order and is also the potential occasion to renew (parts of) the same order. Evaluation has the same double function. And so has a "critical" discussion of evaluation.

No one can say in advance which of the present-day alternative critiques will lead to constructive answers in the future. Critique of evaluation has often led to new and perhaps better evaluation. The field of evaluation has a remarkable ability to renew itself. When the sharp fronts of the past are softened and more polyvalent, pluralistic fronts are found, then an analytical contribution must also enter into this polyvalence. There is no longer a clearly demarcated front with "the system" on one side and "critique" on the other. Evaluation has absorbed the social critique while also being incorporated into predominant formulas for management and organization that are otherwise in constant development.

I have therefore decided in this book not to decide how "critical" the book should be. Instead, I present some analytical perspectives and premises and draw some conclusions. How critical they are remains to be seen.

The Structure of the Book

Evaluation is an important part of modern life. The evaluation wave is complex and dynamic; it includes many mysteries and ambiguities. No one theory can help us understand it all. Yet the analysis in the remainder of the book must be clearly structured.

The central thesis of this book is that if we want to understand many of the norms, values, and expectations that evaluators and others bring, sometimes unknowingly, to evaluation, we should understand how evaluation is demanded, formatted, and shaped by the two great principles of social order in modernity called "organization" and "society." Through this maneuver, we will also be in a better position to understand many of the mysteries, tensions, and paradoxes in evaluation, as well as the use of evaluation, which is often much more or much less than what is officially claimed.

The structure of the book is a result of the general theoretical idea that evaluation can be understood through organizational and sociological analysis.

The book consists of two parts, devoted to organization and society, respectively. In each part, the implications for evaluation are drawn.

The first part of the book, Chapters 1 and 2, is devoted to an organizational analysis of evaluation. Chapter 1 describes three models, called rational organization, the learning organization, and the institutionalized organization. The rational organization is chosen because it provides an underlying ideal for the very phenomenon of organization in modern society. The learning organization is chosen because it describes an ideal that many evaluators share. The institutionalized organization is present because it delivers an insightful, and perhaps surprising, critical contrast to those ideals. Chapter 2 is therefore reserved for an in-depth analysis of what institutionalized organization means for evaluation.

The second part of the book, Chapters 3 through 7, delivers a sociological analysis of evaluation. It is also structured around a tripartite theoretical apparatus. Certain aspects of evaluation as a dynamic, social phenomenon are analyzed through the sociological lenses of modernity, reflexive modernization, and the audit society. In Chapter 3, I describe modernity and its evaluation imaginary. Chapter 4 deals with reflexive modernization, and Chapter 5 with evaluation under reflexively modern conditions. Chapter 6 covers the next phase, which can be called the audit society, characterized by neorigorism and evaluation machines. Chapter 7 discusses the implications of evaluation machines in society.

Finally, I discuss issues that are important for the future of evaluation and for the work of evaluators, if the previous analysis is correct.

The book thus culminates in a critical and constructive discussion of dominant evaluation practices characteristic of our times. It would be a cheap critique, however, if I had not accounted, step by step, for the organizational and societal pillars on which this discussion rests. Both the structure and the content of this book thus reflect an ambition to take the evaluation society seriously.

PART I

An Organizational Analysis of Evaluation

1   Organizational Understandings

Rational, Learning, and Institutionalized Organization

In this chapter, I discuss evaluation from the perspective of organizational theory. There are three reasons for this.

First, a steadily greater proportion of the lives of modern individuals is structured by organizations. Our minds are becoming organizational. The mentality that dominates work organizations diffuse into society (Berger, Berger, and Kellner 1973), and to an increasing degree workplaces such as schools, hospitals, and universities are defining themselves as enterprises, and they must be managed as organizations.

Second, as organizations they take on the culture of evaluation. Organizations are themselves objects of evaluation, and therefore they seek to organize evaluation. They constitute the characteristic social arena in which the evaluations of our day take place. The organizational element in evaluation is in fact becoming more evident. Today, an evaluation should not only be *used* but be *mainstreamed* into an organization and lead to organizational learning. As a corollary, some of the most influential ideas in evaluation today are organizational ideas. When modern ideas about rationality and autonomy are executed in practice, this occurs most often in organizational form. Ideas about goals, plans, abstract rationality, management, bureaucracy, and organizational learning are important for understanding every modern organizational phenomenon. As we shall see in this chapter, elements of the modern organization are gaining ground through the history of evaluation. The attempts to bureaucratize evaluation are innumerable, and they constantly reappear in new forms. In this respect, we have never abandoned the idea of modern organization. Instead we cultivate the idea of organization in evaluation, too.

Third, organizational theory casts a fresh and renewing light on how evaluation actually works. Organizational theory, especially its recent elements, challenges fundamental understandings of what we mean by goals and objectives, evaluation criteria, and learning. Organization theory casts new light on how knowledge is used. If evaluation in contemporary society has become an institutionalized practice, organizational theory can help us understand why this occurs and with what consequences. Evaluation in organizations is our focus now (even if organizations are embedded in social-historical contexts). However, we will not unpack those parentheses until Chapter 3 onward.

"Organizationalization" of Evaluation

Some of the earliest contributions to evaluation viewed it as a technical-methodological tool, a form of assisted sense making, more reliable the more separated it was from human practice and ongoing human interaction (Schwandt 2002, 13). Even though some scholars continue to maintain this idea, several are increasingly aware that evaluation is strongly dependent on its social and organizational context. Context matters. There has been a movement from a naïve instrumental view of evaluation to a more sophisticated acknowledgment that both evaluation and its use are conditioned by organizational processes.

Management and organization have responded to this development. The ideal today is that evaluation must be integrated into all of the general processes in the organization: strategy, resource allocation, in-service training, and day-to-day management. Evaluation must be mainstreamed; this means "moving evaluation to the forefront of organizational thinking and behavior" (Sanders 2002, 2).

Many who work with evaluation think organizationally and sell organizational recipes for good and proper management. Evaluation embodies organizational thinking. Notice, for example, the difference between saying "Hi, my name is Lisa. I'm the evaluator" and the more contemporary approach: "Hi, I come from the quality department. I have management's backing to come and facilitate a joint process about development of capacity for organizational learning."

Several developmental features contribute to the fact that organizations now embrace evaluation. Early on, evaluators with participatory tendencies figured out that the organizational context of evaluation is of great importance. This led to an interest in organizational learning processes. In this way, the official side of management and organization also acquired an interest in evaluation. Evaluation must not be too haphazard; if it is simultaneously integrated into the organization's general operations, perhaps it will succeed in channeling pressure for change so it is used constructively in the organization's development.

That management and organization must begin to master evaluation is also connected to organizations themselves becoming evaluands. It is hardly coincidental that implementation research—the sister discipline of evaluation research, because it concerns itself with how policies are implemented in practice—has discovered that factors at the organizational level play their own role in the actual formation of public policies. Implementation of policy takes place in a complicated interorganizational context (Sabatier 1985; Winter 1994). Organizations add their own dynamics and motives to the implementation process. Fieldworkers employed in organizations experience constant pressure but also exercise their own judgment and thereby form the policy implemented in practice. If evaluators want to understand what results from public policy, they must look inside organizations.

Evaluations have broadened their perspective on the "content" of interventions directed toward clients and patients. The content cannot be separated from the organizational conditions under which it is provided. In a hospital, for example, an evaluation is carried out with the purpose of assessing not just how individual doctors do their job but whether the various specialists as a group have the capacity to provide coordinated, managed health care. We no longer evaluate teaching, but rather the learning environment. Organizational factors such as teamwork, cooperation, paper trails, organizational procedures, and management systems must be susceptible to evaluation, too. The more complex an evaluand, the more evident the need to study how its organization is managed.

This means organizations today must be aware that they are held accountable in evaluation terms. Control over organizations must therefore translate into control within organizations. The organization must adapt itself to evaluation. Therefore managers must also take responsibility for evaluation. A manager who wants to be taken seriously must master a vocabulary that includes terms such as *quality, indicators, benchmark-*

ing, auditing, accreditation, and *documentation.* Management must be able to convert these terms into organizational practice. Managers must make their organizations evaluable and must organize their evaluations accordingly.

The ideal, therefore, is an "organizationalization" of evaluation. Evaluation becomes an important organizational function that cannot be left only to coincidence and to individuals.

As a corollary, we must also change our view of the evaluator. In much evaluation theory, this person is referred to as a fairly autonomous-thinking subject who has ideas and responsibilities in the same way as a natural person (even if the evaluator role is naturally a specific role). However, when evaluation is organizationalized, this idea of the evaluator dissolves, insofar as evaluation becomes an organizational functional entity. It is subsumed under the structures, values, and rules of the game. It is also institutionalized in the sense that, like other structurally defined organizational roles and functions, it can be exercised by interchangeable persons.

Modern sociologists have concerned themselves with what happens when such functions, formerly left to natural persons, become "organized." Bauman (1989), for example, talks of the "adiaphorization" (exception from moral assessment) that characterizes modern organization. Herein lies a structuring of human relations on the basis of formal rules, procedures, and organizational principles, where following them is seen as a goal in itself, or in any case a necessity. In this connection, the organizationalization of evaluation can imply that moral considerations are made irrelevant to evaluation.

This is one of the far-reaching implications of the organizationalization of evaluation. In the following discussion, I delve more closely into three organizational theory models to trace some of the more specific possible effects of organizationalization of evaluation.

On Organizational Models

By an *organizational model* I refer to a particular way of thinking about organizations. Here, organizational models should not be confused with organizations or types of organization.

Models of organization incorporate both analytical, normative, and sociohistorical ideas. They are analytical, like other scientific models or abstractions; they simplify reality. Through simplification, they emphasize certain specific conceptual features that help us understand life in and around organizations. Without simplification, we would see only chaos.

Like other specifically modern types of knowledge, organizational thinking is born almost automatically reflexive, for it has evolved in close interaction with the practical "doing" and "living" of "organization" in society. Practical organizational problems encourage development of organizational models in order to come up with new ways of thinking that would help solve management problems. In turn, new ways of thinking are immediately marketed as new, better, and more-modern types of organization. Organizational and managerial models of good organizations have constantly imposed themselves on reality. Organizational models are theories *of* organization and theories *in* organization at the same time.

Organizational models both describe how organizations function and prescribe how they ought to function. In other words, organizational models are analytical and normative. We constantly behave in organizations with the expectation that what they do is fairly rational, even if our daily life experience tells us they are not.

This creates a dilemma as to how much complexity can be contained in the model. Every conceptual model must be fairly simple if it is to be heuristically useful. But without respect for complexity, descriptive models can be misleading. For example, formal models can ignore and suppress everything that informal organization does to make organizations function. Used prescriptively, simplistic models can have unpleasant and inappropriate consequences in complex reality.

On the other hand, this is exactly what organizations do. They seek to simplify reality so that it becomes manageable in some way according to particular values, norms, and procedures. Because values, norms, and the whole cultural fabric in society change over time, organizational models are sociohistorical symbols at the same time as they are analytical and normative ideas.

Here I describe three organizational perspectives, each of which operates with its own view of evaluation. In principle, one can analyze an organization with the help of a combination of several models, and perhaps in this way achieve a more complex understanding of the world than any single model would make possible. However, in this presentation I have chosen to treat each model separately. I present three models, which I call the "rational," the "learning," and the "institutionalized system" models. They are presented in a sequence of increasing complexity. This means I do not treat the three models equally. The more complex the model is, the later it is presented, and the more is written about it. (Only later may it turn out that the simple rationalistic and bureaucratic model of organization presented first also has a large imprint on today's evaluation.)

In brief, the main features of the three organizational models and their view of evaluation appear in Table 2.1.

Rational Organization

No organizational model illustrates the social embodiment of the modern ideals of mastery of the world better than that of the rational organization. Rational organization aims toward maximum predictability. Once a set of objectives have been determined, the best possible arrangements are made to achieve predictable realization of these objectives.

The organizational characteristic that best expresses this approach is analyzed by Weber (1978) in his ideal-type definition of bureaucracy.

The proper way to do things is defined as a specific procedure. A procedure is a formalized way of ordering specific abstract components temporally (Berger, Berger, and Kellner 1973). The components are abstract in the sense that they can be treated in the same way by the procedure, regardless of their substantive content. Bureaucracy thus succeeds by means of organizing coordinating actions across distance, in time and space.

Documents and handbooks with scales, typologies, rules, and decrees lend assistance to rational organization. It will demand too much organizational attention if several cases are not handled in the same way. Conversely, the demand for mastery of the world leads precisely to abstract homogenization and standardization of the problems in this world, and the organizationally defined solutions to these problems, such that the world becomes manageable with the aid of organizational procedures.

As much as possible, management is carried out using written documents. This applies to both the procedure itself and the treatment of individual cases. Literacy is important for ensuring consistency and continuity over time and through space.

The procedure as form avoids, to the greatest possible extent, personal considerations, emotions, and histories, among employees and among those whom the organization encounters (for example, clients). Decisions are taken according to generalized rules. Optimally, technical and professional tools rather than human judgment are used. In

TABLE 2.1

	Rational Organization	Learning Organization	Institutionalized Organization
Definition of organization	System that loyally implements plans decided after description of objectives and calculation of alternatives	System of knowledge that corrects itself via feedback after actions	Loosely coupled system of metaphorical understandings, values, and organizational recipes and routines that are imitated and taken for granted, and that give legitimacy
Most important theoretical insight		Limited capacity to manage future alternatives and to make plans	Confrontation with logic of consequentiality
Exemplary evaluation advocates	Rossi and Freeman (1985)	Patton (1997); Preskill (1994)	
Evaluation function	Instrumental	Instrumental, learning and enlightening	Ritualistic use of evaluation; constitutive effects of evaluation

other words, the client is viewed through the lens of a bureaucratic typology.

If one uses Schutz's terminology (1973) regarding interpretations, organizational typologies are characterized by a low degree of "indexicality" in comparison to other typological systems. Indexicality refers to the specific meanings that can be connected to a typology when it is applied to a specific personal and contextual practice. Most organizational typologies are formulated in a jargon of management, finance, administration, or law.

Berger, Berger, and Kellner (1973) compare the mentality of bureaucracy with another large, typically modern form of mentality, the technocratic, which also includes manipulation with abstract components. The bureaucratic form of consciousness distinguishes itself, however, in that the technocratic form must give more consideration to substantive properties of the tasks it is dealing with. Construction of a bridge, for example, requires attention to the physical properties of the materials as well as the load capacity of the bridge. Bureaucracy is much less constrained by limits of the physical world; instead, it creates its own kind of world. The objects dealt with are defined in abstract terms on the basis of bureaucracy's own classification systems. Indexicality is low.

In the world of bureaucracy, special value is connected to the procedure itself. If a technocrat, for example, wants to produce a passport document, it does not matter how it is produced, only that it looks genuine. For a bureaucrat, though, how the passport is produced is critical (Berger, Berger, and Kellner 1973).

To ensure maximal predictability, the organization's total work tasks are divided so that the organizational structure reflects the classification of tasks. In this way, each task obtains a corresponding specialized competence to carry out precisely this task. The competencies are divided in the organizational structure, corresponding to the task division. This means that planning of tasks and implementation of tasks are separated. In any individual place in the modern organizational structure, there are skills and competencies to execute only a single specialized task, and there is often no total overview of the entire organization's mode of functioning (Berger 1964). Only in one central place in the organization is it assumed that this overview exists. The remainder of the organization is reduced to being an instrument for this central, rational brain.

This process—making the organization into an instrument—naturally entails a degree of value ambiguity. The tool can evolve into a social form in itself that becomes its own purpose. As described here, the modern bureaucratic organization embodies what Weber called formal rationality, which is expressed in a procedure that gives the impression of calculability, predictability, and efficiency (Ritzer 1996, 138). Formal rationality is thus abstract rationality. It appears separated from substantive values and instead relates itself to "universally applied rules, laws, and regulations" (1996, 136). In rational organization, there is always a risk that the organization as instrument and its legitimate procedures become a social form maintained for its own sake, independent of other substantive values.

Evaluation in the Rational Organization

When rational organization pursues the greatest possible predictability in operations, there are great advantages of operating entirely without evaluation. In a pure, classic modern organization, it is appropriate to operate with plans, not with evaluation. But if evaluation is to function within the frameworks of rational organization, the latter ensure incorporation of the former into predictable procedures.

Evaluation must be planned to the greatest possible degree, and be in accordance with the organization's objectives. A rational organization cannot risk being evaluated on the basis of unpredictable criteria. For evaluation to be used as rationally and predictably as possible, several strict demands are made on the evaluation process. The evaluation criteria must be set up in advance and in strict accordance with the approved organizational objectives. The evaluation process should follow a predefined rational plan and not be open to surprises and complexities discovered after the plan has been made. According to the logic of rational, if not bureaucratic, organization, all activities are carried out in compliance with a strict division of labor. Evaluation is a specific task separate from the doing of other things; whether those who actually perform activities under evaluation also find the evaluation relevant is not important.

The use of evaluation must be purely instrumental. One way of ensuring this is to prospectively calculate advantages and disadvantages of certain alternative actions (as we know from cost-benefit analysis). The alternatives can eventually also be tested under strictly controlled conditions (as we know from the idea of an experimenting society). Here again, both the evaluation criteria and their application must be as well planned as possible.

If evaluation is to be used predictably, it must be reported back to well-defined parts of the organizational structure responsible for follow-up. There must be a clear connection between the structure of problems to be evaluated and the structure of the organization. In this sense, the organizational structure seeks to embody a whole worldview according to which the world is preferably organized. Representation of complex and dynamic problems may be difficult to incorporate in that structure, but if the organizational structure is powerful it may seek to impose its own view of the world upon the world instead.

Critique of the Rational Organization

Critique of the rational organization has been comprehensive and comes from many quarters. In his earlier diagnosis of bureaucracy, Weber captured many of its core features and presented a social critique. With this very form as ideal, bureaucracy becomes purely formal and ends as an iron cage for the modern individual (Weber 1978). His critique is especially strong because he shows that bureaucracy is not a random historical event but a product of dominant modern values. Weber thereby illustrates, as sociologists like to point out, a fundamental ambiguity in modern life: institutions that should master the world in the name of rationality and autonomy end up having their own tyrannical properties.

In the wake of the Second World War and horrific experiences with totalitarian regimes, several sociologists point out that some of the properties of modern organizations, including the individual's displacement of moral responsibility elsewhere, considered a virtue within the rational organization, can under certain circumstances lead to brutal patterns of conduct (Bauman 1989; Milgram 1974). Barbaric behavior is thereby not the diametrical opposite of the modern rationalistic way of life, but on the contrary an uncomfortable potential, the source of which lies in the very form of the modern organization itself.

Philosophers criticize modern bureaucratic mentality as an expression of a technocratization of the entirety of human life. The fact that the bureaucratic organization can function just as effectively to achieve the most inhuman objectives stimulates reflection on the entire division of means and ends in the modern culture of rationalism. The technocratic and bureaucratic mentalities are criticized for masking political contradictions and blocking the road to human emancipation.

Early in the 20th century, an artistic and existentially based critique of bureaucracy was also initiated. Bureaucracy is alienating, anonymous, and powerful. At the same time, there is an element of absurd theater about it. The word *Kafkaesque* has remained an epithet.

After 1968, there emerged a renewed critique of bureaucratic organization. The organization was characterized by rationality, but the individual worker experiences division of labor, specialization, routinization, dehumanization, and loss of control over everyday life. The social and humanistic critique has found allies among progressive managers, consultants, and organizational researchers who point out that project-based organization, horizontal "flat" structures, management by objectives, self-administration, teamwork, etc., can operate in a humanizing way while still being efficient.

In a similar vein, the rational organization has adopted the idea of evaluation. But evaluation in the rational organization is built on problematic assumptions. Does the organization really have a set of clearly defined, unambiguous goals that are so stable over time that they can be used for control? Even if yes, are these goals easily translatable into measurable evaluation criteria? Is the organization's data processing capacity large enough to project the outcomes for all relevant alternatives? Is there always order in the temporal sequence such that everything begins with clear goals? Are spontaneous actions and preferences that cannot be made clear in advance always unthinkable? Can rational procedures be carried out relatively undisturbed if there are essential changes in expectations and demands in the organization's environment? And last but not least: Do people allow themselves to be subordinated to the organizational typifications and procedures that the rational organization prescribes for them?

The rational organization must answer these questions affirmatively. Even in those cases where the rational organization clearly has not succeeded, the ideal of formal rationality appears to thrive. As creatures of organization, we are able to maintain ideas of continued future rationality in organization, even when our everyday prior experiences indicate something else (Kreiner 1989). As a prescription for life in organizations, formal rationality reappears in perpetually new garb. Therefore the model has an important analytical role to play, even though it builds on strange preconditions that other organizational models regard with skepticism, and even though we know the model does not describe the actual world. But it is an important model of organization because it constantly seeks to mold the world according to an image of rationality. If organizational rationality in evaluation is a myth, it is still a myth that organizations recite to themselves as they seek to manage what they officially think is reality. This continues to happen even if people at the top and the bottom of the so-called rational organization experience reality in completely different ways.

The Learning Organization

In real life, said Lindblom as far back as 1959, decision making in organizations is not rational. There is disagreement about goals. But actions must be taken, so values and goals are only partly and temporarily clarified along the way. Some policies are agreed on even if goals and values are not consistent, and many alternatives are not considered. Instead, actors in organizations muddle through on the basis of limited reflection on previous actions. The capacity to process information is limited. Adjustments happen mostly at the margin.

In this spirit, the learning organization presents itself as an alternative to the rational model. Learning theory poses much fewer demands on human calculation. It acknowledges that what and how much we learn depends on what we already know. Most importantly, our knowledge is dependent on our prior actions. Information capacity is limited, and learning often occurs only gradually. We learn with reference to a few, important events. As a matter of course, we assume that the world is connected in a certain way. We can be forgetful, tired, or mistaken; but the possibilities for learning are present. The key to learning is not planning but feedback.

Organizational learning concerns how organizations react to the feedback they register as a result of their own actions (Hedberg 1981; Levitt and March 1988). The idea of organizational learning obtains its inspiration from the way in which individuals learn. The metaphor for an organization is the individual human brain; this model is then used on organizations, albeit with various modifications. It is clear that organizational learning must have some collective aspects not found in the learning of individuals.

Because of the centrality of feedback, learning processes are often depicted in the form of a learning cycle (Morgan 1986, 88). Although contemporary theories of organizational learning have reached a high degree of complexity in their understanding of the interplay between tacit and explicit knowledge, referring to psychological, cognitive, and organizational factors including structures, cultures, and processes (Nonaka 1994), I maintain that the learning cycle continues to bind together elementary particles on which organizational learning theory is built. The cycle is referred to in classical, often-cited works on learning (Argyris and Schön 1978; Morgan 1986), and it is used by evaluators who want to promote organizational learning (Preskill and Torres 1999). It is illustrative in demonstrating the differences between learning organization and other organizational models such as the rational one (above) and the institutionalized organization (next section).

Schematically, the cycle consists of three phases (Dunsire 1986). First, organizations register states in their environment through a detector. These states are then compared with a director, which represents the organization's norms and standards of how reality ought to be. If there is a

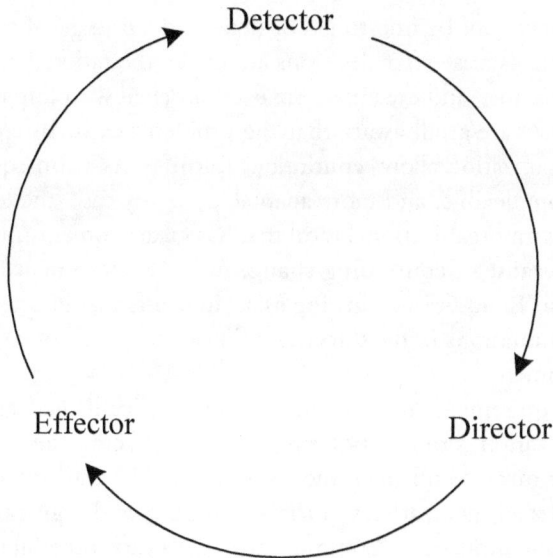

FIGURE I.   Single-loop learning.

discrepancy between ideal and reality, then in the third phase the organization executes an action, an effector, in order to reduce the gap. It is
the connection among the three phases that constitutes learning. Hence
learning does not consist simply of acquisition of new knowledge. Knowledge must be converted into new action; otherwise the cycle is not complete. The learning cycle continues endlessly; it is constant and implies
self-correction.

This basic diagram of learning is extremely simple. Nevertheless, it has
a certain charm due to both its organizational-theoretical points and its
practical advantages. In this way, the theory of organizational learning operates with a more humane image of the human being than does rational
organization.

The learning organization wins out—as it likes to say—over other
organizational forms because it is adaptable to the demands posed by a
changing environment. It also wins out because it permits learning to occur in relation to decisions already taken. In the rational model, there exist only plans decided from above, plans that are then faithfully executed
via set procedures. This means potential adaptation is slow (because it
must pass through the top of the organization), and because at lower lev-

els the plans cannot be fine-tuned or details added to get them to work. If new problems arise after decisions are made, the rational organization becomes inflexible, and executives are overburdened with implementation details, if they are at all aware that the problems exist. In contrast, the learning organization allows continuous learning. As a consequence, it is quicker, more flexible, and more adaptable. In any case, the learning organization is an organizational ideal that has great momentum and seems attractive because of continuing change in the environment around the organization. In addition, learning as an idea offends no one and offers positive connotations in the direction of individual and collective growth and development.

Several requirements must be fulfilled in practice if the learning cycle of an organization is to function properly. The effector, the detector, and the director must be on the same wavelength. The learning cycle operates only if the organization's objectives, inputs, and registration of the effects of these inputs can "communicate" with each other about a given situation.

Several organizational conditions must also be in place for the learning cycle to be complete (March and Olsen 1976; Morgan 1986, 89ff). In other words, using the learning cycle as an ideal, it is easy to see how many organizations have barriers to learning.

If we consider the arrow running from the director to the effector, a number of factors are important:

- *Organization of the information flow in the organization.* The arrow remains intact only if those who perceive that the reality is not as it should be undertake action themselves or can and will inform those who do. The division of tasks, specialization, and hierarchy, however, can lead to a situation whereby those who have knowledge are unable to take action and those who can act do not have the necessary knowledge.

- *Organizational memory.* Is it primarily individuals who maintain experiences in the organization, or are there generalized ways of storing knowledge about possibilities of action? If there is a change of personnel, how is organizational memory ensured?

- *Motivational factors.* Does the individual worker believe it helps and benefits to call attention to the fact that problems have been observed?

- *Reward structure.* Does the organization reward, or punish, those who call attention to problems? Will a manager believe an employee is incompetent if he or she reports difficulties within their area? How are actors held responsible in the organization? Does the manner in which a principle of accountability is respected prevent actors from ever mentioning problems within their area, simply to avoid having to be held responsible?

Does the organization tend to use rhetoric as a buffer against experiences? If one expresses oneself in the form of "espoused theory" (i.e., official explanations of the connections in the world), while experiences do not become "theory-in-use" (Morgan 1986, 90; that is, do not become the actual ideas controlling the organization's actions), this prevents experience from being converted into learning. If, for example, there is a great difference in what can be said in public and in private, in the board room and in the coffee room, there can be a learning-impeding gap between espoused theory and theory-in-use (Spencer and Dale 1979). Thus individually espoused theories can impede organizational learning (Argyris and Schön 1978).

Decision-making processes are often complex. For example, in March and Olsen's "garbage can model" of decision making (1976), there are very loose linkages between problems and decisions. Problems can fester in an organization for a long time, and actors have limited attention. When something finally happens, the problems are linked to "solutions" from outside, to what is fashionable at the moment. It is a logic of timing and coincidence, rather than a logic of predictable professional expertise, that regulates decisions.

What are the barriers between the effector and the detector?

- *Routines* for when and how information about the environment is collected can mean that results are registered slowly, or not at all.

- *Organizational hierarchies and reward structures* can make it too difficult for subordinates to report problems back to their superiors (Morgan 1986, 90).

- *Reality is often so complex* that it permits divergent interpretations as to which actions have worked in which situations. Interpretations indicating that a problem for the organization is caused by the actions of others can operate as a vaccination against learning.

· *Actors have their own stake* in certain interpretations of cause and effect. Advertisers tend to believe that advertisements are effective. Some teachers tend to believe that there is no cause-and-effect relationship between teaching and children's performance in school, but that there is such a causal relationship between children's social background and their school performance. Managers tend to present the world so that successes are attributed to themselves, while failures are due to external circumstances (Levitt and March 1988). If the organizational learning cycle is to be complete, such differing interpretations must be correctly dealt with in a joint process. It is central to organizational learning that understanding of problems and solutions be coordinated in collective sense-making processes.

Finally, how can the arrow from detector to the director be broken?

· *Unlearning is difficult.* If money, resources, and prestige have already been invested in a certain strategy or procedure, it can be intolerable to accept the negative consequences and change course (Nystrom and Starbuck 1984).

· *If objectives, norms, and standards are unclearly conceived* or entirely hidden by rhetoric, one may never reach the point where they are assessed against the actual data. Edelman (1977) notes that rhetoric can sometimes help an ineffective organization survive, especially in a political world. In any case, it is more difficult to be subsequently held accountable for specific results if one has to live up to only vague and unclear objectives.

All these factors can impede organizational learning but are not fatal to the model. On the contrary, proponents of the idea of organizational learning view these factors as obstacles to learning that exist in order to be overcome. Reforms are needed. It is a matter of keeping information channels open, creating cross-cutting forums for learning, and fostering a culture where mistakes can be dealt with openly, thereby promoting individual and collective learning processes. For learning-oriented organization researchers and consultants, there are no limits to optimism and eagerness for reform when it concerns belief in the benefits to be gained by opening toward learning.

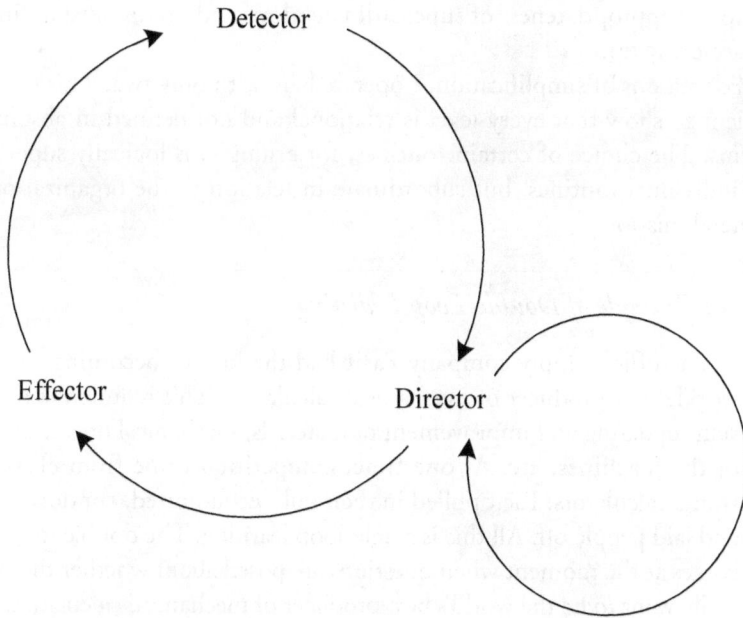

FIGURE 2. Double-loop learning.

Nevertheless, it is sometimes the organization's own fundamental assumptions that prevent learning from taking place. Learning theorists have figured out that this adaptation by way of learning must at times occur at a deeper level than within the circle shown in Figure 1.

The process depicted in Figure 1 is single-loop learning. It is one fundamental cycle, and there occurs continuous adaptation to a set of criteria. This is not the case for double-loop learning (Figure 2).

Here an extra circle is added, connoting a revision of the norms and standards from which one operates. Something is learned about the director rather than about reality "out there." In double-loop learning, strategies for effective performance are questioned, and the organizational norms defining effective performance are reflected on (Argyris and Schön 1978, 22). One learns something about one's learning. Some scholars operate with three levels of learning (Coopey 1996), to include learning about the learning of learning. In principle, every learning process can intervene at ever-higher meta-levels, where questions are asked as to the appropriateness of superordinate ideals and pre-understandings (Bateson 1972).

For reasons of simplification, I operate here with only two. This is sufficient to show that every level is relational and not defined in absolute terms. The choice of certain routines, for example, is logically superior to individual routines, but subordinate in relation to the organization's general mission.

An Example of Double-Loop Learning

The office supply company Facit had the idea of becoming the world's best producer of mechanical calculators. This required constant updating and improvement of materials, mechanical operation of the machines, etc. At one time, competition came from electronic calculators. Facit pulled in their sails, economized, cut down, and laid people off. All this is single-loop learning. The double loop comes at the moment when questions are posed about whether they really want to be the world's best producer of mechanical calculators or perhaps something completely different (Nystrom and Starbuck 1984). The challenge is to achieve double-loop learning, before they die in any case, if they begin by defining themselves as a producer of mechanical calculators.

The discovery of the possibility of double-loop learning has given interesting insights and a more differentiated view of learning than is possible within single-loop learning alone. Double-loop learning is holistically transformative for an organization and requires a psychologically difficult departure from familiar practices, values, objectives, and ways of thinking.

The paradox is in fact that skilled single-loop learning can *inhibit* double-loop learning. This occurs, for example, in the case of a competency trap, where an organization achieves marginal benefits through ceaseless, narrow mastery of a certain technology, but where, from a larger perspective, other forms of working would be better (Levitt and March 1988). The organization's existing adaptation damages its long-term ability to adapt (Weick 1976) if it invests all its energy and attention in a certain type of single-loop learning. The organization may place so much emphasis on measurement and supervision of results in a single-loop

---

perspective that it becomes difficult for the employees to ask questions or discover errors. If the organization views every instance of relaxation as a waste of resources, it can become an obstacle that "slack" is used for creativity and experiments (Geppert 1996). A strict result-based system for measuring performance can have precisely the same effect: promoting single-loop learning and preventing double-loop learning.

The QWERTY System: An Example of a Competence Trap

What is the QWERTY system? If you look at the keyboard of a typewriter or computer, the sequence QWERTY appears toward the upper left. The system indicates the placement of letters on the keys, a layout to which we have all accustomed ourselves. Why do we have precisely this layout, seemingly haphazard, and not some other kind? There appears to be no apparent logic in the QWERTY system. If the letters had been alphabetical, it might have been easier for us to learn to type. It is said that the QWERTY system was developed by American typewriter manufacturers to solve a specific problem. The early mechanical typewriters had "arms" with letters on them, which moved up onto the paper when one pressed a key. If one typed too fast, the two arms would interfere with each other and jam because they were both trying to hit the same place on the paper. The problem is made worse when two arms lie close to each other in the semicircular array. To combat this problem, the first typewriters had to be designed to minimize the statistical probability that letters used in sequence in the language would also be located next to each other. It is said that the QWERTY system was the solution to this problem (if we keep to the English language!). After the transition to electric typing technology, there was no longer any justification for the QWERTY system, except that it takes time to learn to type using another system even if it were easier on the fingers and easier to learn. However, we have inherited a system developed on the basis of an obsolete writing technology (and for some of us on a language not our own). When we try to improve our typing speed, it is the QWERTY system that we try to get into our fingers. All known keyboards symbolize an investment in

> the QWERTY system. Even though an alternative system would
> be better in principle, we must continue with single-loop learn-
> ing within the QWERTY system. This is how a competence trap
> works.

Reforms intended to promote a learning process thus have a tendency
to expand outward, perhaps becoming infinite. There is a large market
for these types of initiatives because there is never enough learning (or
never enough double-loop learning). This fits into a cultural ideal of ever-
evolving personal and social development.

Theories of organization do not stand still. The theoretical reasoning
in this chapter so far has been based on the learning cycle and its comple-
ment, double-loop learning.

Some argue that cyclical models of learning are reductionist, implying
an idea of correction or self-correction based on a problematic assumption about correctness. Some forms of organizational learning lead to incorrect conclusions, which are internalized by managers and others in an
organization (Levitt and March 1988). Even such superstitious learning,
however, presupposes an ideal of correct learning as an alternative. Nonaka (1994) breaks with this idea *in toto* and talks about dynamic knowledge creation in organizations rather than learning. Knowledge creation
takes place in a complex interplay between tacit and explicit knowledge.
It incorporates the intentions and enactments of the creator of knowledge
(Weick 1979), and it is sympathetic to self-organization and multiperspectivity. In this more complex paradigm, the concept of learning may lose
whatever sharpness it had, but not the optimism connected to it.

At the same time, interventions in organizational learning—and processes of knowledge creation—cannot be limited to a few well-defined
cognitive processes and a few important decisions. Because learning and
knowledge creation encompass practically every activity and process in
the organization, a vast territory is open for interventions related to the
improvement and development of these phenomena.

Evaluation as a Link in the Learning Organization

The ideal of learning is hard to resist. Organizational learning is a positive and friendly vision, difficult to oppose; an opponent would appear

to be against intelligence generally or personally incapable of growth and development. Organizational learning creates a positive vision by linking together evaluation, learning processes, and change, which promises benefits for both the organization and the individual. From the perspective of evaluation, the idea of organizational learning sends a fine message about how one can incorporate insights into the organizational context for evaluation into positive contributions to practical work.

Evaluators have therefore been eager to acquire this ideal, explicitly or implicitly. This applies, for example, to Michael Quinn Patton (1997), Preskill and Torres (1999), and several participatory evaluators. There have been few qualms, and only minor changes were needed, to rebrand one's evaluation approach as "participatory" or "learning-oriented."

The bridges between evaluation and organizational learning are many. Evaluation is both an occasion and a tool for learning. Evaluation findings can be the necessary, uncomfortable facts that trigger learning in an otherwise rigid organization. In addition, learning-oriented evaluation generates positive effects not directly related to findings—something referred to as "process use" (Patton 1998; Forss, Rebien, and Carlsson 2002). Process use includes gaining self-confidence for the future, improving understanding of the program and its context, becoming more attentive to the views of others, and preparing to engage in a dialogue with external stakeholders. Preskill and Torres (1999, 190) add that increased responsibility, better sharing of work, an enhanced work climate, and more rapid adaptation to change may be among the effects of being involved in learning-oriented evaluation processes.

Whether it is the results or the process of evaluation that is the most critical trigger for learning, the spirit in learning-oriented evaluation often emphasizes the importance of collective sense making to create a feeling of ownership, common understanding, and shared responsibility for follow-up.

What has the experience been with learning-oriented approaches? The general picture offered here (adapted from Dahler-Larsen, 2009) is moderately positive, with some contextual modifications (Nevo 2002). Referring to both a survey and multiple case studies, Cousins (2003, 258) as well as Preskill and Torres (1999, 191) have found that participatory evaluation produced results used both instrumentally and conceptually.

Dahler-Larsen, Andersen, Hansen, and Pedersen (2003) found that evaluation helped raise questions or clarify assumptions underlying the activities of schools and helped reorganize obsolete data-collection practices so that more aspects of school life would be in alignment with the overall mission of the school. Evaluation also led to discussion about the very nature of schools in their capacity as commercial entities, pedagogical environments, political institutions, and deep-seated cultural communities. Especially when schools were understood as communities of values and cultures, evaluation came into confrontation with the identity of the school as perceived by some actors (Schwandt and Dahler-Larsen 2006). Most participants found the evaluation to be a largely positive experience.

Evaluators experienced in learning-oriented evaluation have also identified a number of problems with the learning approach, or at least difficult situational factors that must be dealt with.

An overall problem is that practitioners often participate under what is perceived as intense time pressure (Cousins 2003, 259; Ryan, Chandler, and Samuels 2007). Practitioners have other pressing tasks and often view evaluation as peripheral to their main mission.

Even under otherwise favorable circumstances, the feeling that evaluation is peripheral to their work tends to impede the motivation of practitioners to participate in learning-oriented evaluation. As compensation for time spent in evaluation, supplementary payments, extra time, or other resources are not always a good solution. These payments may be misperceived as pressure, and once the extra resources are spent evaluation activities may not be sustainable (Monsen 2003). This is unfortunate, because the ideal of organizational learning is that it should be continuous. Advocates of organizational learning processes admit that since these processes are all-encompassing and continuous, they can also be time-consuming and sometimes exhaustive (Nonaka 1994, 31).

With limited time and funds, the technical and methodological quality of the evaluation may be in jeopardy. Cousins (2003, 257) identifies a trade-off between technical quality and responsiveness. Cousins and Earl (1995) suggest that if technical quality is not to be sacrificed, a careful division of labor should be established between the participating practitioners and an external evaluator. Although practitioner participation may be extensive, certain technical and methodological decisions are better left to the professional evaluator. Without intensive training of practitioners or assistance from outsiders with methodological expertise, the technical quality of evaluation may be in jeopardy.

Some methodological expertise is still expected of the evaluator, but an engagement in organizational learning vastly changes and expands the role of the evaluator (Levin-Rozalis and Rosenstein 2005).

Critique of the Learning Organization Model

The model has been criticized by organization theorists for ignoring relations of power and conflicts of interest. Instead, the organization is depicted as a collective brain engaged in common cognitive processes. These processes imply a progression; learning is for the better.

On this point, organizational learning often reveals neglect of its overlap with the rational organization model, to which it otherwise sees itself in opposition. The rational organization is also about how to optimize something. The optimization idea has been inherited by the proponents of the learning organization model. It is also constantly proceeding to find the "best" possible way forward. It obtains its self-confidence and optimism from the notion that it is always working for improvement.

Is the idea about more learning always for the better? One can show a conceptual problem with this idea by bringing a critical and reflexive attitude to the idea of double-loop learning, which has been seen as the culturally most progressive form of learning and the "solution" to the problem for organizations that have brought themselves into a blind alley by virtue of their single-loop learning. But what happens after the double-loop learning? More of the same, which amounts to fundamental challenges to objectives, values, and paradigms in an organization. Will there not be limits to how much and how frequently double-loop learning can occur without it being clearly counterproductive?

The question can be put this way because the learning concept is perhaps beginning to dissipate and lose attraction. This is the assertion from those who offer a profound philosophical and cultural critical reflection on our contemporary ideas about learning.

According to a postmodernist view, the meaning of "appropriate" or "worthwhile" knowledge breaks down as learning becomes an all-encompassing codeword for *performativity* (a term for how smoothly someone turns an input into an outcome, devoid of any content or moral meaning; Edwards 1997; Lyotard 1984). Knowledge is "up for grabs" (Edwards and

Usher 2001, 279), and learning becomes still more disconnected from its earlier connotations of rationality, progress, and science-based knowledge. Furthermore, the learner is decentered. Since learning demands flexibility, learning subjects must make themselves endlessly flexible. What were formerly regarded as sociological "havens" (family life, personal character) are now subsumed under the regimes of flexibility and fluidity (Bauman 2000; Sennett 2002).

If a sense of moral integrity is to be maintained, not all aspects of life can be turned into a flexible object of any given learning process. The ever-increasing demand for flexibility in workplaces leads to what Richard Sennett calls "the corrosion of character" (2002). We should also listen to the critical voices of researchers who study "development," a phenomenon close enough to learning in its sociohistorical typicality. Feminist researchers (Klouzal, Shayne, and Foran 2003) maintain that, in the abstract, development only loosely describes the actual destinies of specific human subjects who are sometimes "caught" under specific circumstances in time and place, always bound to personal histories and to specific personal relations. In each situation, development manifests itself as a sometimes ambivalent, painful, and inevitably uneven process. There is no such thing as "free development." The same is true for learning; a general, smooth, and overly optimistic use of the term *learning* is thus misleading.

Nevertheless, some evaluators remain committed to the ideals of learning-oriented evaluation, even if learning becomes more and more diffusely defined, perhaps because it is perceived to be the only show in town. One of the problems with this commitment is that through the optimistic lens of the learning model it is not possible to see more problematic aspects of evaluations as they unfold in organizations. This would require a more analytical and less prescriptive model.

Institutional Organizational Theory

A fundamental point of departure of institutional theory is that the human being cannot understand itself completely. Collectivities keep something sacred that is not up for rational calculation and reflection (Nisbet 1966). Not everything is transparent and reducible to purpose and function. From the institutional perspective, people's worlds are not so transparent for humans themselves, as is the case in the rational and learning-oriented organization models. Life in organizations cannot be understood merely with reference to rational calculation or optimizing cognitive processes. Institutional theory therefore offers insightful possibilities to understand the limitations of the two other organizational models.

Institutional theory emphasizes that cultural constructions such as rituals, myths, language, typologies, norms, habits, values, and routines become objectified, which is to say they appear for people as givens and in this sense become realities in themselves. Even though they are created by humans, they no longer appear to be human constructions (Berger and Luckmann 1966). Institutionalization takes place when the socially constructed character of culture hides itself behind objectification (Castoriadis 1987b). From this moment, institutions have their own logic. Individual persons can come and go, but the institutions continue. They have considerable strength to maintain themselves and the reality they constitute.

Under an institutional logic, there is no guarantee that institutions and their development will allow themselves to be determined by anything functional (Sahlins 1976). This is due not only to the fact that there is much inertia within institutions. As a rule, they change slower than do their environments. Therefore they are often functionally behind the times (March and Olsen 1984, 737). A more fundamental explanation is that institutions in general are initially created from a logic of meaning rather than a logic of function (Sahlins 1976).

The concepts of ritual and myth give us a deeper understanding of this logic of meaning. For some, the concept of ritual covers a special type of action concerning a narrow sacred realm within a given culture. However, one can also consider the ritual as an especially symbolic aspect of social actions generally. Ritual is a symbolic transformation of human experience (Langer 1979, 49). The ritual can be repeated, thus maintaining and confirming a specific kind of understanding of the world. Ritual orders are experiences within a given interpretive framework. This framework is mythical; the ritual plays through mythical themes. A myth is a narrative presenting the socially constructed as given by nature and unavoidable. It naturalizes the social (Barthes 1972). The myth illustrates what is socially defined as necessary and possible: "The mythical consciousness appears as a kind of confrontation with the human potential or necessities" (Gusdorf, cited in Bouchet 1989, 40).

According to classical sociologists such as Durkheim, ritual is primarily to be understood on the basis of its function, namely to reinforce collective identity and enable society to be cohesive, organized around the myth. Ritual "does" something. But ritual also "says" something. Speeches and songs at a festive occasion say something about what the good life is.

What ritual says in a modern, complex, and dynamic society can certainly be ambiguous in meaning (Rabo 1994). There are different interpretations, all according to the participants' engagements and experiential backgrounds, which are increasingly diverse in modern society. The possibility of multiple interpretations affects in turn what the ritual can "do." Under complex conditions, one cannot in advance be certain that the ritual will achieve a practical objective, such as social integration (Langer 1979, 48). Therefore, rituals and myths are much more than simply a confirmation of a collective identity in our society. Rituals in modern society allow something to be shown for various groups of actors, and their differing interpretations can be a part of the game around evaluation. An organization can also perform a ritual with the intention of demonstrating what the organization wants to be toward others in society, even if this ideal is expressed only in vague terms. Ritual and myth thrive on vagueness and ambiguity.

Durkheim, whom many read as a functionalist and integration theorist, has also been read by Boltanski and Chiapello (2007). They point out, with Durkheim, that the web binding a society together is a moral one. This also means that common myths and rituals are sometimes assessed on the basis of criteria of justice and fairness. This is why we can discuss verdicts, hirings, firings, and evaluations. Among them, the question of interpretation of common myths and rituals is therefore a dynamic matter, constantly subjected to tension. Rituals can therefore be seen as an attempt to conjure up certain interpretations, where other interpretations, especially in the modern society, are always possible. Ritual is more processual than a finished result.

Institutions, however, have a number of mechanisms suited for keeping interpretations of reality in place. Seen in Scott's words (1995), institutions rest on regulative, cognitive, and normative pillars. The regulative pillar consists of several sanctions and rewards; there are economic rewards, legal sanctions, and a range of informal sanctions that can be deployed. The cognitive pillar sets down what counts as true, and how truth is to be discovered. The normative pillar defines what it is good and right to do. When institutions function best and operate under normal conditions, they function by remaining out of sight; one takes for granted what reality is and how actions are to be undertaken. In other words, institutions can often hold the regulative pillar in the background, while the cognitive and normative pillars sustain normal life. The mythical delimitation of human potential and limitation is thus already determined by an institutional set-up.

March and Olsen (1984, 1995) state that although much rationalistic and functionalist theory explains human actions on the basis of their consequences—the "logic of consequentiality"—institutional theory operates according to a "logic of appropriateness." Actions are carried out because they are seen as appropriate, legitimate, and worthy of recognition by certain actors in certain situations.

Seen in an institutional perspective, many actions are performed in an intuitive, unreflective, and routinized way. As Durkheim notes, he awakes in the morning and does not contemplate which language he will speak that day. A great many of our organizational actions have the same character. This perspective on action does not mean that institutional theory cannot embrace actors who reflect on their actions. On the contrary, someone who executes an action can read a unified meaning into the action by placing it in a meaningful context. To this context, of course, belongs the idea of how other actors are routinely expected to react to the action (Weick 1979). The decisive aspect, however, is that the end point of the action—what gives the action its characteristic unified meaning—is defined in interpretive terms (Schutz 1973). It is not exogenously given as rational or functional. On the contrary, there are interests, preferences, goals, and functions, to which the actions must be directed, that are socially constructed within a certain institutional framework (Sahlins 1976; Wildavsky 1987).

"Actors" and their "interests" thus do not exist prior to the formation of institutions but are established within these institutions (Berger and Luckmann 1966; Meyer, Boli, and Thomas 1994). An important function of institutions is to equip actors with dispositions to act in certain ways.

In this profound way, institutional organization theory confronts theories that regard organizations and their structures and actions as a result of needs, interests, and consciously calculated choices on the part of human subjects, and thereby also as "optimizations" of something. On the contrary, the most "rational" aspects of organizations, such as plans, strategies, structures, and decisions, are themselves the expression of ritualized myths. The organizations depicted by institutional theory as well as the actors in them are pervaded by norms, values, attitudes, and routines that are common to organizational fields. Such a field is a normative environment held together by agencies (e.g., the state or other larger organizations) that have common interaction and connections and maintain such practices as holding conferences, dealing with the media, using consultants, sending newsletters, recommending particular ideas and innovations, etc. (Powell and DiMaggio 1991, 65).

Strang and Meyer (1994), for example, state that organizational theory has kept an exaggerated focus on microvariation between organizations and ignored the essentially common features shared by organizations in the modern Western world. Isomorphism (common form) is the institutionalists' label for these common structural features.

Organizations do not exist simply because of their technical problem-solving ability. They depend on legitimacy, support, and recognition from their environment. To have adequate internal support, organizations must also tell themselves they are undertaking legitimate and recognizable activities. They gain recognition and legitimacy by linking themselves to those values and expectations found in their social environment.

The common cultural material in modern societies, however, is of a highly abstract character. Modern society is characterized by division of tasks and differentiation. Consequently, it is only quite abstract values that can obtain the status of supporting the collective consciousness (Durkheim 1968). In the modern world, rationality, individualism, legality, justice, and nationalism exemplify such values.

Organizations in the modern world share several abstract, rationalized, organizational models; this "disembodied management" reflects the modern world's widespread myth of rationality. These models are postulated to be effective and valid, cross-cutting whatever specific task the organization carries out (Meyer 1994). Organizational recipes are standards for good management that are taken to be modern, effective, rational, and appropriate (Røvik 1998).

When institutionalists attempt to understand a given diffusion process, they look at a number of issues.

Who are the carriers of the institutional norms (Scott 1995)? All carriers have their own recognition and power. The state sets out a range of rules common to many organizations; international organizations are also increasingly setting general standards. Education disseminates theory and organizational images with many common features. Management training and a comprehensive diffusion of codified and abstract organizational recipes pull organizations in the direction of isomorphy (Sevon 1996, 10; Strang and Meyer 1994). Specialized organizations contribute to creating images of "good practice" within their fields. Consultants travel from one organization to the next, carrying norms, values, and recipes with them.

Røvik (1992) has carried out an interesting analysis of the role of consultants in diffusing organizational recipes. The analysis showed that consultants represent contemporary fashions, and that they import certain standards, values, and understandings of the problems in organizations at the same time that they sell "solutions" to these problems. The analysis also showed that the same solutions are sold to organizations that otherwise have very different organizational characteristics.

This contributes to the diffusion of organizational recipes, such that they are projected as solutions to problems, but those who spread these "solutions" do not have any responsibility for how the solutions actually work when they are applied in practical life (Meyer 1994). Perhaps the lack of responsibility for how organizational recipes actually work helps explain why they are diffused so much in modern organizational fields.

Which norms, metaphors, values, and structural elements, etc. are operative in the organizational recipes? Elements in harmony with modern society's great myths about rationality generally have a good chance of diffusion. Diffusion is promoted if a certain recipe is integrated into general and abstract theory so that it can more easily travel in time and space (Strang and Meyer 1994), that is, if it is expressed as a link in what we have earlier described as modern technological mentality. Furthermore, Røvik (1998) shows that organizational recipes that are oversimplified, optimistic, in harmony with the spirit of the times, and promising advantages to all (both management and the individual organization member) have the greatest chance of survival and diffusion.

Organizational Recipes with Great Diffusion Capacity

Why have *vision, culture, ethics,* and *quality* been some of the most frequently circulated terms in the organizational recipes of the last decade? Because they are positively loaded words that no one could oppose; they are without ideological opposition. For exactly the same reason, they have become so abstract that they mean virtually nothing.

How do diffusion mechanisms operate? Powell and DiMaggio speak of "coercive," "mimetic," and "normative" isomorphism. By forcing organizations (e.g., through laws or other binding measures), several can end up adopting the same recipes. But they will remain foreign elements in the organization as long as they are incompatible with its own cognitive and normative framework. Mimetic isomorphism occurs when an organization imitates other organizations held in high esteem; the prestige might, for instance, come from the admired organization having been innovative and pioneering. As a strategy, however, mimetic isomorphism is uncertain. Others have paid the costs of developing a new organizational recipe, and it might well be that one can perhaps borrow a bit of status by using a recipe that is fashionable. But whether the recipe also works for one's own organization is uncertain. Prestigious organizations certainly have good reason to present themselves as if everything they have done has worked well. In addition, the effect of taking over a fashionable recipe can decline if other organizations do the same. Imitators often discover that the fashion has changed precisely while they think they are keeping up with the fashion. Status and prestige can thus be an especially motivating factor, but also a capricious one. Normative isomorphism is encountered when an organization in fact believes in the new recipes because it takes on the norms and values that support them.

Expressed in terms of the three pillars supporting institutions—the regulative, normative, and cognitive—our hypothesis is therefore that the diffusion supported by the regulative pillar gives the highest certainty that a new recipe will in fact be assimilated, but the least certainty that it also will be integrated into organizational practice. Diffusion with support from the normative and cognitive pillars produces less security that the recipe is assimilated, but a greater chance that it will be used with conviction. The latter, however, is not without reservations; a new recipe is certainly not necessarily coordinated with other already institutionalized elements, no matter whether they are cognitive, normative, or regulative.

To varying degrees, organizations can translate an organizational recipe to their own identity and mode of operation. In Meyer's and Powell and DiMaggio's editions of institutional organizational theory (1994 and 1991, respectively), the main interest is to explain isomorphy, that is, the similarities between organizations. Other variants of institutionalism emphasize that the organizations use rules of editing (Sahlin-Andersson

1996) to adapt recipes to their own identity (Czarniawska and Sevon 1996).

The outcome of diffusion of organizational recipes varies. The normative and regulatory institutional environments around organizations are complex and composite. The same goes for the elements an organization has institutionalized over time. Even if an organizational recipe has been adopted by an organization, not much is known about the extent to which this recipe influences other aspects of life in the organization.

It is not surprising that concepts such as "inconsistency" and "loose coupling" play a large role in institutional theory. There are often contradictions between the elements assimilated because of external coercion, legitimacy, and imitation on the one hand, and the organization's daily operations on the other. The organization's tradition becomes a rich inventory of cultural debris, which can be recycled on numerous occasions. No comprehensive organizational consequences are drawn from the fact that the parts of the organization only marginally affect one another. Loose coupling in an organization means there are very loose connections between top and bottom, between speech and action, between yesterday and tomorrow, between decision and implementation, and between functional parts (Weick 1976).

Loosely coupled systems can respond to the changing demands of a heterogeneous environment, while certain functions and values are retained as stable. The loose couplings are perhaps a more elegant and more advantageous solution to the organization's problems than a tight, integrated adaptation. In loosely coupled systems, change and experimentation can occur locally, without a demand for total, systemic change. A breakdown of particular elements has no total implications. A loosely coupled system is ensured against changes in the demands of the environment because the focus is not on a single value or competence (Weick 1976). Faced with new demands, a loosely coupled organization can often find something in the embedded institutional stock of knowledge (i.e., recipes, scripts, and competencies) that can be polished and recycled. A loosely coupled organization can satisfy this year's changing and symbolically presented demands in the environment without sacrificing key values.

The ideas of translation and loose couplings represent only some of the contributions that have renewed the theoretical image of institutions as being rigid, stable, and taken-for-granted. Through translations, an organization can define its own version of general organizational recipes. With loose couplings, it can live up to inconsistent expectations. But the idea of loose couplings also opens up instability and change. If actors in and around the organization begin to take on organizational promises, even if inconsistent with other statements, norms, values, structural elements, and recipes, then the inconsistencies may become obvious. Elements in organizations that were newly adopted for mostly symbolic reasons may thus have a very real effect in the long run. Røvik (1998) talks about a virus effect. In the beginning, the virus appears to be innocent, but after some time it spreads and the patient is seriously affected.

The inherent contradictions embodied in some loose couplings may in themselves be sources of instability, conflict, and perhaps change. For example, concern for external legitimacy may be so costly and take up so much energy that it undermines an organization's functional effectiveness. Conformity with broader social expectations may be in conflict with the interests of important stakeholders in and around the organization (Seo and Creed 2002).

Recent research in institutionalism has focused on the communicative processes that are necessary to the meaningful and taken-for-granted character of institutions present in a given situation. In discursive institutionalism, there is an important distinction between the background of ideas, norms, and values constituting the institutionalized world on the one hand and, on the other hand, the foreground of discursive abilities of the actors involved (Schmidt 2010). Discursive institutionalism thus attends to how tension in institutions is debated, discussed, and mediated through discourse. Although important aspects of institutions remain taken for granted on the one hand, there are as well translation, loose couplings, and discourses to help us see that institutions are much more than frozen cultural landscapes.

The implications of the institutional model of organization for an understanding of evaluation are so far-reaching that they deserve a whole chapter, the following one.

2 Evaluation in the Institutionalized Organization

Consider two metaphors for an evaluation process. One is the children's train in an amusement park, where kids can take a ride. Since the tracks have already been laid out, the route of the train is predictable.

Another metaphor is the bumper car, where the trajectory is fairly unpredictable; there is no overall plan for where the car is going. What happens depends to some extent on the intentions and skills of the driver, but all the other bumper cars are more important. After each bump, the car goes in a new direction, and the overall image is one of disconnected elements, continuously trying to find their way. Overall planning and rationality have limited effect. In the institutionalized organization, evaluation processes are more like driving in a bumper car than riding a toy train.

We now consider evaluation as an organizational recipe adopted to be a generally accepted ritual legitimized by expectations in organizational environments, but looking more closely at the phases of the evaluation process in the organization. We will look again at the previously presented learning cycle but interpret each of its three points on the basis of the institutional model of organization. The detector, director, and effector are "charged" with norms, habits, expectations, and demands from the surrounding environment, which can give each of them many other tasks and roles than simply being part of a learning cycle. In fact, the moments in a more or less perfect learning cycle are now understood in a completely different theoretical light: as loosely coupled elements in a complex institutional order, each obeying their own logic.

In the detector's place, we find certain ways of knowing that are institutionally sanctioned. With ways of knowing, we aim toward the rules of the game defining what counts socially as knowledge. This often involves assumptions about ontology (what is real), epistemology (what the conditions for knowledge are), and methodology (how we can know in practice; Shadish, Cook, and Leviton 1991), even though these assumptions are, of course, usually implicit to the evaluator. Every institution creates structures of relevance and credibility that regulate its knowledge (Berger and Luckmann 1966), as well as specific procedures for how knowledge is actually created. In modern institutions, systematic investigation generally counts more than prejudice, feelings, or revelations. In medical institutions, randomized controlled experiments count as an especially legitimate form of evidence. In some institutions, self-experienced statements from experienced practitioners traditionally play a great role. Every organizational culture and every institutional regime recognizes particular forms of knowledge.

The director known from learning theory is replaced in the institutional model by heterogeneous values. The organization is dependent on the legitimacy achieved by appropriating itself toward legitimate, dominating values in the environment. But values can be mobilized according to the occasion. They can be more or less explicit, more or less subject to interpretation. The more openly they are formulated, the greater are the hope and social trust they may embody, perhaps without leading to disappointment over lack of goal fulfillment later on.

Instead of an effector, we will speak of organizational prescriptions, routines, scripts, action plans, and policies. Each effector is initiated on institutionalized grounds, primarily because it is seen as legitimate in relation to the expectations of the surrounding society. The legitimacy of each initiative is more important than the coordination between several of them. Neither is it important how well initiatives are coordinated with values and goals otherwise held in high regard. Therefore many activities are also initiated without being coordinated, and without learning taking place from one initiative to the next.

By seeing the learning cycle not on the basis of learning theory but instead by institutional theory, we secure three decisive changes in the theoretical perspective on evaluation.

The first is that the learning cycle is radically opened in relation to the organization's environment. Recipes for values, criteria, and procedures are imposed from various social environments around organizations, and the very idea of evaluation as a legitimate if not necessary organizational procedure is socially constructed and expected by societies that furnish resources and legitimacy to organizations. As an implication, organizations may carry out evaluation not because they think evaluation will help them but because they see no other choice than to evaluate.

The second is that each of the three individual stations in the learning cycle has become normatively charged, or "bewitched," if you will. They are there not primarily because they are helpful in the learning cycle but because they have values, norms, and meanings connected to them. Each can thus have its own institutional logic setting it apart from the other parts of the so-called learning cycle.

The third is that as a result of the normative and institutional charging of these stations, the idea that they are connected by a neat, chronological, and closely connected learning cycle is dissolved. There is no reason to expect that they line themselves up in a coordinated sequence and act neatly in relation to a learning cycle.

In the following, I look more closely at moments in evaluation processes that may have such institutional logics. To reiterate, the central idea is that an element is taken for granted because it is supported by norms, values, and other sources of legitimacy. Institutions work at every moment in evaluation. There is no guarantee of any overall consistency or coherence.

To begin with, the very decision to evaluate may not really be a "decision" that is made in awareness of its consequences. It may be a recipe or ritual that is simply obvious because everybody does it and it appears to be a good thing for modern organizations to do.

Evaluation as an Organizational Recipe

Modern organizations are expected to use information rationally (Feldman and March 1981). It is an integral part of organizational effectiveness to be able to explain one's effectiveness (Gaertner and Ramnarayan 1983). Some kind of procedure leading to production of data is thus necessary.

Even before results are present, evaluation may have great institutional or organizational advantages. Tasks that organizations carry out are sometimes complex and uneven, and they are associated with risk. Risk is a result not only of unforeseen events in organizational environments but also of the inability of any organizational structure to handle all the problems as well as the uncertainties of organizational technologies. Since all these risks are substantially difficult to describe or measure, there is a need for a socially acceptable way to report that things are under control. A procedure that absorbs risk and signifies that things are in good hands is in great institutional demand. Evaluation is such a procedure.

Adopting evaluation as an organizational procedure may also be a way of gaining time or some internal freedom in an organization, because things are apparently under control as they are being evaluated. In the meantime, reforms can be promised, and maybe things will improve more or less by themselves.

In addition, even if no such cynical calculation is made about the benefits of evaluation, it is an attractive organizational recipe because it signifies good management and because all good organizations today are evaluating. For all these reasons, evaluation may be a wonderful institutional gift even if it is not unwrapped. (Or perhaps especially if it is not unwrapped. In fact, if it is unwrapped, then problems begin to appear.)

To a large extent, evaluation is therefore generally consistent with the normative and cognitive pillars of much institutional life in modern society. Increasingly, it is also mandated by the regulative pillar. This happens when some evaluation system is required by law, when evaluation is built into administrative policies, and when foundations support grantees only on the condition of subsequent evaluation. If regulators do not know what to do, they often install evaluation systems.

The Choice of Evaluation Topic

On first sight, it may appear as if evaluation includes all types of activities and programs. Everything seems to be subject to evaluation nowadays. However, this is not correct. An evaluation selects an evaluand from a larger political, organizational, and social context. The choice of evaluation topic sends a double signal: the topic is important enough to be evaluated, but also it is problematic enough to deem an evaluation necessary (Weiss 1998, 313). The choice of evaluation topic cannot be institutionally neutral.

At a given time in a society, there exist ideas and institutions that succeed in evading skeptical considerations and investigations. As a classical historical example we can cite the French strategic reliance on a defense fortification, the Maginot Line. Even though it had some notorious weak points, which would be revealed in all their historical clarity with the Nazi invasion, French society was unable to observe these weak points and rectify them. The Maginot Line was such a critical feature of French national self-understanding, and its possible collapse so inconceivable, that they were unable to consider it in objective, practical terms. Today as well, policies related to national security seem to escape rational evaluation, even if there is an evaluation mania in society.

Institutionalized elements in a society that are given great historical, ethnic, national, or cultural significance can avoid evaluation. But the boundary between the evaluable and the non-evaluable is pushed when a culture favorable to evaluation expands. In Denmark, an evaluation project was recently initiated of the peculiar Danish Folk High Schools, a group of nondegree-granting residential schools with a tradition of popular enlightenment and citizen education that address themselves to adults on a voluntary basis. According to a new law, the schools should evaluate their activity according to their own declared value statements, as a kind of compromise between entirely avoiding evaluation on the one hand and subordinating the schools to modern demands for efficiency on the other. But a certain spell was broken; the school could begin to see itself as not necessarily having value simply by virtue of its existence. The values and tradition were no longer an entirely secure defensive fortification against ideological challenge. Instead, evaluation could question some of the fundamental assumptions that held the schools together as cultural communities (Schwandt and Dahler-Larsen 2006). They now had to be evaluable.

Institutions in society that are given great power and authority can often entirely avoid being evaluated. As mentioned above, there is very little evaluation of the military or the judiciary. In Denmark, military education is the only publicly funded education that does not have to publicize its evaluation results.

In addition, there are more generalized modern ideas, recognized and legitimate, if not institutionalized, that can succeed in avoiding evaluation. A current example of an idea that is seldom evaluated is New Public Management. Even though NPM has helped to spread the norm that public inputs must be evaluated, the ideology of NPM is remarkably exempt from evaluation, as noted with some degree of sarcasm by Pollitt (1995).

On the other hand, evaluation can also be stimulated by a new, socially recognized interest in a specific topic. A norm-based interest in the psychological working environment, fibromyalgia, crib death, stress, or incest cannot be explained solely on the basis of objective manifestations of the existing problem. For these problems to have public attention, there needs to be some institutional focus on the new labels or typifications describing them (Beck 1992). Once new diagnoses are institutionally recognized, society can focus on solving problems related to these diagnoses, and on evaluating the interventions.

Selective attention to various potential evaluands continues down through the institutional hierarchy. In a development project for Danish charter schools (called "free schools"), the schools could themselves choose the evaluation topic. They all selected something about the general life of the school beyond specific educational activities. A Christian school, for example, found that children of non-Christian backgrounds did not feel entirely welcome at the school compared to children from Christian backgrounds, something the school deemed surprising and instructive (Dahler-Larsen et al. 2003). Nevertheless, none of the schools chose to pose evaluative questions regarding the pupils' scholastic performance. On the basis of the schools' identity and self-understanding, this topic was not self-evident, as it might have been for other schools.

Certain organizations can have particularly explicit rules for what should be the focus of their evaluation work. An internal evaluator in one county was asked to evaluate a program with intense difficulties in management and organizational cooperation, but he was told at the same time that in this county it was not possible to attribute poor evaluation results to a specific manager in writing. There were institutional limitations on where the focus could be on this point.

In other words, before evaluation can have any effects (positive or negative), institutional filters and limitations often contribute to regulating which topics are focused on in the first place. Even though evaluation attempts to operate transparently and systematically, imposing its own logic of clarity, the choice of evaluation topic is not necessarily so transparent. An organizational interest in evaluation topics can come and go, for institutional reasons.

Evaluation Criteria

The institutional environments in which modern organizations live are large-scale and sometimes global. Certain evaluation criteria circulate in worldwide landscapes of ideas. There is a remarkable isomorphism in the types of institutionalized evaluation criteria. Commercial organizations must compete for market share; nations must increase their gross national income per capita. In a number of policy areas, nations must also score well on specific indicators defined by international organizations. Indicators describe, for example, tertiary enrollment or the number of Ph.D.s per 10,000 citizens. Indicators also describe the placement on international league tables on the basis of standardized student assessments. Such figures are evaluation criteria to the extent that they are used in statistical operations to achieve judgment about how well the policies of different nations work. Their function is to create a common international, institutionalized, socially constructed space in which policies can be defined, conceived, and evaluated (Lawn 2007). The evaluation criteria operate with the assumption that they represent values and goals valid for all.

From an institutional perspective, the world is full of such organizational fields with already institutionalized evaluation criteria. In a more specific analysis, it is useful to make a distinction among the value catalogue in an organization, program goals, and evaluation criteria.

By the term *value catalogue* we refer to the totality of fairly abstract visions of what is good for collectivities or individuals (Nisbet and Perrin 1977). These values are not translated into specific norms or standards. An organization is often bestowed with legitimacy precisely because of its commitment to such broad values. In modern society, most organizations remain committed to the values of rationality, justice, and individualism (Meyer 1994). However, the total catalogue of values often consists of multidimensional, or partly contradictory, elements. It is especially public organizations that must justify themselves with reference to normative vectors that, if not balanced against each other, would pull the organization in opposing directions. Compromises between them must be made in particular situations (Harmon and Mayer 1986, 34).

Because of the complexity of the value catalogue, there are often many control systems in and around an organization. The systems sometimes partly overlap or are redundant. They represent different parts of the total value catalogue, although a strict division of labor among them may not be explicitly made. The balance may be dynamic or situation-dependent.

Most organizations do not have the time or energy to focus on the whole value catalogue. Still, to be legitimate the organization must display some sort of commitment to the whole value catalogue. A common strategy in organizations, especially public ones, is to express several values as abstractly as possible (Edelman 1977; Eisenberg 1984). This sometimes secures broad acceptance and protects against critique. Another approach is to deliver long lists of value statements without explaining how they should be prioritized.

These strategies can sometimes lead to confusion, capacity problems, or both. They may surface when program goals have to be chosen. Goals are more concrete and specific than values, and they cover only a narrow segment of the total value catalogue. Program goals are expected to guide the behavior of those implementing the program. Even at the level of program goals, confusion may arise. Goals can be more or less clear; two contradictory goals can be stated. Confusion may also arise as to whether a goal was really a goal or just an argument to support a particular activity.

Sometimes organizations focus on a few goals at a time and implement programs correspondingly. Each program covers a goal representing a small segment of the value catalogue in turn. This is sometimes called "sequential attention to goals" (March and Olsen 1976).

Sequential Attention to Goals at the University

During my early years as university lecturer, the highest goals were those connected to achieving international publications. Then came some years with a political focus on the quality of teaching, which seemed to have been forgotten. Systems of evaluating teaching were installed. After some years, the interaction between the university and the surrounding world was a major issue; we should document external grants, interaction with journalists, and dissemination of our research results to the public. In recent years, a new indicator system for publications is being implemented. Thus there has been sequential attention to goals attached to different parts of the overall value catalogue of a university. It is a good thing that I have not put all my energy in any of the goals that were institutionally highlighted at a given time. The time span of a particular goal is much shorter than the time span of my whole life at the university. Today the most troublesome minister of research and his ideas are gone, but I am still a university professor.

Is a goal really a goal? It is sometimes institutionally useful to maintain some ambiguity and confusion among values, goals, and criteria.

Is a Goal Really a Goal?

In Denmark, there was a debate after the invasion of Iraq about whether identification and elimination of Saddam Hussein's weapons of mass destruction was really a goal. Danish government officials claimed that although the assumed presence of such weapons was an argument to support Danish engagement in the war, it was never really an official goal. If it were a goal, it could be converted into evaluation criteria. A potential evaluation, which in fact never took place, could demonstrate negative results. Hence, it might be useful to say that it was never really a goal.

Program goals are sometimes ambitiously stated in an application for funding. After the funding is received and the money is spent, and evaluation is necessary, it is tempting to modify evaluation criteria so that they are less ambitious than the goals. Even better is the situation where there were no goals, only broadly formulated values.

Although faulty memory in this situation may be beneficial to those implementing a program, the problems of interpreting goals or appealing to broad values are not always a result of cynical speculation. Sometimes, political values or goals are stated in ambiguous terms because this is the only form in which they can be backed up by a political majority or a dominant coalition of interest groups. Somewhere down the implementation chain, in the organizational machinery, it is necessary to interpret values and goals and translate them into practical activities (Baier, March, and Sætren 1986).

Especially in these situations, delineation of specific evaluation criteria may be complicated. Evaluation criteria are those used to make actual judgments about the merit, worth, or value of the activity. The criteria constitute an interpretation of what the goals might mean, unless goals are very clearly stated. If there is a gap between goals and evaluation criteria, the detector in the so-called learning cycle does not send information on the wavelength defined by the director, and the learning cycle becomes incomplete or broken.

In the rational organization and in the learning organization, it is often assumed that the differences among the value catalogue of the organization, the program goals, and the evaluation criteria are insignificant. It is assumed—or hoped—that what is important is what is measured. In the institutional model of organization, the differences among values, goals, and criteria are substantial. Each follows its own organizational logic. Each of them can draw the organization in a different direction. Evaluation criteria, in contrast to values and goals, must surface empirically. In a sense, evaluation is the critical moment when something very specific and operational must be said about what constitutes a good organization, program, or activity. The moment of evaluation therefore triggers a particular organizational game different from the game that is played when values and goals are espoused.

Theories of measurement take varying standpoints on these issues. Some approaches assume that what is important in the value catalogue can more often than not also be measured as an evaluation criterion. Relevance does not necessarily imply lack of measurability (Kelman and Friedman 2009). Others argue that the logical move from the metaphysical and imaginary (values) to mundane measurement of something empirical always implies an interpretation of the phenomenon in focus, and thus a potential change of meaning (Bereiter 2002).

Those following the rationalistic school argue (not very rationally) that once we start measuring things, even invalidly or incompletely, our measurements will improve over time. Institutional theorists would maintain that a gap—or at least confusion—usually remains between values and goals on the one hand and evaluation criteria on the other.

One of the genuine tensions in selecting evaluation criteria is that some constituents in or around the organization may insist on maintaining the broadly based value catalogue, or highlight those values that are difficult to measure or that are not measured in a particular evaluation.

In many human service organizations, such as aid groups or those working in social services, it makes sense to appeal to broad human values because concrete results are difficult to specify or measure (Hasenfeld 1983). At the same time, there may be legitimacy to be gained by carrying out an evaluation regardless of criteria, or by demonstrating loyalty to particular evaluation criteria mandated by important institutions in the organizational environment.

For example, sometimes outputs are far more specifiable and measurable than outcomes, but organizations are expected to measure their outcomes because this makes them look more effectiveness-oriented. A common solution to this problem is just to relabel classical process variables or output variables and begin to call them outcomes.

The tension between what is measured and what is claimed to be measured, or between broad goals and narrow criteria, will remain through the entire evaluation process. For example, in evaluation of public sector services, the criterion of user satisfaction has been around for years, legitimized by consumerism in society. When this criterion is institutionalized as an evaluation criterion, it is both appropriate and inappropriate at the same time, because many public services are not designed to please consumers. This is true, for instance, for much public sector regulation and inspection, which is largely control activity rather than service delivery.

As another example, a municipality wanted to evaluate activities aimed at assisting the unemployed. User satisfaction was believed to be an appropriate criterion. However, some of the activities for unemployed people were designed to make life so miserable for the participants that they would be motivated to exit the unemployment rolls and pursue an education or get any kind of job. It was believed that well-off and fairly privileged young people would sometimes choose unemployment benefits, even if they were in fact able to work or be enrolled in an educational program. The unemployed people's *dissatisfaction* with the unemployment system was thus a criterion of success, because it would help push them out of the system. Nevertheless, user satisfaction was chosen as an evaluation criterion, perhaps because it was the most common and taken-for-granted criterion at that time.

Consultants play an important role in transporting and selecting ideas of evaluation criteria. Røvik (1992) has shown how consultants bring with them particular criteria and standards to analysis of public sector organizations. These views are often imposed regardless of the type of institution at stake. Hospitals, schools, and agencies are all seen as organizations with the same generic types of problems, and they all become objects of consultative treatment according to the same fashionable recipes for good modern management.

In addition, what is practically measurable within a given institutional order sometimes influences or defines what qualifies as evaluation criteria. Various arguments sometimes work together, such as legal arguments, managerial concerns, fashions, or "practical arguments," to define what is institutionally possible in an organization.

Simple Things Can Be Difficult to Measure

In Denmark, a large-scale indicator project is being developed for all major diagnoses and services in the hospital sector. In birth clinics, midwives come and go because of their work hours and the many tasks they have to attend to. However, expectant mothers find it confusing to relate to new persons during this stressful time. An important criterion from the perspective of the mother-to-be is whether it is possible to be served by the same midwife through the entire birth process. This never qualified as an evaluation criterion in the indicator project. Despite the enormous amount of complicated measurements taking place in health care institutions, birth clinics offered no way of measuring the number of midwives involved in a birth process. Institutionally, conducting this measurement was simply out of the question.

Research has added to our understanding of institutional logics by influencing how organizations choose evaluation criteria over time. Meyer and Gupta (1994) suggest that if a set of criteria are used over time, the ability to discriminate between good and bad evaluands is likely to diminish. This is true, for example, when competing programs adapt themselves to the evaluation criteria in the same way. At that point, it is necessary to shift criteria, if discrimination between good and bad programs is to be maintained. In this sense, the choice of evaluation criteria is not independent from the choice of previous evaluation criteria. We are far from the ideas of the rational or the learning organization, where criteria spring out of predefined goals or the subject matter itself. In the institutionalized organization, the measurement regime has a logic of its own. This observation changes our understanding of where problems reside in measurement; they are hidden not just in methodological problems but in the measurement system itself.

Because of the broadness of value catalogues and because of the many institutional logics influencing the choice of evaluation criteria, evaluators often find themselves confused about exactly which evaluation criteria should be applied in a given evaluation. The evaluator must make priorities and interpretations. Here we are reminded of Karl Weick's idea (1979) that people often make sense of activities after the fact. Goals and purposes are reconstructed as part of a subsequent sense-making process. Polemically, one can say that one reason this is often an enormous task is that the goals and purposes never existed in the first place. Activities unfold as a part of a large institutional logic. The same is true of interpretations of these activities. There never was a master plan that needed to be "reconstructed." From a rational or a learning perspective, it is difficult to explain why it is so problematic to establish suitable evaluation criteria. From an institutional perspective, however, the sources of this difficulty become more obvious. Evaluation itself is due to a normative expectation that evaluation must be done. It is evaluation that requires a clear explication of goals and purposes, because they are necessary for exact delineation of evaluation criteria. Before evaluation, the institutionalized organization was marred by inconsistencies, paradoxes, hypocrisy, and lack of rational goals. Perhaps it lived happily under these circumstances. Evaluation criteria are sometimes controversial because they insist on transparency in a situation where some degree of opacity might be normal, and even functional too.

Precise delineation of evaluation criteria has political and institutional implications. The probability that a given activity will be judged a success or failure depends, of course, on which part of the value catalogue the evaluation criteria seek to represent. This is especially true if potential evaluation criteria corresponding to some parts of the value catalogue are negatively correlated. If there is a trade-off between legality and speed in processing administrative cases, a given program cannot score well on both. In many public sector organizations, the value catalogue is so diverse and multidimensional that at least some of the potential evaluation criteria might be negatively correlated. This is often forgotten when clear and unambiguous evaluation is called for. However, it does not follow that the broad value catalogue has disappeared. It is still supported by institutional arrangements, and it continues to create tension in the selection of evaluation criteria, or further down the road in the evaluation process because of the discrepancy between narrow criteria and broader values.

Broad Values and Narrow Criteria

In Danish universities, researchers are expected to make publications. In the era of evaluation, the quality and quantity of publications are expected to be incorporated in a monitoring structure that has financial consequences for the universities. How the publications are to be counted constitutes a major problem. A new system is being developed in which researchers in all areas take part in defining high-ranking and not-so-high-ranking types of publications. Each type is then attributed some points, which can later be used to allocate financial resources to the universities. No matter how publications are counted, the system is criticized for being narrow compared to the many values and goals researchers must take into account. Most high-ranking journals are in English, but why should Danish taxpayers not want publications in Danish? How important are books compared to articles? At the end of the day, is it really better to count publications than to read them? It will take us too far to discuss the potentially disturbing effects on publication patterns here. Suffice it to mention that a number of problems flow from the discrepancy between the many concerns and values researchers seek to live up to, and the narrow criteria that any evaluation system of bibliographic counting must be based on. The institutional choice of such criteria perhaps raises more problems than it solves.

According to their roles in an institutional arrangement, various stakeholders such as politicians, managers, professionals, and clients typically emphasize different types of criteria (Scott 1992, 342–362). They also have differing interests in presenting an activity as a success or a failure. If they commit too early and too clearly to a given evaluation criterion, they may lose a basis for argumentation because their expectations about how the evaluand actually scores on that criterion may disappoint them, even if they continue to hold a particular positive or negative view of the evaluand. This is especially true for politicians who are held publicly accountable.

For this reason, they may suspend their commitment to specific evaluation criteria until they see the actual evaluation results and what difference they are likely to make. If the results are institutionally discarded and not used, who cares about evaluation criteria? In this sense, evaluation criteria may be loosely coupled to goals, and stakeholders to criteria, and outcomes of evaluation to evaluation results.

Understanding these connections helps explain why some evaluators feel they have a large amount of discretion—sometimes too much—in defining evaluation criteria. Only after the evaluation unfolds, and it is seen how little difference it sometimes makes, do evaluators really know how much or how little influence they have.

An evaluation of chiropractic treatment, for example, demonstrated effects in terms of reduction of pain and better functioning in daily life activities for patients. The program had no demonstrable effect on the amount of sick leave or the consumption of medicine. The terms of reference for the evaluation stated that all these criteria should be included, but not how they should be prioritized. Rhetoric and political factors determined whether the program was a success.

Two Sets of Criteria in Two Institutional Regimes

It has been a long-standing ambition in Denmark to establish a set of common, accepted standards for quality measurement of the performance of all hospitals using evidence-based criteria. Various pilot projects have offered their solution as to how to construct such an evaluation system. In one project, an American joint commission was asked to accredit a Danish hospital. It operates with about 360 criteria for accrediting hospitals in many countries. In another project, recognized representatives for professional groups were asked to select a maximum of 10 relevant indicators for each diagnosis. The two projects came up with very different criteria, reflecting the institutional regimes under which they each had evolved. In the accreditation project, many criteria focus on the question of risk and security. These are important topics for the joint commission because accreditation has historically been necessary in order for insurance companies to insure privately financed hospitals in the United States. These institutional considerations were exported to Denmark, even though the context here differs, since hospitals do not have to convince anyone as to whether they can be insured. In the indicator project, the indicators were specific to diagnoses and therefore professionally based, together with the fact that they were also formed by the rules defining these criteria. It was determined, for example, which professional groups participated in the groups, how fast the indicators should be made, that there must be only 10 indicators, that existing data should be used to the greatest possible extent, and that patients should not be represented in the process (Dahler-Larsen 2006b).

Evaluation Criteria Can Become Goals in Themselves

Once evaluation criteria are established, institutional logics unfold. People react to them as something formal, real, and given. If evaluation criteria are repeated in several evaluations, and if sanctions follow from them, the institutional mechanisms connected to them will be more forceful.

Messick (1989) is said to be the first to introduce the idea of consequential validity; that is, the validity of a test system should be judged on the basis of its practical consequences. The issue is perhaps mostly researched in educational testing, where test scores become goals in themselves and teachers "teach to the test" (Doran 2003; Greenwald, Nosek, and Sriram 2006; Jennings and Rentner 2006; Jones and Olkin 2004; McNeil 2000).

There is a rich literature in evaluation on how evaluation criteria have unintended or constitutive effects (Dahler-Larsen 2007; Munro 2004; Smith 1995; Tilbury 2004; van Thiel and Leeuw 2002). We will get back to this fascinating topic in Chapter 7, but the present chapter looks specifically at the *organizational* aspects of evaluation systems.

It has been a classical observation for more than 50 years in organization theory that behavior is affected by what is being measured, regardless of whether the measurement is dysfunctional for the organization (Jasinsky 1956; Ridgway 1956). Sometimes even "surrogate measures become reified and guide future performance" (Lipsky 1980, 52).

A Tragic Example: Dead Bodies as an Indicator of Success

During the Vietnam War, the reported number of enemy dead was used as an indicator of success by the U.S. Department of Defense. The institutionalization of this criterion had tragic consequences. It ignored costs and casualties on the American side, and it paved the way for a biased conception of the strategic development of the war as well as for escalating commitment without any real victory in sight. On top of that, there were serious reliability problems, because military units were encouraged to report high numbers that in fact could not be checked.

There are three specific organizational mechanisms that help explain how evaluation criteria can become goals in themselves.

The first has to do with the organizational meaning of evaluation criteria. The criteria become objects of sense making. People interpret what they do in light of official evaluation systems. They also measure their own status in combination with how they score on organizationally defined indicators. In this process, people compare themselves to others or develop subcultures having their own norms and values in opposition to official organizational criteria (van Maanen and Barley 1984). Whether competition, coordination, or conflict best describes life in the organization, interpretation of the meaning of evaluation criteria is thus an inherently collective and interactive process.

The second mechanism is reporting systems. Once groups, departments, and organizations learn that upward and outward reporting refer to evaluation criteria, it becomes important to score well on these criteria. They become goals. This organizational mechanism is powerful even if those who report do not consider the criteria fair, relevant, or valid.

The third mechanism is reward systems. If the score on evaluation criteria constitutes a basis for organizational rewards, then symbols of achievement, cleverness, status, and personal worth begin to circulate in the organization. This is also true for people who think that particular evaluation criteria may lack fairness, relevance, or validity. They have to accept that people who live up to the criteria think they are smart and may conspicuously reveal the material and symbolic rewards they have won. In institutional language, there are no longer just subjective interpretive differences attached to the evaluation criteria; instead, their effects become objectified. This strengthens and sustains them as being organizationally relevant.

Overall integration of these mechanisms takes place through institutionalization. As organizations repeat and routinize particular evaluation criteria, transport them through reporting, and solidify them through rewards, they become part of what must be taken as reality.

One important effect of a particular evaluation criterion, no matter how apparently small or insignificant, is that it may attract attention and thereby influence the overall balance in the total set of overlapping, conflicting, or redundant control systems in an organization. For example, when evaluation of teaching was introduced at my university, the younger teachers were confused about its importance. The most important promotion decisions were still made by external review boards, which looked almost exclusively at research publications. The exact status of evaluation of teaching remains unclear, although most teachers are aware that it is not a good idea to consistently score low on these evaluations for a long time; university management will have to take measures, such as identifying factors behind the low scores and consulting with the teacher. Consequences are not completely known, and some remedial measures can continue for a long time. Whether students' assessments of one's teaching have any substantial influence on important formal decisions at all is still unclear. Yet the students' informal influence on a teacher's motivation, self-confidence, reputation, etc., may be substantial. Unclear consequences of this sort constitute an important part of life in the organization.

At the same time, the fact that control systems in public organizations are often multiple, overlapping, and partly contradictory prevents a specific new evaluation criterion from having a revolutionary effect on behavior in the organization. Sometimes the effect of an evaluation criterion will be limited by other concerns, such as informal collegial or professional values, which prevent the rational, managerial evaluation system from running amok. In this respect, the success of an official, managerial evaluation criterion may depend on values not recognized by rational, managerial ideology. Organizations may tacitly hope that people behave responsibly and are driven by professionalism and good conscience, even if the official monitoring system recognizes only a few performance indicators.

Following Messick's idea of consequential validity of a test (1989), a simple question can be asked before introducing an evaluation criterion into an organization: How will the organization perform if the criterion is used as a goal? Suppose X occurs if we have quality; does it also mean that we have quality if we achieve X (Tilbury 2004)? Can we use X as a goal and then be on the safe side? Do we have a good university if the students are satisfied? Do we have the right number of caesarean sections if all clinics conform to the national average? More often than not, this simple test will reveal substantial weaknesses in the practical effects of a criterion that is institutionalized.

Evaluation Design

Apart from evaluation criteria, the evaluation design itself may be institutionally determined. As with evaluation criteria, the design may help define what is seen as valuable, real, and important in an organization.

The timing of evaluation plays a role, especially if evaluation is repetitive. Images of activities and their effects vary, depending on the rhythm of evaluation and on the time span of data collection within an evaluation.

Timing of Evaluation

Soon after completing a harsh marathon run in the sands of Western Jutland, one of my friends was given a questionnaire about how well the run was organized. Not surprisingly, his need for water and rest made it impossible for him to take the evaluation seriously.

When students are asked to evaluate teaching, the results will depend on whether the evaluation form is distributed before or after the final examination.

Like budget periods, evaluation periods may be characterized by hectic activity right before the deadline, with the period after the deadline being spent on preparing the organization for normal life. There is a tendency for people with low status to be evaluated with short time intervals (such as trainees in hairdressing), whereas people with high status are evaluated only rarely or not at all (such as queens after a lifetime on the throne). For this reason, the timing of evaluation is indicative of the status of the people under evaluation. Evaluation meta-communicates about status. Meta-communication is communication about communication; it refers to the relations between those involved.

Meta-communication is also involved in the choice of the unit, agent, collectivity, or institution to which evaluation results are attributed. For example, research can be attributed to universities, schools, departments, groups of researchers, and individuals. The informal networks that are crucial for many researchers are often not coterminous with the formal units for evaluation that are recognized by official organizational structures (Christiansen and Hansen 1993, 18–19). If, however, the evaluated unit begins to behave as someone who must be evaluable, then the evaluation design has been instrumental in constituting particular social patterns of coordination and cooperation, if not solidarity. In this sense, evaluation meta-communicates about who should be held responsible.

The probability of institutional recognition of some form of evaluation design or evaluation data is not equally distributed across institutional landscapes in time and place. Some forms of evaluation, such as the randomized experiment or statistical indicators, are more recognized than others in particular institutional or professional milieus. They may be chosen not because they are always methodologically superior but because they are institutionally legitimized as the proper method of conducting an evaluation in a given time and place. Once chosen, a particular design allows only those aspects of reality that are portrayed through the lenses of the design to enter into the evaluation's account of reality. Randomized experiments, for example, tend to favor the idea of causal links over other aspects of reality. In this view, there is a preference for those interventions considered to be instrumentally isolated from the context in which they work. If randomized experiments are institutionally sanctioned as a superior evaluation methodology, but practically or ethically impossible for some reason, it becomes difficult to achieve useful evaluative data, because all sources of information other than the controlled experiment are a priori regarded as illegitimate. For this reason, there is often an institutional struggle to have other designs fully or partly acknowledged. Both the European and the American evaluation associations have recently been engaged in debate about whether it is reasonable to institutionalize randomized controlled experiments as a golden standard for all evaluation designs.

Institutional aspects of evaluation design also surface in the debate between advocates of qualitative and quantitative methods. The latter have had a general privilege in modern, rational culture. Quantitative data have been regarded as "hard," although they are not hard at all; what is hard is perhaps their social implications (Hastrup 1993). Sometimes it is institutionally sanctioned that this and that group of stakeholders need to be heard so they are interviewed. This part of the evaluation is decided on even if it does not fit into an overall plan for an evaluation design.

Qualitative evaluators have done a lot to pave the way for qualitative evaluation in various institutions. Among other things, they argue that qualitative methods, under the umbrella of understanding, relevance, participation, and dialogue, help solve the ever-evolving problem of the lack of utilization of evaluation. Quantitative evaluators argue that only more rigorous research will ameliorate the utilization problem. The fact that two contrasting methodologies offer to solve the same problem suggests that the problem of evaluation impact lies not in methodological technicalities but in the legitimacy with which it is bestowed. In a given situation, the credibility of any method is a social construction that depends on the organizational and institutional setting as well as the specific configuration of stakeholders all with their own institutional bonds (Weiss 1984).

In this way, evaluation designs and their credibility are deeply institutional phenomena. The same is true when a combination of institutional factors in a particular situation make it difficult to remain loyal to one design or type of thinking only—or even to choose a design altogether.

To Be Evidence-Based . . . or Evidence-Based?

A large public health campaign aimed at increased awareness about skin cancer resulting from sunburn. Based on existing evidence from international studies, the campaign recommended, among other things, that people should wear hats, respect the siesta, and use sun screen. A survey carried out by the young, dynamic, and evidence-based campaign team documented that the use of hats and siesta were negatively correlated with sunburn, and sunscreen was positively correlated with damage to the skin. Of course, this could be explained. People who use sunscreen are intentional tanners who want to spend more time in the sun than other people. On the other hand, how can we know that intentional tanners do not apply sunscreen inappropriately and get a false sense of protection when they use sunscreen, even though it has been directly recommended by the campaign? How much evidence should the campaign collect until it will no longer recommend sunscreen based on evidence?

The question was a real trap for the campaign, because it needed the legitimacy flowing from evidence-based medical research and public health research. The solution for the time being for the campaign is a classic trick described by institutional theory (Meyer and Rowan 1977). The campaign makes a *promise*. It will remain true to evidence, and more research is needed in the future.

Institutional Support for No Evaluation Design

A foundation supports security and safety in society in many ways. More than 200 initiatives are supported in a given year. For example, the foundation finances health promotion campaigns, puts up life-saving equipment on beaches, and gives away life jackets to sailing clubs. Members of the board want to know that good initiatives in their local area, even small and uneven ones, are supported. They also want a report on the effect of what the foundation does every year. (*Effect* is a fashionable word in the social environment of foundations these days, and so is *reporting*.) The administrative staff is uncertain about how to measure the effect of 200 initiatives, all of different scale and embodying various types of support depending on the context. So the foundation calls in an expert (another classical institutional strategy for gaining legitimacy under uncertain circumstances). The expert suggests making program theories about how the interventions work in certain situations. Self-evaluation by grantees is considered, but they often have no evaluation expertise at all. Initiatives to strengthen the evaluation capacity of grantees, such as a handbook and support from the foundation staff, are considered next. The expert has no magic bullet; for each proposal, limitations in time, capacity, or expertise block the way forward.

It is decided that each grantee should write a couple of lines about the estimated effects of the grant. It will then be up to some staff member in the future to summarize these 200 uneven statements into a passage in the annual report to the board. This approach hardly qualifies as an evaluation design, but it is the best answer the foundation can come up with under the present institutional circumstances, with a demand for more than 200 disparate projects and a conclusion about the effect of all of them. The subsequent annual report mentions no effects. But in it the foundation can say it has initiated an initiative about describing effects.

Benefits of Nonuse

The analysis described here of the institutional logics involved in evaluation themes, evaluation criteria, and evaluation designs offers hints as to why an evaluation may not always be perceived as relevant or important. People involved in the evaluand may in their daily life be focusing on those segments of a value catalogue that are not well represented in the particular evaluation. Sometimes an institutionalized and approved evaluation design is not regarded by all as the best one. Sometimes the choice of a convincing and consistent evaluation design is not possible.

Furthermore, an evaluation will produce its own institutional effects going beyond just checking the evaluand. Evaluations may make a point, and set an example. These effects may create anxiety for those who think the criteria are inconsistent with important parts of what they hold as the value catalogue.

For this reason, it often makes sense for organizations not to take evaluations too seriously. Given a broad value catalogue, no organization can afford to regard a small set of evaluation criteria as representative of the entire set of the organization's goals and values. The expectation among some evaluators that each evaluation be used directly and instrumentally will often be frustrated. Among the most frequent ways to undermine the importance and usefulness of an evaluation is to claim that it is methodologically inadequate, that the evaluator has misinterpreted the terms of reference, or that the evaluation does not respect the true mission of the organization. All these arguments would be consistent with predictions made by an institutional theory of organization, and all of them could explain why evaluations lead to resistance or are followed by inaction. The organization can live with a loose coupling among goals, values, and evaluation criteria, but *only if it also maintains a loose coupling between the evaluation and its use.*

A common strategy in organizations is to promise reforms (Meyer and Rowan 1977). Evaluation can be a functional alternative to action, delaying the promised reforms, which are always on the horizon. Promises can also be made that more evaluations will take place in the future. Any of these strategies can be combined with sequential attention to goals. There is limited attention and cognitive capacity in the organization, so little is done at a time. Support from various stakeholders can be mobilized at different times, as the organization moves around in the overall catalogue of values. If this is cleverly done, the most attention-getting stakeholders will be served at the right time, while other stakeholders look in the other direction or receive promises that their concerns will be attended to later.

Routines Are Difficult to Change

It is often difficult to terminate an existing program. Start-up costs are high, institutional inertia is substantial, and it is easier to see the benefits of existing activities than of future ones. The literature on the difficulties of program termination (de Leon 1978) draws to a great extent on institutional arguments. Existing programs are supported by identifiable stakeholders with interests in the programs, and by such resources of theirs as staff, computers, positions, networks, and information.

Even whole institutions can display a surprising ability to survive, either from their use of inherited symbolism (such as the U.S. cavalry) or from redefinition of their purpose. For example, schools and prisons have rarely been dismantled, but their purposes are constantly "reformed" (Foucault 1980). When preservation of the royal family as an institution in my country, Denmark, is debated politically, one of the arguments in favor of royalty is that it is not a threat to the political system; it has no real political or constitutional function. It is quite interesting that the lack of function of an institutional arrangement can be used as an argument for its continued existence, but so it is.

Even if evaluations sometimes demonstrate serious flaws in some activity, program, or institution, institutional arrangements may hinder dramatic change. Sometimes incremental change is the only option. Or reorganization or training is preferred to genuine termination. Or low-ranking employees are fired rather than senior members of staff. Since younger people are often more innovative, the rate of change is slowed down through this strategy. A degree of inertia or stability is inherent to the very idea of institution.

Almost No Activities Were Terminated

In a survey of 601 evaluations in Danish municipalities (Dahler-Larsen 2000), I found out that only 0.7 percent of the evaluated activities were terminated. Many activities were legally mandated, and many were obviously difficult to terminate for a number of reasons. Maybe the evaluations were used to improve services. In any case, the small termination rate is entirely consistent with how institutional theory views most organizational activities: they are routines.

Action Programs Are Set in Motion Regardless of Evaluation

Many action programs are institutionalized in the form of organizational recipes adopted because they are legitimate. Sometimes they come with particular problem definitions. There is often a simultaneous growth in the socially available attention to a problem (stress, battered children, harassment) and the organizationally adopted recipes to ameliorate the problem. Organizational recipes are often implemented by people who have an eye for precisely the type of problem to which the recipe is supposed to be a cure. Depression and impotence (or at least some fabricated ways of registering these phenomena) became more frequent after pharmaceutical firms began to market drugs to fight these illnesses.

Sometimes a whole institution embodies an ideology that views the world in such a way that what is needed is more of what the institution has to offer. For example, the World Bank produces myriad reports about economic sectors in dozens of developing countries, but they are said to be strikingly similar in the sense that they tend to diagnose problems such that a need occurs for the type of initiative the World Bank is ready to support or finance. Some organizations are skilled at combining an ideology with an interpretive device that makes the organization highly operational. They institutionalize a view of the world that justifies action programs that in turn legitimate the existence of the organization and the "solutions" it offers.

There is a close relationship between what organizations do and how they view problems. As Foucault says, prisons are dependent on crime. They do not eliminate crime.

In an organizational setting, the repertoire of actions that are possible is often limited, which is due to legal, financial, or cognitive restrictions. The choice of instruments in policy settings depends to some extent on policy styles in various countries (Howlett 1991). In many health care settings, if a new problem arises the immediate response is "Let's make a campaign."

Some initiatives in organizations are legally mandated. Others are fashionable recipes, which are institutionally legitimate, promote optimism, and mesh with contemporary fads. Still other initiatives are supported, as we have seen, by inherent organizational ideologies. As a consequence, organizations initiate action programs for reasons other than their purported technical superiority. The vast majority of activities in an organization would never pass a formal evaluation.

Many people in organizations are intuitively aware that this is how organizations work. They assume that when an evaluation process begins, there is little likelihood that the result will have any effect on core activities. They respond to evaluation in a similar fashion, knowing that before the evaluation is over many initiatives will be started for reasons other than rational evaluation results.

One frustration connected to reform in public organizations is that new reforms are often imposed before previous reforms are fully implemented, not to mention evaluated.

To sum up: new initiatives in organizations are justified on a number of normative and institutional grounds. These new initiatives are often not the result of evaluation. For these institutional reasons, learning cycles in organizations are inherently incomplete, and many people know this intuitively. This is why their enthusiasm for evaluation is limited, especially if they are not evaluators.

Reactions to Evaluation in the Institutionalized Organization

It is possible to distinguish various organizational strategies of handling a new organizational recipe such as evaluation—rejection, decoupling, taming, and colonization. In rejection, the organization simply refuses to have anything to do with a particular recipe. This may happen if the recipe is seen as completely inconsistent with fundamental organizational values, or if nobody in the organizational environment insists that the new recipe is important or legitimate. If some part of the organizational environment suggests or demands that a new recipe such as evaluation be adopted, and where the institutional logics embedded in values, goals, and action programs make it impossible to comply with its requirements, decoupling is an appropriate response. Taming is used to describe a situation where the organization more seriously integrates evaluation into its practice, but only in a moderate form, largely consistent with traditions and existing procedures in the organization. Colonization happens when a new organizational recipe such as evaluation is integrated into organizational routines and fundamentally reshapes daily practice. Although it may be difficult to draw sharp distinctions between, say, decoupling and taming, and between taming and colonization, the set of categories as a whole remains a useful frame of reference for understanding how organizations respond to a demand for evaluation.

In the preceding sections, I have used a number of institutional arguments to suggest that decoupling is a likely, and sometimes even functionally appropriate, response. It may be beneficial for organizations to be hypocritical (Brunsson 1986). Organizations may adopt evaluation because it is modern or because they have to, yet refuse to allow the results of the evaluation to have any serious consequences for the organization's long-term goals or routine operations. Decoupling is likely when evaluation is fashionable but considered functionally inadequate or unnecessary compared with the totality of organizational values, concerns, structures, and procedures.

On the other hand, whether decoupling, taming, or colonization occurs remains an empirical question. We can imagine a number of factors leading to revision of the decoupling hypothesis. One such factor is the role of internal evaluators. If they are hired or appointed, and they self-identify as such, they may see themselves exposed to a "show-me test" (Mathison 1991), which challenges them to prove their worth. It is unbearable for internal evaluators, and for their reputation in the organization, to have their work constantly rendered useless or forgotten because of broken learning cycles and inconsistent institutional mechanisms. Someday, some people will find out, and they will react to hypocrisy as they see it. This phenomenon, called the "virus effect," can be grasped within neo-institutional theory itself. Even if new organizational recipes are adopted because of their external legitimacy or for purely symbolic reasons, they can have considerable effects once people who implement them start taking them seriously. After some time, the organization will be infected—hence, the virus effect. Expressed in more theoretical terms, a seemingly symbolic gesture in an organization is never purely symbolic. It is through symbols that we understand the world and act on it, and there is no sharp theoretical distinction between the symbolic and the real world (Tompkins 1987). Although the organizational world may be contradictory and inconsistent, it does not follow that ritualistically imported recipes have no real consequences. If this is the case, we should look for taming and colonization more seriously instead of just assuming decoupling.

Another hypothesis has to do with how the external world's demand for evaluation is formulated. In the early versions of neo-institutional theory, Meyer and Rowan (1977) predicted that most organizations would simply avoid evaluation to protect their productive core and their central values. When Meyer and Rowan wrote their famous article, evaluation had not yet manifested itself strongly as a fashion in managerial circles and among consultants. It was not yet a part of widespread New Public Management ideology, or a conventional part of policy making in most countries (Furubo, Rist, and Sandahl 2002).

If, however, the demands for evaluation from governments, funders, and other important partners in organizational environments become more frequent, more articulate, and more supported by financial or legal requirements, evaluation will be adopted by organizations in ways that do not permit simple rejection, or even decoupling. If educational evaluation (for example, in the form of accreditation) is coupled with the financing of educational institutions, or with the very survival of these institutions, we can predict that evaluation will play a much more invasive role than suggested by Meyer and Rowan (1977).

A key point here is whether evaluation is supported only by cognitive and normative institutional pillars, or whether it is also promoted by the regulatory one. More raw power may be invested in the latter. If the regulatory pillar is involved, we can expect the sanctions following from evaluation (or lack of evaluation) to be stronger, but also expect the local meaningfulness of evaluation to be less clear. Evaluation will be adopted because it is necessary—what Weiss, Murphy-Graham, and Birkeland (2005) call "imposed use." This will increase the organizational propensity to keep evaluation disconnected from everything else the organization is interested in. On the other hand, if imposed use of evaluation also makes tight, institutionally defined demands on evaluation processes and how they are used, it will be more difficult to keep evaluation loosely coupled from the rest of the organization. (In this way, how organizations can "use" evaluation depends on the specific character of the demands made by organizational environments. This is an important theoretical insight, which we will fully explore in the second part of the book.)

More work thus needs to be done, and perhaps organizational energy expended. Some of the newest contributions to discursive institutionalism would still argue that when there is pressure and tension, such as what arises from external evaluation demands, some space is open for the discursive abilities of the actors involved. It is up to them to explain (or explain away) what they think needs to be done with evaluation, given the institutional circumstances.

Critique of the Institutional Organization Model

The stable and taken-for-granted character of institutions is a central part of the logic in institutional theory. The strength of the institutional view is that it shows organizations are not nearly as rational as they claim to be. Organizations do what organizational environments expect of them, and fairly isomorphically. Norms, values, scripts, procedures, and rituals constitute the fabric of organizational life. Organizations mostly do what is in accordance with the cultural environment in which they operate, even if it leads to ineffectiveness or inconsistency. Evaluation is thus chosen as a ritual because it is an accepted recipe for good modern organization. All the components in this ritual may be derived from different norms and values, even if they do not amount to a coherent evaluation process.

However, the focus on the nonrational, taken-for-granted, and sometimes rigid character of ritualized institutional life is also the weakness of the institutional model, at least in its classical version where it tends to ignore differences, ambiguities, struggle, change, and controversy.

For this reason, institutionalists themselves have gradually revised the model, allocating more conceptual space to translation, tension, loose coupling, virus effects, and contradiction as sources of change. There is also a new focus on how debate and reflexivity over institutional norms can be promoted through communication and discourse. Others would argue that the institutional model loses its sharpness and explanatory power when it hands over more space to local meaning production, negotiation, and discourse. Perhaps the model also comes closer to the real tensions, debates, and struggles over the various purposes and uses of evaluation processes in real life.

With respect to evaluation and its outcomes, the institutional model suggests that evaluation may lead to colonization, taming, or hypocrisy. But it is not specific enough to suggest which of the outcomes occur under which particular conditions.

Radical critics of the institutional model would argue further that institutionalists overestimate the importance of norms, values, and meaning and underestimate the importance of differences in power and resources between the actors involved.

Finally—and this is our most central critique of the institutional model in relation to evaluation—human beings in general are not institutional puppets, and neither are evaluators in particular. Many good evaluators know already that the world in which evaluation takes place is fragmented, inconsistent, and disorderly. But just because knowledge is produced under strenuous social circumstances, it cannot be concluded that the producers of knowledge do not seek some sort of order and rationality (Longino 2002). Evaluators and others associated with evaluation will develop responses to organizational inconsistency and hypocrisy in evaluation when they meet it. In the remainder of the book, we therefore remember not only the insights from the institutional perspective on evaluation but also that some evaluators are cunning, and as well that the field of evaluation has a long tradition for responding to challenges posed by the social, political, and organizational contexts in which evaluation operates, and to which it allocates an increasing amount of attention. Still, the institutional model is promising because it reminds us about the importance of the larger social, cultural, and normative climates in which the demand for evaluation is shaped. The institutional theory of organizations, however, describes how organizations are depending on their environments, but it take these environments as exogenous. It is not a theory about the creation of these environments. To find such theory, we must turn to sociology.

The Organizational Formation of Evaluation

It is time to sum up the two preceding chapters on how organization as a form of social order imposes purposes, ideals, and formats on evaluation. We should remind ourselves that the models of organization are just that: models, not reality itself.

Yet from the perspective of each organizational model, evaluation is formed differently because it fits into varying images of organization. In the rational model, evaluation must be clearly based on preexisting organizational goals, and evaluation processes must be predictable. This model has been criticized for its overly rationalistic and sometimes inhumane assumptions. The learning model has attracted many evaluators because it is seen as more humane and because it is full of optimistic promises to both individuals and organizations. As we have presented it here, however, it does embody a particular pre-understanding of how learning processes should be conceived and structured in organizations. To be successful, it also requires comprehensive and sometimes time-consuming and exhausting efforts as the concept of learning becomes more and more diffuse and practically everything that happens in organizations has to do with learning or dynamic knowledge creation. The learning model continues to be optimistic; perhaps it does not offer the necessary analytical insights to understand the many reasons for which the learning paradise is so difficult to make real in actual organizations.

The institutional model has provided a fresh and alternative perspective on evaluation. It explains why evaluation is sometimes in social demand even if there is little desire to use the evaluation instrumentally. Evaluation is fashionable, or required, or expected, even if there is little interest in actually learning from it. The institutional perspective accounts for why many evaluation processes consist of elements having little to do with each other; for example, evaluation criteria, the timing of evaluation, and evaluation designs sometimes obey differing normative logics that make it difficult to connect the parts into a coherent evaluation process. The institutional model also explains why organizations hesitate to use evaluation results.

The key to the institutionalized organizational explanatory mechanism is that organizations seek legitimacy and embody taken-for-granted norms, values, and expectations. The institutional model invites a deeper sociological analysis of evaluation.

We must therefore turn to those factors in society that may affect the legitimacy of and institutional support for evaluations. We must analyze the societal environments to which evaluating organizations respond. Hence, in the second part of this book we now turn to a sociohistorical analysis of the role of evaluation in society. Only after that analysis can we fully understand the sociohistorical significance of evaluation as an organizational phenomenon.

PART 2

A Sociological Analysis of Evaluation

3   Modernity and Its "Evaluation Imaginary"

Many evaluators and evaluation theorists view evaluation as a self-evident rational, conceptual, and methodological tool. However, it is a mistake to believe that this tool has emerged *ex nihilo* (Schwandt 2002, 60). On the contrary, the rise of evaluation has several historical, social, and cultural prerequisites.

Only in modern society have we come up with the idea of evaluating. Even though the emergence of modern society long predates the rise of evaluation, we must include the history of modernity in order to identify the sociohistorical conditions of evaluation.

This strategy is, of course, also in line with the conclusion of the organizational analysis in the first part of the book, which is that organizations to a large extent do evaluation in ways that reflect norms, values, and expectations in the social environment around them.

In this part of the book, I analyze the changing society around evaluation more systematically. I present three outlines of sociohistorical stages of modernity corresponding to different social conditions of evaluation over time. The three outlines, as we have seen, are entitled modernity, reflexive modernity, and the audit society. Each headline describes a particular set of social imaginaries. (Imaginaries are configurations of meanings that define a particular society.)

Each of these imaginaries corresponds to what Thomas Schwandt calls "evaluation imaginaries." These imaginaries define the purpose and meaning, if not the whole taken-for-granted character, of particular forms of evaluation in light of the society in which they unfold. In this way, it is possible to talk about the norms and values evaluators sometimes un-knowingly bring into evaluation as a result of their societal embeddedness.

The three outlines can be understood simply as epochs, each with a beginning and an end. A better understanding, however, can be obtained if one views the three outlines as social historical configurations that have dominated in various times and situations but that also overlap.

None of the earlier epochs has simply disappeared. Each subsequent epoch is in dialogue with earlier ones and repeats some of their tenets. Each of the three outlines, in its own, new way, takes up something that has been touched on earlier. Yet every imaginary is characterized by its own constellation of questions and answers concerning key problems of evaluation. Even so, no answer is perfect. Although our present-day society exemplifies the audit society and its neorigorism more clearly than other epochs, it is unfinished and full of tensions in its evaluation imaginary. As such, our contemporary society is not exhaustively described by just one single determinant (Morin 1992), and the social-historical conditions underlying evaluation in our present-day society are not one-dimensional. Our contemporary society comprises various layers of a complex social-historical formation. The principles characterizing different epochs are thus at any moment in tension with one another (Beck 1992).

Let us first examine modern society as a general precondition for evaluation being able to emerge at all. Subsequently, Chapters 4 and 5 will be devoted to reflexive modernity and its consequences, while the audit society and its evaluation are dealt with in Chapters 6 and 7.

Modernity: Progress Through Knowledge

Modern society is characterized by an attempt to replace tradition, prejudice, and religion with rationality and autonomy—the two key components in the modern configuration of ideas (Castoriadis 1987a). Rationality entails that human beings should not subordinate themselves to illegitimate authorities who function on the basis of prejudice. Autonomy entails people's responsibility to govern themselves.

Rationality and autonomy follow from a decisive modern discovery: the order of society is determined not by transcendental forces but by society itself. Modern society distinguishes itself precisely by bringing the category *society* out into the open as a perspective on common life (Wagner 2001). *Society* denotes strong and complex forces at the common collective level that are decisive for people's lives but are nevertheless man-made. It is therefore our own responsibility to master society, if we want to take responsibility for our common destiny. Nothing should be beyond critical democratic questioning, since a modern democratic society is one that seeks to institute itself explicitly and self-consciously (Bouchet 2007, 4). A modern political mentality is one that has unlimited interrogation as its ideal (Bouchet 2007, 7).

Consequently, modern mentality finds it difficult to accept anything as inevitable. It wants to fix things. A technological mode of thinking is thus an essential trait of modern mentality. From a technological perspective, the world—also the social world—is viewed in principle as consisting of abstract components whose relations can be manipulated according to the purpose (Berger, Berger, and Kellner 1973).

Nothing is more illustrative of modern mentality than how this world-view is accompanied by abstract systems for measure and weight (Nisbet 1980). Earlier anthropocentric and sociocentric units of measurement—a foot, an inch, a stone, a day's journey, the harvest season, etc.—were connected to intuitive human experiences and with the local community's forms of interaction and rhythms of life. With the introduction of the metric system, and coherent scales for distance, volume, and weight, the abstract and strongly productive idea arose that very different conditions can be measured in the same way across local human experiences.

Modernity seeks to prevent metaphysical ideas from being collectively obligatory any longer. The modern project becomes one of mastering nature and the social order alike, with reason and autonomy as guiding principles. In the modern, one imagines that a disengaged subject can deal with the world instrumentally, while society is dealt with as its atomized, abstract, and manipulable components (Schwandt 2002, 61, refer-ring to Taylor 1987).

At its base, evaluation carries the idea that the quality of human activities, projects, and institutions can be measured on abstract scales. Evaluation carries with it the idea that the evaluand (the object of evaluation)—what-ever it might be—can be divided and decomposed into inputs, activities, programs, criteria, and outcomes so that it can be managed and reorga-nized. Without this specifically modern cosmology, evaluation could not have been invented. Without this cosmology, it would not have been pos-sible for modern evaluation to establish itself as one way in which people obtained access to their own society's organization (Bouchet 2007, 12).

Society's exposure of itself based on the ideals of autonomy and rationality, however, is not without a significant amount of ambiguity. The modern idea of where society is headed could not be divorced from metaphysical ideas, even though society did precisely this in its own self-understanding (Vattimo 2004). No sooner was the category *society* laid bare than its space was filled with ideas about progress. It has been too difficult for society to imagine how little the opening to itself might really be determined. Therefore, society continues to cling to myths. In modernity, one of these is the myth of progress.

The grand narratives that have legitimated the modern project practically all coalesced around narratives of progress. They have had variations on the theme of the rational or the human subject's elevation or emancipation, or most recently, in more vulgar visions, the human subject's future in wealth (Cooper and Burrell 1988; Lyotard 1984).

The ideas of progress have been inclusive enough to be able to communicate quite diverse definitions of the content and meaning of progress at the individual and social levels. Common to them all, however, has been a narrow linking together of the timeline and a better life. Time contains mechanisms for improvement, be they technological, organizational, or political. Visions of progress have thereby resembled teleological religious ideas more than modernity would admit. Their function was to promote excitement, enthusiasm, or confidence in the projects of the modern social formation.

Evaluation, which is genuinely modern in its ambition, therefore has an optimistic belief in the possibilities of improving society via rational data gathering and decision making.

Various schools of thought conceptualize the link between evaluation and societal progress. One of them is the experimenting society, in which evaluation has a key role to play in determining which of the alternative strategies—based on experimental or quasi-experimental data—solve social problems most effectively (Campbell 1988). This and other ideas related to how evaluation could make society better were conceived within a cleverly elaborated division of labor between political decision making and evaluation, which was designed to transform rational knowledge directly into rational collective decision making.

The overall ideological framework around the idea of societal progress through evaluation was soon to be criticized for its emphasis on social engineering, its almost superstitious belief in the power of scientific methods to produce unequivocal results, and its reduction of political questions to technical questions (Albæk 1988). Studies of political systems, decision making, bureaucracies, and organizational logics soon made it obvious that the official political machinery did not behave according to the assumed rationalistic model (Albæk 1988; Weiss 1983). Early rationalistic evaluation was also criticized for its elitist perspective and for producing statistically complex results that were irrelevant for people working with concrete programs. It became clear, as it did generally in social critiques of modern society, that society is a result of complex human action, not of deliberate and transparent design (Bouchet 2007, 13). In evaluation, it was found that the underlying assumptions about the ease of transmission of knowledge into rational decisions were apparently too naïve. And the very idea of knowledge as objective and generalizable has been questioned. Instead it is acknowledged that it is naïve to attribute to knowledge the kind of certainty and indebatability that characterized the religious beliefs of earlier epochs. If scientific thinking had attempted to usurp an authority similar to earlier religious authority, it had made a mistake.

Many contributions to the field of evaluation today are reflections of the difficulties evaluators encounter with the early modernist mandate for evaluation, that is, improving society through objective knowledge and rational feedback. Whether they slightly revise the mandate or revolt against it, this mandate is still a part of the history of evaluation.

In recent years, however, the general social and cultural context around the mandate has changed.

Significant changes have occurred in the social imaginary (Castoriadis 1997). Progress is no longer considered certain. It has lost its status, and the collapse has brought many other consequences (Nisbet 1980).

According to the Italian philosopher Gianni Vattimo (2004), the diverse interpretations of the world we find today are a sign that the West's dominant narratives to itself about progress (and thereby the West's narrative of its own sovereignty in relation to other worldviews) have been mythical. The narratives of progress, though asserting that they were abandoning myths, simply perpetuated them. Instead, says Vattimo, each perspective must acknowledge its "weakness" as being but one of several ways of interpreting the world, whereby none has an indisputable metaphysical foundation. There is no certain direction for so-called progress any longer, and the very idea of progress has been weakened and replaced by ideas of development and change. Development and change appear to be everywhere, necessary, and unavoidable, but they do not attract the same enthusiasm and excitement about the future as does the idea of progress.

Things have come to this point because of a complicated interaction between the two main categories in the specifically modern configuration of ideas: autonomy and rationality. When the desire for autonomy is expressed through institutionalization of rational, modern forms of control and organization (political systems, bureaucracies, markets), these systems quickly show themselves to have their own counterintentional logic. Their reproduction becomes a goal in itself, and they entail much more than could have been imagined by any type of ideal brain constructing such systems. A classic theme in sociology is that manmade institutions can become reified. They can turn against their creators. The modern epoch has brutally demonstrated the power of manmade institutions over people. For a sociologist such as Zygmunt Bauman, the Holocaust is illustrative of a potential lying within the modern rational organization as such. Hence, the entire modern effort toward autonomy and reason is always ambiguous.

This has to do with the fact that the instruments people choose in the name of autonomy and rationality make possible the institutionalization of new "false gods," which at the same time deny the very principles of autonomy and rationality (Bouchet 2007). As such, the modern, rather than being a completion of a predetermined project, is a continuing struggle with and against modernity's own ideals.

The theme of how our own modern institutions can turn against us is a continuing *leitmotif* in this second part of the book. Constructions dominate us. On the other hand, they are our own constructions. We will highlight that modernity has opened up a thematic that can be called "society," which even though it is seldom consciously designed is constantly the object of critical interrogation and of human construction. Even though modern society's own ambitions about rationality and autonomy have shown themselves to be naïve, modernity has opened up a space from which we cannot escape, one that evaluators have struggled with from the onset of modernity and something we continue to struggle with. The space from which we cannot escape is a society made by human beings.

To do evaluation is to live in that space. To do evaluation is a form of "societizing." We now look at how evaluation has developed in a society that is specifically modern.

Evaluation Proceeds Gradually from Progress to Reflexivity

Evaluation contains certain fundamentally modern features. It requires that the social relations in society be laid bare as something that can be investigated and debated. Evaluation is a child of the rationalist belief that by the use of reason, including systematic investigation, we can rationally improve societal arrangements.

It demands at the same time a certain view of the social as something ordered. Evaluation would not be possible without a typically modern form of mentality that Berger, Berger, and Kellner (1973) call "technological," meaning that certain areas of life under evaluation are viewed as abstract evaluands that can be controlled, ordered, regulated, or "fixed" through manipulation of relations between abstract components.

Evaluation transports modernity. In the understanding of many people—including that of the evaluator herself—the evaluator is often a kind of torchbearer for modernity. With the help of modern reason (methods, data, processes), the evaluator can help sweep away ignorance, prejudice, traditions, and inefficient practices (Schwandt 2002, 16).

Many factors had to be in place in modernity, however, before evaluation could emerge. One obvious factor is the development of social science methods and analysis, and the education of a sufficient number of people qualified to collect and analyze social science data. But many years were to pass from the development of such methods and their introductory application to elucidating social problems (Easthope 1974) and to their application as instruments of *planned social intervention*, an object that becomes really important only with initiatives such as the Great Society programs in the United States in the 1960s and in Europe with the expansion of the welfare state. Developments in the European countries, however, were uneven in scope and speed. The degree of social consensus varied, as did the size of the welfare state as well as the role of scientific research in the development of the welfare state.

It is only when social science methods are used for the investigation of modern, consciously planned, and targeted initiatives that modernity begins to systematically use research methods on itself. This occurs in close connection with the emergence of visible ruptures in faith in progress. It is with the recognition that political interventions intended to produce progress in fact may fail that we realize the need for evaluation. When evaluation is in place, it calls attention to the fact that progress does not come automatically. As large public interventions are investigated, it becomes easier to identify mistakes and shortcomings than successes. Hence, there is a close association between early evaluation research and the emergence of the field of implementation research (Winter, in Dahler-Larsen and Krogstrup 2001). The entire spirit in implementation research is to show a range of factors that have impeded political initiatives from achieving their ambitions.

In its early phases, however, evaluation research succeeded in maintaining essential modern characteristics. As a significant example of this, we can mention the idea of the use of experiments and evaluation as part of policy making. One of the leading spokesmen for this ideal was Donald T. Campbell, who wrote important papers on this topic in 1969 and 1971 [1991]. (They are also discussed in a much revised edition in 1988, and in an interesting way by Shadish, Cook, and Leviton 1991.)

The idea here is that different types of intervention are tested experimentally. Their effect is assessed with the help of randomized experiments. Subsequently, there is a rational application of this knowledge in policy making.

The idea entails a closely respected division of labor between politics and evaluation (Albæk 1988). In politics, collective societal goals for interventions are established. Decisions are taken as to which policies will be carried out. In this process, evaluation helps to determine the effects of alterative interventions with the greatest possible certainty.

In ideal terms, the experimental society carries out reality testing of its own interventions. The ideal of the experimental society builds on a range of assumptions about social rationality and about the ontological characteristics of the world in which the interventions take place. Among the key assumptions here:

- Political determination of goals is relatively uncontroversial and basically stable before, during and after the experimental period.
- Alterative interventions are proposed in a cool, rational fashion on the basis of a genuine interest in determining which of them work best.

· Questions of impact are the most important ones to pose (not questions of value).

· Knowledge based on the experimental design will show itself to be more important and relevant for decisions about an intervention than other forms of knowledge.

· Participants in a program have their primary role as subjects of the intervention and thereby for an experiment, the purpose of which is to collect socially useful data.

· Implementation of evaluation unfolds cool and rationally, with the primary purpose being collection of knowledge about the potential policy consequences of the evaluation.

· Evaluation creates relatively certain and uncontroversial knowledge that most rational persons would accept.

· Indicators have stable meanings and are equally valid before, during, and after an experiment.

· Knowledge from a randomized experiment is generalizable.

· Rational extension and application of knowledge from a randomized experiment is uncontroversial.

Each of these applications has subsequently been called into question (Albæk 1988; Shadish, Cook, and Leviton 1991; Vedung 1997). In the eyes of its subsequent critics, the idea of the experimenting society represented a particular methodological monopoly of knowledge; a negligence of multiple, alternative points of view; and consequently a technocratization of policy.

It is characteristic of the modern character of this early ideal in evaluation, however, that proponents of the ideal of the experimental society saw themselves as supporters of free, open, and democratic decision making based on the highest possible degree of knowledge collection, regarded as free of prejudice (Campbell, cited in Shadish, Cook, and Leviton 1991, 136–138). Society should be marked by scientific ideals with reference to open critique and willingness to change otherwise-established favorite theories when confronted with experimental and other evidence (Campbell 1988, 295). There must be public access to documentation of how societal decisions are made (ibid.). Campbell himself, in several statements, was skeptical as to the practical possibilities for realizing this ideal.

Nevertheless, the ideal of the experimenting society is inherently modern: "It would be honest, committed to reality testing and avoiding self-deception and defensiveness, open in its self-representation to the world" (Campbell 1988, 295, cited in Shadish, Cook, and Leviton 1991, 140).

In this sense, the ideal reflects a continuation of the key modern visions. The only breach in the modern faith in progress that this ideal shows is that social interventions do not automatically succeed. If they evince some degree of success, they must be subjected to an experimental test before they can be made into a general policy in society. Even the relatively reliable theories of interventions are potentially falsifiable. In this way, Popper's idea within the philosophy of science—that every theory is empirically falsifiable—is both a strong rationalist idea and a declaration of the opportunity for a more reflexive way of thinking, as soon as it is diffused as a societal principle of control.

In sum, although the experimental society is still a rationalist society, progress is no longer entirely automatic. It must be qualified by evaluation, which, however, must also contribute to solving precisely this task. The practical and ethical controversies here will nevertheless continue to spread.

In this section, I describe the evolution of the critical discussions of the rationalist ideal, of which the experimental society is an expression. I organize the discussion along the four main domains of evaluation theory: utilization, the evaluand, knowledge, and values. I have chosen these four domains because, as we saw in the Introduction, they are common elements in most contemporary definitions of evaluation. In practice, these domains have provided arguments that mesh with each other.

Sociologically speaking, one can understand the discussion as how modern evaluation struggles with its relation to its modern ideals. These reflections of modern evaluation upon itself unfold in parallel with the gradual societal transition from modernity to reflexive modernity. The full-fledged version of the latter is unpacked in the next chapter.

Utilization

Very early in the development of evaluation, it was observed that serious problems arose in having them used instrumentally (Weiss 1972, 11; Weiss and Bucuvalas 1980).

Instrumental utilization of the immediate results of evaluation is limited because politics does not function nearly as rationally as is assumed. Preferences are unstable. There are many decision makers, dispersed among various institutions with differing points of view. Each category of decision makers has its own interests and expectations for evaluation depending on the maturity of the program (Shadish, Cook, and Leviton 1991, 336). Together, they constitute a "policy-shaping community" (Cronbach et al. 1980) rather than one societal agency for rational policy making.

The decision makers have many official and unofficial interests in public activities. Their desire to undertake special efforts (or not undertake them) may be based on completely different grounds from the evaluation's results (Weiss 1990).

This problem generated several interesting reactions. The first is to undertake evaluation only in situations where a preliminary calculation demonstrated that it is sensible. The second is to have patience with the fact that evaluations are used in ways other than purely instrumental. The third is to work more consciously to reform evaluation so that it is directed toward instrumental utilization. Let us examine these issues in turn.

"Evaluability assessment" refers to the process of deciding whether it is sensible to evaluate under given circumstances. The idea of evaluability assessment is practical and useful in trying to determine when to evaluate and when not to. However, evaluability assessment is not nearly as popular today as it was in the 1970s (Smith 2005, 137). In fact, the emergence and decline of evaluability assessment is a significant development in the history of evaluation.

The main question in evaluability assessment is not whether evaluation can be done, but whether it is the most rational thing to do in light of the costs and benefits (Shadish, Cook, and Leviton 1991, 237). Evaluability assessment highlights several factors relevant to an evaluand and the evaluation situation, factors that should be clarified before evaluation is undertaken (Shadish, Cook, and Leviton 1991, 237; Rossi, Freeman, and Lipsey 2004, 137). For example:

· Is there a clear description of the program? If not, resources are better spent on clarifying the program than on evaluating an unclear one.

· Is the program fairly well implemented? If a preliminary assessment already reveals that it is not, it may be wiser to improve implementation of the program before evaluating it. The ability to draw clear conclusions about the impact of a program improves dramatically if implementation problems are addressed so that the risk of pro- gram failure can be reduced.

· Is there a good program theory? If not, it is better to clarify the logic of the program and perhaps improve it before undertaking an evalu- ation.

· Are there well-described and realistic goals? If not, the outcome of the evaluation can be predicted without evaluation, and resources for evaluation can be saved.

· Are relevant data within reach? If not, an evaluation effort would be unreliable, if not impossible.

· Are opportunities to improve the program identified? If intended users of the evaluation appear unwilling or unable to use the results, there is no sense in commencing an evaluation in the first place.

In essence, the idea of testing a program's evaluability is highly rational. It assumes that evaluation can be deliberately applied in those situations in which it can make an instrumental difference. Evaluation should be carried out only when appropriate. Factors affecting the appropriateness of evaluation are fairly straightforward, as we have seen. However, perhaps precisely because of the assumptions of strict rationality, the popularity of evaluability assessment has declined since the 1970s (Smith 2005, 139). The waning interest in evaluability assessment also reflects the interests of evaluators, who would find it disadvantageous to decline a lucrative evaluation contract—which they should do if their evaluability assessment leads to a negative result (Shadish, Cook, and Leviton 1991, 237). But the very idea of evaluability assessment constituted an interesting discovery relevant to the sociology of evaluation, namely that maybe evaluation was not a perfectly rational solution to all problems in all situations. The idea was even codified in a procedure called evaluability assessment. For evaluation to continue to grow, though, this idea had to be kept under strict control—or even better, forgotten. In a sense, it is therefore good for the evaluation industry that the idea of evaluability assessment has declined since the 1970s.

The reactions of the evaluation toward the problems with (lack of) instrumental use took other directions.

Weiss's reaction to the observation of limited instrumental use was to have patience because she identified alternatives to instrumental use that perhaps took longer but were of great social importance. According to Weiss, evaluation is not entirely wasted even in the absence of instrumental use. Several evaluations together can contribute to "knowledge creep," that is, gradual development and diffusion of knowledge. Evaluations thus have an enlightenment function (Weiss 1977). This function, by the way, is not dependent on evaluation being carried out on the basis of assumptions and values held by decision makers at the time. The evaluation results might themselves create debate or produce innovative thinking. Good ideas can gradually replace bad ideas. But the road to this enhanced knowledge is full of detours and obstacles. Nevertheless, over the long run evaluation does more to enlighten us about social realities than to obscure them. Weiss is thus a moderate optimist in terms of seeing evaluation as a contribution to progress. Progress here does not refer to the individual evaluation but hopefully to long-term progress in all areas where there is tension between knowledge and politics.

In an oft-cited debate between Carol Weiss and Michael Quinn Patton (Alkin, Patton, and Weiss 1990), the latter insists that the ambitions of evaluation for utilization must be higher than a general enlightenment function. Evaluation as enlightenment is laudable, but evaluators themselves have a responsibility to ensure that their evaluations are used for the purpose for which they were intended—for instrumental utilization. This motivates Patton (1997) to recommend several pragmatic strategies for utilization, including close cooperation between evaluator and the other "primarily intended user(s)" of evaluation. Subsequently, Patton was criticized for politically and philosophically unsophisticated pragmatism.

In the wake of the utilization debate, other scholars have developed strategies for participatory evaluation, a model that includes a somewhat broader scope of stakeholders than Patton's primary intended user. The idea here is that inclusion of various stakeholders produces a broad sense of ownership and relevance and thereby increases the chances for utilization. As noted in Chapter 1, proponents of participatory and learning-oriented approaches report moderately positive results, but also new tensions as a result of these strategies. Practitioners who employ participatory processes often come under time pressure. Participatory processes demand special methodological attention, if the methodological integrity of evaluation work is to be maintained. Participatory process can generate a positive dynamic in an evaluation situation otherwise characterized by political conflict, but it does not eliminate these conflicts. Evaluation utilization is thus obviously dependent on the social, political, and organizational context in which the evaluation takes place (Cousins 2003; Cousins and Earl 1992), but it cannot eliminate the tension in these contexts.

There can emerge considerable ambiguity regarding who "owns" the participatory strategies, and who should be included, the degree of inclusion, and why. Proponents of participatory strategies, such as Greene (1997), reflect on tensions internal to these strategies between the utilization purpose, which speaks pragmatically for close dialogue with leaders and other power holders, and those with a political agenda who seek to have underprivileged groups included because they are not otherwise heard (Guba and Lincoln 1989).

A special group of utilization-oriented evaluators, especially in extension of the ideas about participatory evaluation, are interested in organizational learning process (Preskill and Torres 1999). By raising the evaluation process to the organizational level, our attention is directed to the necessity of common learning forums. At the same time, this builds on the participatory evaluators' earlier observations regarding the importance of the organizational context in which evaluation takes place.

The organizational strategies for learning distinguish themselves by thinking in a more cyclical fashion than linear. Learning in organizations must be a permanent process of continuing reflection. Evaluation must become a part of the organization's general life; hence the interest in mainstreaming evaluation and building the organizational capacity to undertake evaluation (Compton, Baizerman, and Stockdill 2002).

In sum, the field of evaluation generates an immense amount of internal reflection in order to promote utilization of evaluation in the most open and inclusive possible way, in acknowledgment that the conditions set by the surroundings for utilization are not structured such that an individual rational decision can be assumed to be carried out without friction.

All this signifies the departure in modern society from the overly rationalistic ideal that there is one great brain in society making all decisions. The departure from strong rationalism can be lamented. But acknowledgment of the fragmented, gradual, and sometimes chaotic decision-making processes in modern society can also be interpreted as a good thing for democracy. The incremental and not overly rational decision-making processes described by Lindblom (1959) and the pluralistic and imperfect knowledge production described by Popper (1969) are indicative of a democracy coming to terms with itself. Since modern society's belief in rationality and autonomy does have a dark side—terribly illustrated by 20th century totalitarianism—and since critics are much concerned with uncomfortable links among rationalism, totalitarianism, and technocracy, a new vision of democracy is possible that accommodates pluralism, incrementalism, and imperfection. Much of what is learned about utilization in the field of evaluation, including the departure from expectations of automatic instrumental use of evaluations, is consistent with these more modest visions of modern democracy.

One final note about utilization: overly rationalistic expectations of decision making are usually based on the assumption that there is only one decision to make and the decision is clearly defined. For example, can we demonstrate such a strong causal link between a program and its effect that further funding of it is justified? As Cronbach and Shapiro (1982) suggest, there is a trade-off in evaluation between fidelity and bandwidth. Even if one such fairly well-defined question could be answered with some fidelity, there may be another broad set of questions that are also relevant, such as how the underlying social problem is understood, how social contexts influence the program, which program processes contribute to outcomes (Shadish, Cook, and Leviton 1991, 338), what the side effects of the program are, and how the program fits into the lives and perspectives of various stakeholders. In a particular evaluation, not all questions (bandwidth) can be answered with the same fidelity.

In a democracy, however, it may be useful to deal with a broad set of questions even if fidelity is far from perfect. Nevertheless, admitting limited fidelity is just an invitation to make the whole utilization problem more pressing. Yet the very complexity of evaluands in modern society is an invitation for evaluators to broaden the bandwidth of their evaluations.

The Evaluand

Modern society is complex—technologically, organizationally, and culturally. In all of these complexities, evaluands are entangled. Under these circumstances, it becomes difficult to define evaluands (policies, programs, program components) such that they are clearly bounded from their contexts. Next, it becomes difficult to identify their effects, and especially their side effects. Identifying effects is not a purely methodological matter; it presupposes some image, vision, understanding, or theory—an ontology, if you will—about the complexity of the real social world in which the evaluand unfolds.

One way in which evaluators have tried to grasp the complexity of an evaluand is through detailed local study. An advocate of this strategy is Robert Stake. Social and cultural contexts, says Stake, evolve more rapidly than do general theories. One must therefore work responsively toward the context in each individual evaluation. According to Stake, we must act according to the American Indian proverb of not judging a man before we have walked at least two moons in his moccasins (Stake 2004, 86).

In Stake's responsive evaluation, evaluation must begin by becoming sensitive to the unique conditions existing in every local context. This sensitizing occurs primarily through long-term residence in the field and through qualitative methods. What counts as quality in this local context is precisely context-dependent. The evaluation results are part of contextualized and nuanced case-based reports, generalization of which is up to the reader.

Stake's importance lies in calling attention to the fact that what takes place in a local context is much more than what is expressed in a score based on general and standard-based indicators. He therefore attempts to open the evaluators' eyes to complexity in the evaluand. Stake inspires a philosophical interest in turning what the evaluation field conceives as an abstract, independent, disembodied evaluand into activity that is a practice based on its own moral and philosophical premises (Schwandt 2002). Standardized criteria derived externally result in a reductionist picture of the evaluand. Stake has inspired those who find philosophically that quality is something that must be sought out, not measured (Stake 1997). Generalizations decay (Stake 2004).

Stake's argument thus questions rationalistic faith in general laws and standardized evaluation criteria, which earlier evaluators subscribed to. He has thereby contributed to reflexivity in the field of evaluation through adaptability to the specific evaluand. Evaluation must be context-sensitive and for this reason tailor-made to the task.

In the footsteps of Stake's responsive evaluation, participatory and constructivist evaluators sought to capture the many perspectives of local stakeholders on a particular program in its context.

From macroscopic to microscopic, evaluators' attention to the complex nature of evaluands thus leads to a questioning of the ability to produce the type of undebatable, certain, valid, and unequivocally relevant knowledge-based statements about evaluands that was assumed under the ideals of rationalistic modern decision making.

Knowledge

The more multiplex vision of evaluands came together with a whole revolution in the very idea of knowledge and how it should be created in the field of evaluation.

One of the first debated points in connection with the modern rationalist tenet in evaluation was the privileging of quantitative, experimental methods, a phenomenon we also observe in the idea of the experimental society.

An essential part of the discussion within evaluation, therefore, was the controversy between proponents of quantitative and qualitative methods. The quantitative group argued that only quantitative methods could describe general cause-and-effect relations. "If we want to have the maximum likelihood of our results being accepted and used," wrote Sechrest, "we should do well to ground them, not in theory or hermeneutics, but in dependable rigor afforded by our best science and accompanying quantitative analysis" (1992, 3, quoted in Schwandt 2002, 191).

The qualitative camp offered several responses, stressing the importance of the local context and of implementation problems, and the fact that side effects and unforeseen unintended consequences are best elucidated via qualitative methods.

Another sales point mentioned by advocates of qualitative methods relates to inclusion of stakeholders, where it is argued that ownership and relevance depend on the stakeholders feeling that they have been heard and that they can recognize their priorities in the evaluation. Expression of the views of the stakeholders in their own language is best facilitated by qualitative methods.

With a basis in a political transformative agenda, some qualitative evaluators assert that qualitative methods are best suited for allowing multiplicity of views and interests to be expressed in an evaluation process. Some qualitative evaluators also criticize the assertions of rationality and quantitative philosophy that they provide assisted sense making from an apparently disembodied and objective position. Instead, they argue that all knowledge is socially constructed and therefore not independent of viewpoints, ideologies, and interests (see, e.g., Guba and Lincoln 1989).

The latter argument can have problematic consequences for evaluation itself. If evaluation in this respect is made equal to every other form of knowledge production in social and political contexts, it can be difficult to argue that evaluation has any special or essential role to play. In this case, evaluation must find other sources of legitimation than its own capacity to create a uniquely systematic or qualified form of knowledge.

In a similar vein, increased attention to utilization in evaluation leads to ambiguities about the validity of knowledge. If the usefulness and social relevance of evaluative knowledge is a dimension in good evaluation in itself, to what extent are evaluators ready to question the aura of fidelity, validity, and rigor that is otherwise associated with what modern evaluation has inherited from modern, rational, scientific knowledge production?

In a refined and comprehensive way, the field of evaluation thereby reflects the conditions for creation of knowledge that have otherwise characterized scientific self-reflection in recent years. At the same time, it entails that the field of evaluation can now contain and absorb a broad gamut of viewpoints on an issue. This helps promote reflexivity in society and advances the field of evaluation. But it also creates tensions.

Values

Under rationalism, evaluation primarily consists of answering questions about the extent to which a given intervention is an appropriate means of realizing the intended goals and objectives. These have per definition been delimited to official policy goals. However, developments within the field of evaluation have gone in the direction of considering a broader range of stakeholders with diverse interests as legitimate players in formulating evaluation criteria (Albæk 1998).

The various models for participatory evaluation help to expand the set of values that must be sought as sources for relevant evaluation criteria. This step alone contributes to evaluation being able to break with the conventional view of progress. In any case, from multiple perspectives, evaluation has shown the capacity to contest the conventional modern understanding of what progress is all about.

The discussion of values is not only about evaluation criteria. The evaluation process itself is an object of value-based reflection. The argument, for example, is that if evaluation seeks to be a democratic process, then it must itself be a model of democracy. Depending on whose view of democracy is operative, this thesis has varying consequences. Vedung argues for classical democratic values such as the rule of law, equality, justice, etc. (Vedung 1997).

For Guba and Lincoln, an exchange of views from numerous stakeholders occurs, and the least privileged are accorded special attention without this being anchored in any explicit theory of democracy. House and Howe (2000) propose procedural criteria for a deliberative, democratic evaluation process characterized by principles of inclusion, deliberation, and consensus. Hence there does not seem to be any logical limit for which types of values can be brought into evaluation.

Schwandt (2002) points out that in connection with evaluation work in practice there are occupational professional ethics, guidelines concerning evaluators' ethics and values linked to the use of evaluation. How do we think more systematically about all these values? Schwandt presents three styles or "frameworks" describing how one can think of the relationship between evaluation and values: an "analytical value-neutral framework," an "emancipatory value-committed framework," and a "value-critical framework." Where the first postulates itself as politically neutral and the second is characterized by advocacy, the last distinguishes itself by the fact that research, investigation, and evaluation do not play any strong or privileged role with reference to "clarifying" the reality and "overcoming" value conflicts. This last position is fundamentally anticriteriological, in that it sees practice, including good practice, as something different from and more than a deductive result of already established criteria. From an anticriteriological perspective, there is no specific set of values or procedure or method that generates the best evaluation. All that a good evaluator can do is contribute to a dialogue that cultivates the practitioner's ability to exercise practical wisdom.

Schwandt's contribution thus exemplifies that not only has the field of evaluation undergone several value discussions that together make it more sensitive to different value-related perspectives; it is itself systematically reflexive about how to relate to the multiplicity of values (which, of course, does not imply that every evaluation always does the same).

The field of evaluation has further demonstrated an ability to convert a critique of earlier models and lively internal debate into myriad alternative evaluation models and concepts, giving individual evaluators and organizations the possibly to select from preferred variants and exploit the flexibility of multiple models. Similarly, considerable developmental work has been undertaken with the evaluation models, so that there is both something to choose from and the possibility of individual adaptation of the model selected (Dahler-Larsen and Krogstrup 2003).

Shadish, Cook, and Leviton (1991, 321) described the development of evaluation theory. They argue that we have now reached a kind of synthesis of the experiences of early years of evaluation. In contrast to earlier, the style should now be "contingency-oriented," meaning that certain approaches to evaluation can be meaningful and appropriate only under specific situational conditions. It is therefore decisive to carry out a thorough situational analysis to determine what kind of evaluation is most appropriate in the situation. They recognize that evaluation theorists can rationally use certain evaluation models because they find themselves in differing evaluation situations. However, this is far from being a happy "synthesis." Evaluation models vary in emphasizing fundamentally different values, and proponents of these models would not necessarily accept their model being defined as applicable to only a narrow category of situations. In a similar vein, evaluators believing in a number of approaches to evaluation do not always happily accept evaluations made from other perspectives, even if produced under situational circumstances that are said to fit them.

No given evaluation situation can be expected to be totally congruent with a given evaluation model. This would require that one and only one evaluation model be determined by the situation. One can just as well imagine that a situation contains tensions that underdetermine or overdetermine the choice of an evaluation model. Different models will respond to the demands of the situation in their own individual style, though without thereby necessarily dissolving the relevant tensions. More simply put, even the choice of the very best evaluation model under the situational circumstances will not put value questions to rest.

Evaluation theory has thus evolved rapidly and entered many areas, but it offers us a cacophony of arguments and approaches rather than a unified and systematic body of theory.

What does this illustrate? That the modern ideals of rationality and clarity have not paved the way for unequivocal and undebatable evaluation. The debates along all the important dimensions of evaluation—utilization, evaluands, knowledge, and values—instead lead to multiple positions if not a fragmentation of perspectives. To the extent that evaluation is a child of modernity, this should in fact not surprise us. As an insightful observer of modernity, Vattimo (1992) noted that the modern ideals of rationality, clarity, and transparence were themselves mythical. What they in fact did was to open up a multiplicity of views of the world. The ideal of transparence has given birth to many ways of seeing.

This development within evaluation thus reflects the coming of a new era in modernity where multiplicity of views is the order of the day: reflexive modernity.

4   Reflexive Modernity

Sociologists describe several changes in society that have made it impossible to maintain the modern notion of progress in its original form. No diagnosis summarizes these changes better than Ulrich Beck's "reflexive modernity" (1994a), even though in this chapter I will not do full justice to Beck's analysis or refer to him exclusively.

In this book, in-depth attention to reflexive modernity is necessary for a number of reasons. Reflexive modernity is not only the result of how modernity struggles with or works through its own ideals. As I shall seek to demonstrate, it gives us an insightful diagnosis of central problems in contemporary society, and it underscores the man-made character of these problems. Its occupation with evaluation is intense, but problematic. It sets the agenda for the types of problems that evaluators have to work with, but it also paves the way for a whole culture that makes evaluation fashionable in a historically unprecedented way. Reflexive modernity thus at the same time makes evaluation more necessary and more ritualistic. This paradox has a number of consequences for evaluation in today's society, as we shall see in the following chapters. This chapter is devoted to reflexive modernization itself.

Let us open our analysis with a symptomatic observation made by academics who study happiness. Up to a point, happiness is positively correlated with income (Eriksen 2008). This is true for individuals as well as for nations. After that point, however, income no longer generates any additional happiness. The conventional modern recommendation to achieve happiness—which is "Make more money!"—simply does not work anymore. This is why individuals who seek to make more money in contemporary Western societies in fact end up with stress, pills, fatigue, and obesity, but not happiness. For nations, a fairly deep disorientation may follow from the recognition that further growth in GDP (for modern capitalist nations) no longer adds to the well-being of the population. In brief, the conventional modern recipe for progress is simply out of order. This situation—that modern initiatives no longer lead to success—is indicative of the social situation we are dealing with in this chapter.

The concept of reflexive modernity, then, can be understood as a phase in the development of modern society. However, it is impossible to operate with a sharp delimitation of its starting and ending points. In a subtler sense, reflexive modernity, like modernity itself, is a set of ideas and social structural forms that make their impact at a certain point of time, while it is superimposed on large remainders transmitted from other epochs. Last but not least, reflexive modernity is a process. As such, "reflexive modernization" is a better label than reflexive modernity. It is both a kind of working through of the modern, a turning of the modern against the modern itself, and a process that, once it starts, has its own logic.

The steam has gone out of the optimism of modernity, as modernity stands face to face with its own side effects. Therefore, a great deal of the energy in the reflexively modern society is allocated to counterbalancing, managing, and allocating the risks and disadvantages of modernity's own products. One of these genuinely epoch-making side effects is clearly foreshadowed by weapons technology, which enables human beings to exterminate humanity many times over—something never before possible in history (Beck 1994b, 180).

However, there are other areas of daily life—work, health, environment, food—where the reflexive modern human being is greatly concerned about risks. According to Beck, these risks are "democratized," in that a broad range of society's citizens are affected. Air pollution and climate changes do not simply strike the poorest segment of the population; stress can burden the highest and lowest social classes. Unemployment can hit bank managers and IT specialists alike. This turns the problematic of side effects into a widespread theme.

As an illustration of the side-effects problem, I decided to collect examples from the media. I regret to say that I quickly obtained so many examples that they could not be on a single page.

- Despite intense preventive efforts, bacteria in hospitals are a significant source of infection in patients. In general, hospitals are a dangerous place to be. We now speak of iatrogenic diseases, that is, diseases created by doctors.

· Chemicals in our everyday life cause many people to suffer from allergy, with no more than a small part of these causal associations having been described.

· Well-meaning mothers, as a result of campaigns for better nutrition, cut down on the fat content in the food they give their small children, leading to malnutrition, because young children in fact require a certain amount of fat.

· Although it has been discovered that high noise levels from rock music are quite harmful, researchers also find that children who are used to listening to loud music are less receptive to noise damage later in life. The theory is that the ear builds up resistance to noise.

· Today we are advised that babies should not sleep on their stomach. This is due to the discovery of a statistical association between this sleeping position and crib death. Not many years ago, however, health personnel recommended precisely that babies sleep on their stomach, and their advice was sometimes followed even though it was counterintuitive for parents.

· The presence of too many cars now prevents us from being transported rapidly from one place to another. Characteristically enough, there is doubt as to whether more roads will alleviate the problem or simply lead people to drive even more. Road pricing is being considered, which will not only reduce the amount of traffic but also make it more expensive for poor people to get to work.

· Alternatives to automobile traffic are being considered. But in some countries taxes on cars and gasoline have been a significant part of the income of the public treasury.

· Charitable organizations sell support wristbands in solidarity with the struggle against cancer, but the wristbands produce allergies. There is now consideration of selling new support armbands in solidarity with the allergy-stricken wristband victims.

· Several diagnoses have been developed as socially acceptable labels for a number of mental illnesses, but also for general stress reactions and hypersensitivity reactions. A diagnosis makes it possible to manage and explain—or perhaps prevent—an illness. But diagnoses also have several disadvantages, notably that they lead to labeling people by their various syndromes.

- For good reasons, there are laws against drug abuse and drug trafficking. However, antidrug laws contribute to pushing up the price of these drugs on the illegal market. Abusers who would otherwise not be criminals are therefore pushed into crime to obtain money for drugs. A considerable portion of petty burglaries are committed by drug addicts who are desperate for cash.

- In connection with preventive efforts against breast cancer, the problem is discussed that screening creates false positives, exposing women to an unnecessary sense of insecurity.

- The welfare state's social policy is said to have led to passivization, clientelization, and dependence on the authorities.

As a result of the multiplication of side effects, progress is in retreat. Several contemporary problems are due not to too little progress but to too much (Beck 1992).

In public policy and in public institutions, the side-effect problem has rightly been among the key themes in recent years. Social policy creates welfare dependency. Psychiatric institutions create psychiatric patients. Users of public services feel like victims of bureaucracy.

Instead of progress, we now talk about "development." The concept of development is a collective label for several complexities of a technological, social, economic, political, and personal nature. In today's social imaginary, development is both important and unavoidable. The historian of ideas, Jens Erik Kristensen, thus speaks of a "commandment of development," but development is there because we cannot dissociate ourselves from its social necessity, not because we are so enthusiastic about its results.

We live in an era in which modern society is under attack by its own effects and side effects. We discover that our actions constantly create problems for us, problems that often come back to us in changing and surprising forms.

The climate discussion is a fine example of this. Whereas in the old days we could speak of the weather as something that came and went and was a given thing, today we are anxious about whether extreme weather might be caused by human effects on climate. In situations where the vagaries of nature strike human beings, we refuse to accept it as something unavoidable. Even in the case of a catastrophic hurricane or tsunami, we do not accept the unavoidable. We debate the failure of warning systems, efforts made by officials, the role of the disaster aid organizations, and organization of reconstruction efforts. The social side of disasters has become obvious in Japan, where the breakdown of nuclear power plants clearly has added to the complexity and severity of already catastrophic natural phenomena.

The Greatest Shortage in Denmark in 25 Years

The greatest shortage situation in Denmark in the last 25 years had nothing to do with bad weather, a poor harvest, or anything that could be traced back to a natural calamity. It was a shortage of yeast, and it was a purely social construction. In connection with a general strike, which included workers in the transport and food processing sectors, many citizens feared they would not be able to purchase food. People got the idea that in the event of a long strike, they would have to bake their own bread. Consumers began to hoard yeast—massive amounts of yeast. When retail merchants noticed how much people were buying, they themselves began to purchase more yeast. It is doubtful whether much home-baked bread actually came out of all this. However, it is certain that there was no actual shortage of food before, during, or after the strike. The food shortage situation existed, nevertheless, as a social construction and with real consequences.

In a situation where man-made organizations are in the broadest sense putting their stamp on the world, it becomes more important to grasp that nearly every problem has a social origin. In any case, reflexive modernity is characterized by having to turn the modern desire for constant improvement against modern institutions and organizations themselves.

Because of internationalization, technology, and coordination problems, however, the side-effect problem has become much more complex. In traditional society, there were face-to-face relations between those who provided a product and those who received one. In industrial society, this and a great many other social relations became anonymous (buyer and seller of labor, buyer and seller of services), but they could nevertheless still be regulated to a certain degree through general agreements, contracts, laws, and policies. In the current era of reflexive modernity, there is a dramatic expansion and rising level of complexity in the interface between an organized activity and its effects. Even real natural disasters spread because of the extension of interface between parts of the globalized human world.

A specific example is that the largest natural disaster affecting Sweden in recent years was the tsunami in Southeast Asia. This was because the web of globalization made it normal for many Swedes to take their vacation on the other side of the globe. No disaster in Sweden had led to so many Swedish casualties for a long time.

If, under conditions of reflexive modernity, we want to obtain an overview of the relationship between the origin of a problem and its effects, we must think in a complex way and across time and space. We must conceptualize a rather intricate web of organizations (the interaction of one sector with another), dependencies in relation to other countries (human rights and child labor), and perhaps the effects on future generations of unborn children (environmental problems). Add to this that many side effects are difficult to formally classify, because many of the products of reflexive modernity concern life politics and body politics, communication, competencies, symbolic considerations, and the experience of not being treated with respect and taken seriously. These themes are extremely open to multiple social definitions (Beck 1992).

What interests us in this context is not any precise reckoning of the objective existence and extent of these side effects. It is instead the sociological significance of side effects as risk. Even though the reflexively modern society is a risk society, this does not necessarily mean that it is more dangerous to live in this society than in others. In the risk society, however, there occurs a special attention to risk and a special construction of it.

Risks become risks precisely by being pointed out. Science thus contributes to constituting risks, for example by investigating and identifying them statistically, and also by naming areas of activities and practices that require our attention, such as "psychological working environment," "preventive health work," and "man-made climate changes."

The fact that risks are socially constructed—and like other social constructions have reality-creating consequences—is illustrated in situations where action is taken concerning a problem that has not yet materialized as anything other than a statistical predictive calculation. For example, women have decided on the advice of their doctor to have preventive breast removal surgery, not because they contracted breast cancer but because these women have a statistically high genetic risk of contracting breast cancer.

Included in the social construction of risks is thus a cultural inclination to attend to warnings about risks, and the associated amount of calculations or surveys as well as the demands and expectations linking themselves to subsequent management or minimizing of the risk. Risk becomes a widespread social structuration principle if there is a cultural basis for it. The risk thereby refers socially to both the authority that has created or investigated it and the authority expected to minimize or manage the risk.

Critique of Authorities

The social basis for risk thus consists not only in calculation of probability but also in norms and expectations that the social order can be renegotiated. Reflexive modernity has created the pathway for a comprehensive critique of authorities, both traditional (family, church, and school) and bureaucratic and organizational. Students, for example, make demands for the relevance of study programs, posing questions about why they should not be able to grade the teacher on the same kind of scale as the teacher uses to grade students.

Parents are subject to strict criticism as authorities, not only in connection with the entire set of ideas connected to post-1968 cultural mentalities but also from professionals who use their knowledge with a reflexive intention.

An Example of the Spread of Risk Consciousness

In Denmark, brochures were distributed to new parents to call attention to the importance of talking with small children. Surveys had shown that children in many "language-deficient" families could incur permanent problems in speaking. No one dared take responsibility to distribute the brochures only to underprivileged families; this might have the appearance of being discriminatory. As parents of newborn children without visible social problems, we were therefore left with the impression that a special effort was required of us, if our children were not to grow up with permanent aphasia. No one called attention to the fact that most parents speak spontaneously to their children, and that most children learn to speak excellently.

This occurred during the years when the task of parenting grew difficult and demanded great public attention. It was in the same years that the path was cleared for the "curling generation," the generation of children and youths who expect that their path forward is "swept" by others so they will not encounter problems with delayed gratification, long academic studies, hard work, or existential problems.

Traditional hierarchical and rule-oriented exercise of authority is strongly criticized both for creating inequality and for being alienating, cold, inhuman, and so on—that is, for hindering human emancipation and development. The modern work organization responds to this critique partly by restructuring the division of work, automating repetitive tasks and appealing to innovation and creativity, partly by developing more inspiring organizational cultures, and partly by substituting rigid hierarchies for flexible project organizations. Considerations of efficiency and profitability were contributing factors. But a critique of the basis of a humanistic point of view becomes more effective as it links itself to an argument that a new and better organization in fact also works (Boltanski and Chiapello 2007).

The feeling of (a lack of) justice and humanity are important social driving forces. Among some of the most important side effects of reflexive modernity are thus not only natural-sciencelike risks but also experienced breaches of social norms and individual expectations.

The authority that, under conditions of reflexive modernity, would keep up with the times must include awareness of the side effects it creates, among which are the experiences and reactions on the part of people with whom the authority interacts. It must take into consideration that reflexive modernity sometimes entails considerable pressure to acknowledge responsibility for its side effects. An important question in reflexive modernity is whether it is possible to make sure that an agency or institution that produces side effects that grow in complex ways in time and space also recognizes and reinternalizes its responsibility for these side effects.

Of course, having this challenge taken seriously by public agencies implies an immense broadening of the scope of responsibilities, since the side effects not only include oil spills on beaches but also experiences of subjectively felt injustice and violation of expectations.

Many Types of Side Effects

Let us take smoking as an example. A key problem in reflexive modernity is how one gets tobacco companies to reinternalize responsibility for the health-damaging effects of tobacco. According to the legal systems of various countries, smokers who contract cancer have the possibility of claiming legal compensation. This still leaves the public and private health systems with considerable costs, and it leaves individuals with personal tragedies.

Lacking perfect mechanisms for backward linkage of responsibility for these side effects, the state power exerts pressure. More countries pass new laws forbidding cigarette advertising, demanding warnings on cigarette packages about the risks of cancer, and placing strong limitations on smoking in public places. These initiatives have a noticeable side effect: smokers begin to articulate themselves as a persecuted minority. They also, in fact, *become* a minority.

Contingency

More social conditions than ever are clearly social. In "The Sims" computer game, there is an interesting feature that reflects something significant in our contemporary society: in the game, one can turn the actors' free will on and off. According to Manovich (2001), it is a general feature of the new media that they attempt to replace constants with variables. It is a reflection of the tendency of our era toward contingency.

As a steadily greater part of our lives appears to be a result of human activity, organizational, political, economic, and institutional activity and change, and as critique comes from many angles, *contingency* becomes a key word. It connotes a situation with a fragile social order, where social relations and determinations could constantly be otherwise. There is an idea and an expectation that the existing social arrangements can be turned on or off, that society is malleable. This results from knowledge about the possibilities for changes being continuously led back to the existing order (Stehr 2001).

Contingency exists, for example, when two women can have children together if they can convince the state to provide the necessary reproductive technology, and where legislation and ethics can also be brought into the game in the proper constellation. At the same time, there is an important ethical problem concerning the child's right to know the name of both its mothers (!), not to mention the name of the father. Hence contingency concerns not the isolated decision-making situation among the two women but the relatively indeterminate character of the entire social, political, organizational, and ethical configuration within which the decision can take place. The sociological perspective in the contingency concept thus articulates itself to the extent that it is the changing social conditions that make the entire question of the two women's children open. Formerly, there was no possibility for any such opening in a decision on this point; a child with two female parents would clearly be presupposing innovative test tube technology. But the technology is now woven into the human world. Choices have to be made about technology, ethics, and the whole social and political regulation of human reproduction. Contingency thrives.

Contingency also appears when it becomes less evident what food one should eat. Travel, immigration, and shops bring new foods and new inspiration all the time. But we are also made constantly aware that the nutritional advice we previously received was erroneous, and new food habits can make us thinner, happier, or healthier. In his book *Menneskeføde* (*Human Food*), Tor Nørretranders (2005) calls our attention to the fact that much of the advice we formerly received as the truth about a healthy diet is in reality historically dependent, influenced to a great degree by the values prevailing at a point in time, and by dominant industrial and commercial interests. Earlier advice came out of a specific social configuration but does not work today. Now, nutritional advice changes with astounding speed. What it is natural to eat becomes, subjectively and objectively, a social construction.

Another example of contingency is the issue of cross-border day care. In the Copenhagen area, where there is a shortage of day care facilities, a proposal was made that children be bussed across the Øresund Bridge to Malmø, Sweden, where day care settings are more abundant and cheaper. In the history of child care, there has never before been a question of which country the daily care of children should take place in.

Contingency means circumstantial and situational conditionality; fewer and fewer parts of social life are determined by their destiny or tradition. Contingency promotes the general idea that life could be lived differently. As a cultural form, it leads to an ongoing feeling of instability, and uncertainty about whether the fundamental dimensions of personal life are stable. For example, American psychologists demonstrate that our persistent viewing of attractive people in films and on television leads us to pose questions about whether we have chosen the right partner. The gradual dissolution of earlier time-space divisions in the modern world exposes us to variations in lifestyles and the need to make new choices, even in our personal lives. We think unwaveringly that life could be organized differently, when the principle task for every individual is to organize life course and personal growth (Giddens 1994). Involving scientific, pseudoscientific, and therapeutic discourses in the individual's daily life does not appear to offer much more than temporary relief. Stability is only temporary. Instead, contingency appears to spread.

Even though contingency thus has psychological implications, it is basically a sociological phenomenon. Nevertheless, this does mean that at the social level a decision can simply be made at will. Individual decisions are woven into larger systems. Hence, although someone in Denmark invents a new type of fuel that can be extracted from straw, and although this fuel could eliminate all known environmental problems caused by petroleum-based fuels, and although the technology could generate great business prospects for Denmark, it is not certain that the Ministry of Taxation would lower the surcharges for such a fuel sufficiently to produce it with commercial viability. The interests of the petroleum industry are opposed to this development. And biodegradable fuels have several unpleasant consequences for food prices, thus affecting poor people throughout the world. In addition, it is not certain that biofuels are as environmentally promising as was once thought. Perhaps more research is needed. This is just one example of how phenomena are weaved into larger contexts in our complex contemporary society. The dependency on larger technical, organizational, political, and international systems has never been greater.

Global dependencies are themselves sources of contingency. Appadurai (1990) offers a complex perspective on the global cultural situation. He speaks of ethnoscapes, mediascapes, technoscapes, financescapes, and ideoscapes—that is, "landscapes," or people, media images, technology, finance, and ideas. He points out that these configurations do not follow the same uniform logic, and that fragments from each one (e.g., certain political or controlling ideas) can obtain entirely new, special, local meaning when disaggregated from the grand narratives of the West and reimplanted under other contextual conditions.

Of course, this leads to even more contingency. We are constantly made aware of how things are done elsewhere, which alternatives exist, how one's behavior may appear from a theoretical perspective, and the kinds of criticism presented. Contingency is increased as we now have the knowledge about, and the possibility to reflect on, myriad feasible alternatives.

To live with contingency is to be aware of the fragility of the social order. To live with contingency is also to attempt to be aware of the side effects that others create for us by virtue of the side effects we created for them. This is why systemic thinking and the idea of complexity theory blossom under reflexive modernity.

As tradition loses its dominant position, it becomes clearer that the construction of society is in fact precisely a construction. If one is struck by contingency, one must acknowledge the practice as variable and justify why a particular practice is chosen over all the others that are possible. Contingency means that traditional recipes for success lose their power. It also means that success can lie in creative utilization of change.

In any case, at both the personal and the institutional levels, contingency sharpens our attention to the necessity of choosing. This is especially true when an organization takes on a task under public scrutiny. Here, contingency creates pressure on the organization to develop ways of orienting itself and showing that it can manage contingency. In this way, contingency generates pressure for explanation and justification. This is why public relations, communication policies, and impression management are especially relevant under reflexive modernization.

In the same fashion, public organizations become more open to restructuring. Reflexive modernization accelerates the need for organizational reforms. New organizational recipes appear, promising improvements and effectiveness. Several recent regulation paradigms within New Public Management (based on contracts, principal-agent thinking, outsourcing, and so on) promote contingency as an instrument in the very organization of public activities.

Sometimes there are several layers of contingency. For example, the experience of grief, war, catastrophe, or loss is understood not as destiny but as a social situation to be dealt with. In other words, the human interpretation and outcome of these experiences is contingent. There are for this reason programs for psychological assistance to help people cope. It is much discussed, however, whether these psychological programs in fact help people—or perhaps make the experiences so much more difficult that they must be talked through, over and over again. The program installed to handle contingency is thus itself dependent on contingent discussion about its effectiveness and side effects.

In reflexive modernization, there is no logical end to contingency.

Research

Science, research, and surveys in general are necessary aids in this connection because they create knowledge about possibilities, costs, and effects. In this sense, they call attention to contingency and even produce it, because they describe social variations across time and space and point to new technological opportunities.

But science, research, and surveys are also ambiguous partners. In earlier versions of the modern society, science could speak with a degree of certainty reminiscent of the voice of religious authority. Even though there is a great demand to conceptualize and control the complexity of reflexive modernity, science and technology cannot maintain a credible, uniform voice. This is not necessarily due to any lack of data but is just as often due to internal contradiction in evidence among researchers. Application of scientific methods such as controlled experiments has up to now failed in the sense that it is able to produce a coherent set of conclusions only to a limited degree (Albæk 1988). Producers of knowledge contradict one another; the very concept of expertise has been compromised (Giddens 1990, 131).

Today there is limited confidence that science and technology can provide unequivocal and reliable overviews of existing social regularities, let alone causal links. Recommendations regarding diet are an excellent example. One week we are advised to eat a certain type of food in order to avoid cancer; the next week we should avoid the same food because it is said to contain pesticide residues.

The competition and contradictions between different forms of knowledge change the social foundations of science and technology. In some cases, the lack of credibility in research is related to commercial interests having paid for the desired results. Or in any case, the research has not succeeded in ensuring its own independence from partisan interests in society (House 2008). However, the problem is far more serious than that. Even when not biased, scientific research is not unequivocal. On the contrary, science has used scientific thinking against itself, with the result being a schism. Critical studies in the sociology of science point out the socially conditioned and particularistic aspects of every research inquiry. It has also been shown that science not only identifies facts and causal relations; it attaches names and labels to phenomena. Under conditions of reflexive modernity, one of science's most important functions is to point out areas and problem domains demanding attention. There has been growth especially in research on issues concerning human reactions to manmade social conditions, on topics such as the working environment, work motivation, stress, consumer behavior, communications studies, effects of chemicals on humans, and climate change.

Developments within science, research, and studies of social conditions show that there is no single correct way to study, or even label, a given problem. On the contrary, the complex society of reflexive modernity offers many possible angles of approach, and science and research themselves contribute to these developments with a growing abundance of paradigms and methods. Instead of being carried out within individual disciplines, science and research are progressively linked to many practical and application-oriented contexts in connection with a variety of stakeholders (Gibbons et al. 1994). This development contributes to making science multiperspective in character. Research is itself affected by contingency; the production of knowledge today cannot be understood apart from the social conditions it originates from and also describes, that is, reflexive modernization.

Governance

These conditions naturally create more complex conditions for governance of society. In earlier times, society could be conceived as a body (Mongin 1982). All parts were seen as integrated into an organic whole. Several modern sociologists could still count on—at least as a vision—establishing a new head in the form of a rationally driven state. Later on, theorists within political science began to describe the state as a complex interaction of partially opposing organizations. In the era of reflexive modernity, the body metaphor has collapsed completely. The feeling that society has a center representing it in entirety and knows what is happening in society as a whole has weakened (Luhmann 1989). None of us, and all of us, want to be at the helm.

The political leadership that could be the center first discovers ideas from the rest of society once they have become banal (Beck 1994a, 39). Instead, the political pops up in new forms and in new areas in everyday life, and among activists and grassroots organizations under such headlines as ethics; the politics of life, health, and death; quality of life; and the political consumer. Society fragments in new ways, but this does not mean that these new areas are not genuinely political.

There is weakening faith that a center can plan on behalf of all of society. Planning as a means of regulation is too inflexible to tackle the side effects and coordination problems of reflexive modernity.

Wagner (1994) sees these steering problems as indicative of the current phase of modern society: it has simply become difficult to have confidence that society as a collective agent can care for itself coherently and sensibly. It almost seems as if today's massive debt problems were foreshadowed in Wagner's analysis.

Planning is appropriate for coordinating decisions, but not for the side effects of action. The movement from a societal model marked by a center to a chaotic, polycentric model is aptly illustrated by the development of theoretical studies of government and governance.

Research in implementation of legislation (itself a child of reflexive modernity) demonstrates how political plans and decisions can change direction and lead to unintended consequences when implemented in complex organizational contexts (Sabatier 1985; Wildavsky 1979; Winter 1994). Explanations are numerous. Among implementers, there is limited local knowledge about what can be done, and limits to what is desired and what one dares to do. Implementers of policy have their own views and limited resources, and they must make a number of choices by themselves (Lipsky 1980). They are not simply the extended arm of the state. A special branch of research is also occupied with the instruments used in executing policy (Lascoumes and Le Gales 2007). It appears that most instruments are much more than just instruments. They are themselves interpretations of policy problems, and they generate their own side effects. An additional approach is that many "implementation problems" are caused by the approved policies being unclear or strongly symbolic. Lack of clarity has been a fundamental precondition for obtaining a majority to support a policy (Baier, March, and Sætren 1986). No wonder implementation problems occur.

Some of the most timely concepts of modern policy implementation have therefore changed from ideas of "governing" to "governance" (Falkner 1999). The idea here is that policy is set and implemented dynamically in composite networks of actors. Several leading policy ideas (e.g., sustainability, innovation, security) are also especially ambiguous and demand local specification and interpretation in practice. The problem is not that implementers are corrupt or lazy, as old-fashioned implementation theory might sometimes suggest. The problem is that under complex conditions political initiatives must be interpreted locally in order to be implemented at all.

The problem of interpretation appears to be gaining significance in connection with policy implementation under the conditions of reflexive modernity. During the earlier period of modernity, raw power in the form of resources was seen as decisive for a policy to be efficient (just as capital was a force of production in industrial societies). Several pressing problems, however, can no longer be solved simply by furnishing more resource inputs (just as wars do not seem to be decided by who has the best weapons or the most soldiers). Therefore disagreement about interpretation and conviction is added to the existing list of the types of implementation problems encountered. Though other implementation problems concern practical limitations and resource limitations in the effect of policy, problems of interpretation concern which problem understandings should form the basis for a policy, and which values should define the solution to a problem.

*An Implementation Gap Supplemented by
an Interpretation Gap*

As an example of a public governance problem with both implementation problems and gaps in interpretation, we can cite the Danish child vaccination program (MFR) against measles, mumps, and rubella.

Before the program, practically all children contracted these diseases and thereby achieved immunity via natural contagion. But in some individual situations, the diseases can have serious consequences if one contracts them as an adult. The authorities assessed that an effective vaccination program would be beneficial. The basis

was a health economics analysis in which the costs of the vaccination program, savings of avoiding side effects in serious cases, and
especially savings on sick days for both children and parents in all
the normal cases entered into the decision.

Because such a program will prevent the natural spread of the disease and subsequent general immunity, a vaccination program must
achieve very close to 100 percent coverage if it is to be successful.
If an epidemic breaks out among unvaccinated adults, they are in a
much worse position than if there had been no program at all. More
than 10 years after introduction of the program, official sources es-
timate that the current rate of support of 85 percent in parts of the
program is so "inadequate" that it might "lead to local epidemics in
the receptive groups" (EPI News, November 19, 1997). Today, more
than 20 years after the introduction, support goes up and down and
is sometimes below 90 percent (EPI News, September 3, 2008).

This is not only a case of a classical implementation problem,
where many parents forget to take their children to the doctor and
where some doctors are a bit uncertain of when vaccination is con-
traindicated. In cases of doubt, vaccination may be omitted. It is also
a case of a more fundamental gap in interpretation, because some
parents disagree with the entire idea of the vaccination program. They
believe that measles, mumps, and rubella are natural diseases, and
that there should be room in society for parents to be able to care for
their sick children. Last but not least, they do not trust the medical
world's assurances that the side effects of vaccinations are negligible.
Even in professional medical circles, side effects are investigated and
discussed, as is the extent to which an allergy in a child should con-
traindicate vaccination (Christensen, Rønne, and Christiansen 1999).
Such a discussion sows doubt among some parents. In other countries, there has also been debate as to how much the pharmaceutical
industry earns when doctors recommend vaccination (Harris 2007).

The existence of such an interpretation gap and the costs of sur-
mounting it hardly entered into the decision behind the program but
are illustrative of the governance problems under reflexive modernity.

Today public authorities acknowledge a risk of an epidemic
of measles. In 2008, six children in Copenhagen contracted the
disease. It was feared that an epidemic could start if Danish
children traveling abroad contracted measles from foreign chil-

dren. Included in the complexity in the problem is that younger
Danish physicians find it more difficult to diagnose measles,
mumps, and rubella because they do not recognize and identify
the symptoms easily because the diseases are now rare (though
not eliminated).

As an alternative to central governing, policy analysts discuss the contours of a polycentric governance model with iterative feedback loops and
self-reflection operating on many levels. In other words, governance is
possible without a centrally located brain doing social planning.

Rose (2003) mentions that attempts are made to manage governance
complexity with various regimes of deregulation and self-regulation. Strict
rule following is replaced by regimes of self-monitoring and self-regulation, or what Rose calls "governing at a distance." The ideal is to install
local self-discipline so that it is sufficient that the monitored persons or
units need to remind themselves only sporadically that they are in fact
being monitored.

Such governing at a distance (embodied in management by results,
contract regulation, etc.) is one way in which modern organizations have
responded to social critique since 1968—a critique saying that large organizations are stiff and bureaucratic and place too much emphasis on
management from the top.

Reflexivity means that one is confronted by the products of a large
number of uncoordinated actions (Beck 1994a, 3; 1994b, 176). Reflexivity
also entails the possibility of forms of governance with less authoritarian
exercise of power. Under conditions of reflexive modernity, however, there
is no guarantee of a "tranquil" outcome of reflexivity. On the contrary,
reflexivity itself can contribute to uncoordinated action. Therefore, the
concept refers to a social order where disturbance, doubt, and multiple
points of view are not put to rest. New forms of organization and governance lead to new dilemmas concerning self-discipline and new issues of
monitoring and control (Boltanski and Chiapello 2007).

The ambiguity in new forms of governance is promoted by the fact
that even though a certain self-control and reflexivity are welcome within
an organizational regime, this very regime is itself contingent. More than
once has a local organization discovered that while it practiced self-regulation, there occurred an intervention in the self-regulation. While it

practiced budget responsibility, the budget was changed. While it practiced evaluating itself, the evaluation results could be used by others, and
for other purposes.

The Concept of Quality as a Typically Reflexive Modern Concept

The concept of quality has been central to many attempts to control
and develop both private and public organizations, their performance,
and their products in recent decades. Think of phrases such as *quality
measurement, quality surveys, quality assurance, quality development, quality reform,* etc. At the same time, the content of the concept and use of
the quality concept under conditions of reflexive modernity are indicative
and symptomatic of this epoch as such. I will therefore look more closely
at the quality concept itself.

Semantically, *quality* is an immensely rich concept, one of the richest in
the language. In terms of content, it has many layers of meaning. Etymo-
logically, it has its origins in Latin, where Cicero (106–43 B.C.) spoke of
qualis in the sense of "what-ness" or "how-ness." Cicero builds on Plato's
ideas of classic epistemological theory. What lies in the things themselves,
and what lies in our view of them? We have in fact ideas about the properties of thing (for example, whiteness), which are distinct from our sense
of the thing. The object is white, but not whiteness. And how is it, by the
way, that people view objects so differently? These simple questions posed
here do not, of course, do justice to Plato's ideas, which are expressed in
a difficult-to-understand and somewhat inconclusive dialogue with Theaetetus (Klein 1977). The decisive aspect, however, is that quality has a
prehistory as an *epistemological* concept.

In the 1600–1700s, the concept obtains a new meaning, and both aesthetic and moral overtones. Here, the first step is taken to free the ideas
of morality from strict religious dogma. One can speak of "a man of quality," where it (naturally) refers to social origins but also to moral qualities.
In the aesthetic domain, the concept of quality develops as well. Quality
comes to mean something fine, elevated, sublime, and rare. One can even
imagine how the new goods exiting from the colonies—silks, spices, and
precious metals—are admired for their quality in this respect.

With industrialism, the concept of quality is again transformed. The
industrial mode of organization, with its separation of the individual

worker from responsibility for the entire production process, sharpens possibilities for mass production of low quality. The industrial organization responds again in the first half of the 20th century by taking on a special organizational function with quality assurance as its area of responsibility. With the aid of modern sampling technology, developed for this purpose, efforts are made to control the quality of mass-produced goods.

The idea of quality control, however, becomes refined to a subtler idea of quality development. It is not appropriate to simply investigate quality and discard the inadequate goods. It becomes especially inappropriate to mass-produce under increasing competition if consumers' desires are not taken into account. Therefore, it is not enough just to test the final products before selling them. A new, organizational approach is needed so that quality is an integrative aspect of the whole production process. This process includes how well the product is conceived in relation to the needs and preferences of consumers.

Naturally, this produces conflicts between marketing people, who define quality as experienced quality in relation to consumer desires, and engineers, who continue to measure objective properties of the produced goods. A classic contradiction re-appears in the concept of quality as objectified versus quality as subjectively experienced.

Conceptually speaking, integrating quality problems by industrialism into statistical and managerial thinking has other interesting implications. Quality now clearly becomes something that cannot be left to chance. It is not God-given; nor is it extraordinary or external. It is a product of good organization and management. It should be statistically present virtually all the time. It becomes simply what can be expected, a new norm that the organization as a whole must live up to.

When quality thus becomes an organizational matter, the quality function must be an overarching and integrating function in the organization, which both listens to consumers and is a spokesperson for the organization's strategy.

As quality becomes a question of how good the organization and its processes are managed and integrated, and no longer a property of the things produced, quality is organizationalized.

In this way, the possibility is opened up for a wide-ranging abstraction of the concept of quality, and as a corollary, colossal expansion of the domain for quality work. General prescriptions for quality can travel from organization to organization, and the influence of quality specialists grows (Power 2005). Quality becomes a property organizations can have in the abstract. In this way, the possibility is given for the concept of quality to travel through time and space and be connected to every conceivable action.

Under conditions of reflexive modernity, the concept of quality ends up bereft of content. It can be connected to every conceivable topic. It continues to have connotations from the epistemological, aesthetic, and statistical domains, but its significance is not fixed because it can oscillate between subjective and objectified quality, and between the extraordinary and the normal.

The concept of quality is suited to all forms of critique, of all things from all perspectives and all forms of "reform work"; but it is not in itself capable of retaining any certain definition in terms of its content.

The quality concept, on the other hand, is well suited to facilitating critique and reflection—reflexivity, if you will—but cannot itself point out any certain values without cheating on the scale (Bauman 1995, 79). Under such conditions, "quality of life" becomes an abstraction that refers to reflexivity as a social form without any particular content. It is solely in its pragmatic function (it facilitates reflexivity) that the concept of quality gains meaning.

The concept of quality is typical for the era of reflexive modernity because it operates as an arena where all sorts of frustrations can be aired, and the multiplicity of subjective viewpoints can unfold. A broad and otherwise uneven range of problems can be raised and discussed, and various remedial initiatives can be instituted as promises of better quality. That the epistemological, aesthetic, and industrial aspects of the quality concept can be mobilized and mixed together relatively freely is but a sign of the concept's multifaceted potential for application today.

Nevertheless, the concept is not free of paradoxes. The centrality of the concept of quality to reflexive modernity is related to the positive ring to the term *quality*, such that there is general permission to desire more. No one is denied the right to quality of life. The concept's openness of content, however, also means that no concrete project to obtain more quality can have the entire quality concept on its side. If specific initiatives are started in order to produce more quality, someone must maintain one among many possible ideas of quality and attempt to generate support for it, at least for a time. This can take place, for example, with the help of some specific and agreed rules of the game for a participatory process, or by political or rhetorical tricks, or by someone using more energy on the case than others and thereby establishing a specific quality agenda. One way to do this is to sell particular definitions of quality where it is made equal to fulfillment of objectives, effects, standards, or fulfillment of user expectations (Dahler-Larsen 2008).

Nevertheless, every specific quality initiative runs the risk that the non-mobilized views of quality that are suppressed to make a place for a specific quality concept in precisely this initiative can be mobilized again. Under conditions of reflexive modernity, the limits on critique are only temporary. In this way, the concept of quality under conditions of reflexive modernity is symptomatic of its time.

Society's Image of Itself: Dilemmas

Instead of modernity's self-confident belief in progress, what is the spirit of reflexive modernization? In light of the collapse of the grand narratives about progress, of the weakening feeling of an omniscient center in society, and of the intensification of complexity and side effects for society, the dominating mentality of reflexive modernity becomes marked by doubt, suspicion, and uncertainty.

Progress has lost its status because of its side effects. Nor is there any great excitement about the merits of progress. Instead, these merits are taken for granted. Generations grow up for whom access to education, cars, washing machines, cell phones, and the internet does not generate any particular excitement; these things are perhaps just regarded as necessary tools for a normal life. The energy may be potentially used to complain about problems of lack of quality in the anticipated goods and services.

The former Western ideas of universal rights connected to the idea of progress have been replaced by an explosion of diverse rights for diverse groups, each seeing itself as the center of the world.

The conditions for critique have never been so favorable, writes Beck (1994a, 12): "Everything must be inspected, cut into pieces, discussed and debated to death, until finally, with a blessing from general dissatisfaction, a decision is reached which no one wants" (21–22).

Although critique and dissatisfaction can come from many sides, reflexive modernization leaves little room in society for a larger utopia or vision about a general societal change. Especially after 1989, there is no alternative to the Western capitalist societal model. The revolutions behind the former Iron Curtain were—in contrast to other great revolutions—not borne by new or heretofore untested visions, and they were not trying to realize a utopia. Neither in the West nor in the East is there any urge to move toward a fundamentally different societal form in the future.

The Western societies themselves are no longer certain they will respect the human rights that they were previously so proud to promote throughout the entire world. In essential areas such as environment, culture, economy, social policy, and international cooperation, the West seems not to appear as competent and happy about its own solutions as it did in earlier times. This is partly because progress has run out of steam, but also because the West criticizes itself as a part of reflexive modernization.

This is a situation that intellectuals such as sociologists and philosophers interpret with differing emphasis. Castoriadis mentions that modern society today no longer desires for itself but simply endures itself (1982, 25). He sees the creative and future-oriented force that marked earlier phases of modern society, both politically and artistically, as having been lost.

Bauman states that society's current organization is characterized by a comprehensive "interface," complicated and opaque connections among people, technologies, organizations, and politics. It is now difficult for individuals to feel, in the phenomenology of their everyday experience, that they are members of society. Consumer society helps to install an existence that amounts to just a series of episodes. We ignore the collective problems that appear, or we respond to them through individual actions that worsen the problem. For example, children get too little exercise, among other reasons because they do not walk or bike to school anymore but are driven there by their parents. Why do we drive our children to school? Because it has become more dangerous to move about in traffic without a car. A great deal of morning commuter traffic consists, by the way, of parents who are driving their children to school. But if others do it, I must do it too. In this way, individual solutions wind up in worse collective problems, and a collective incapacity for solving the problem is exposed (Bauman 2002). In Bauman's perspective, there is a close and reciprocal connection among increasing interface, society's invisibility, an incapacity to produce sustainable collective solutions, and lack of societal ambition.

Vattimo (2004) would here emphasize that if we take modern ideas about progress as our standard, we demand a metaphysics that the modern otherwise promised to abandon. We must instead recognize and accept that the modern does not contain any guarantee of a better world. For him, the departure from ideas of progress is instead an occasion to take up new, collective forms of handling what it means to live in a modern society.

As is shown, philosophers and sociologists present images of contemporary society with very different nuances. What I would like to underscore here, in conclusion, is the dynamic and dual character marking reflexive modernity.

Reflexive modernity is an extension and reworking of modernity. In early phases, there was greater excitement about the new possibilities for the critique of authority and increased individual emancipation and development. After a certain point, however, the critique of authority can presumably no longer create undivided excitement. Ziehe (2004), for example, mentions how de-traditionalization has falling marginal utility, and youths are now also longing for "momentary stylizations"—areas of existence and ways of life that recapture the advantages of rituals and something that is not constantly up for discussion.

Reflexive modernity has praised doubt and critique, but it does not contain any prescriptions for how limits on reflection can be set. There is no solution offered as to when there has been enough doubt, enough learning, enough restructuring, enough critique. One can image that at some point fatigue, lack of enthusiasm, and problems with the capacity to reflect may occur.

5   Evaluation in Reflexive Modernity

The purpose of this chapter is twofold: to illustrate what evaluation looks like when it is culturally compatible with reflexive modernization, and to identify the problems and weaknesses in evaluation in this era as it points toward the next.

In a reflexively modern society, organizations must evaluate. They must show that they are up to date with the times. They must appear to take the issue of side effects seriously, be able to listen, and be capable of adapting themselves to changing conditions. They must handle contingency. Whether they in fact do so in practice is difficult to determine, and it can also be debatable from one situation to another. Whether an organization has legitimate procedures in place to signal that it is up to date with the times, however, is far more evident.

Evaluation thus becomes the manifest sign showing an organization is in line with present cultural expectations in society. It demonstrates a reflexively modern mentality.

The fact that organizations, under conditions of reflexive modernity, must evaluate means that whatever function evaluation has, it is overlaid by a strongly symbolic element. Evaluation becomes a procedure ritualistically required by society.

The first and most fundamental theoretical movement we must undertake in order to understand evaluation as an organizational remedy in the age of reflexive modernity is therefore to abandon the idea that an evaluation must always be explained on the basis of its intended consequences. A "logic of consequentiality" must be replaced by a "logic of appropriateness" (March and Olsen 1989). Evaluation is not undertaken primarily for its utilitarian benefits, but rather because it is expected and demanded—because it represents a confirmation of organizational remedies and scripts in a social configuration of reflexive modernity.

Evaluations are initiated primarily when organizations expect that they will be carried out. There have been a large number of contributing *carriers* of the idea of evaluation. The state makes increasing demands for evaluation, in some countries with a high degree of regulatory content, that is, legislation stipulating compulsory evaluation or the linking of evaluation results and budget allocations. Many countries have now established evaluation institutions to undertake evaluation themselves and ensure that others do so. International organizations have allied themselves with evaluation and conduct quite spectacular evaluation (an example is the PISA studies), which leads to more evaluation work. National PISA studies often lead to more detailed evaluation regimes at the subnational level, such as those of evaluation centers, performance management systems, and school self-evaluation. Evaluation has been facilitated not only by education systems and courses but also by consultants, along with the proliferation of professional evaluation associations having the goal of promoting the benefits of evaluation.

As an organizational recipe for good management, evaluation offers benefits that, on the basis of institutional theory, would lead to predictions of expansion. Evaluation builds further on the ideas of modern rationality about improving the social, manmade world. With its continuing feedback loops, it has undertaken the necessary modernization to which modern attitudes about rationality and progress are gradually being subjected. Evaluation builds on the recognized norm that decisions in responsible organizations must be taken on the basis of solid information (Feldman and March 1981). Evaluation, at least in many of the variants we have discussed up to now, also seeks to market itself for the benefit of both the individual and the organization, as in the form of collective learning. Evaluation has been so positive and beneficial that it can be considered a meta-recipe. This means it can operate as a heading for several other solutions (management by results, contract management, quality assurance, accreditation, auditing, etc.). It links itself to any and all of these techniques, which only further facilitates its diffusion. Clever consultants also understand how to sell evaluation or parts of it under the label of other organizational recipes such as "reality testing" as part of "leadership development" (if a specific situation makes it more marketable using these particular buzzwords).

The mechanisms for the spread of evaluation are numerous. The demand can be mimetic, as when prestigious organizations evaluate and others copy them. The inspiration to evaluation can be normative, such that it is now expected that modern organizations will "listen" to their employees, users, or partners and be capable of responding to side effects and reactions from various stakeholders. We have already cited examples (education, training courses, associations, books), most of which can be classified as normative and mimetic sources of the institutional spread of evaluation. As evaluation becomes institutionalized, partly with the assistance of state intervention, the number of regulatory mechanisms rises so as to ensure the continued diffusion of evaluation. Hence a broad range of mechanisms contribute to the spread of evaluation.

In addition, evaluation is aided by international and fashionable trends. An international study shows that the spread of evaluation has primarily taken place in two major waves: a rationalist, data-based, and experimental first wave beginning in the late 1960s, and a second in the 1980s in the wake of New Public Management (Furubo, Rist, and Sandahl 2002). The evaluation cultures in individual countries were marked by both national preconditions and the international developments dominant at the time. That the entrance of evaluation is differentiated does not detract from our main observation, however, that evaluation to a great extent is understood on the basis of large organizational fields setting norms for individual organizations, nationally and internationally.

These mechanisms, however, emphasized ensuring that evaluation is established as an organizational recipe. Demands for the actual *use of evaluation* have not been institutionalized in the same way, or in any case not in an early phase. On the contrary, we can apply a new, radical, openminded, and less ambitious view of the utilization of evaluations if we recognize that evaluation begins primarily because it is expected as part of organizational routine, not because it is known to produce certain results or solve specific problems (unless, of course, building organizational legitimacy is a problem in itself). For this problem, evaluation is a cure under reflexive modernization.

Evaluation is particularly useful in relation to complex problems that must be handled by organizations. It may be a good functional answer to a central problem in reflexive modernization: How can organizations that produce side effects (including their material and symbolic effects on users of services and other stakeholders) as part of an ever more complex society be made sensitive to these effects so that they can internalize their social function and better live up to their responsibility (Power 1997b)? Contemporary forms of evaluation that incorporate side effects and the many views of stakeholders may be a fine functional response to this challenge.

However, for a person or agency in need of knowing whether an organization handles the complexity and contingency posed by the problems in reflexive modernity, it is extremely difficult to specify what it is necessary to know.

Trust in the organization is thus in jeopardy, unless some respected and fashionable procedure can be put in place to help assure these persons and agencies that the organization does at least what other sensible organizations would do in order to check and follow up on their achievements. Evaluation is such a procedure. If organization A has to tell organization B that organization C can be trusted, it may do so by saying that C is evaluating itself, or A is evaluating how C is evaluating itself.

Our main argument here is not entirely functional, although we might argue that evaluation sometimes helps organizations manage complex problems. Our main argument is that evaluation is so much in line with the dominant cultural mentality in reflexive modernization that it may be a shorthand symbol for the best procedural assurance we can get under the circumstances. As such, it is a powerful ritual.

Hence millions of questionnaire surveys are sent out to users, students, and clients, not because their replies necessarily make any practical difference but because the exercise of authority under reflexive modernization must include an attitude of listening and reflection, because the respondents are accustomed to being asked their opinions, and because evaluation signifies proper organization.

The basic attitude of reflexive modernization toward evaluation is, therefore, "The more the better." It is especially when it becomes unconscious and unreflective that a certain practice begins to act like an institution, and this is precisely what has occurred with evaluation.

Reflexive Modernity as an Explanation of the Evaluation Wave

Many explanations have been given for the emergence and growth of evaluation. The education of a sufficiently large number of social science graduates who were prepared to use their knowledge in a practical way is one factor. This explanation is not entirely irrelevant, but it does not take into account why evaluation was in demand in the first place. Financial restrictions on public expenses are another factor. This explanation is not necessarily irrelevant either, even though evaluation in fact emerged in an era of economic growth and with great hopes for social progress. Furthermore, if the purpose of evaluation is to save money, evaluation should be extremely careful with its own costs, which it often is not (Hansen 2005; Power 1996), and evaluability assessment should be increasingly used, which it is not (Smith 2005; Dahler-Larsen 2010).

A third explanation is the rise of New Public Management and its mobilization of neoliberal ideas. Yet, as we have mentioned, evaluation entered the scene before the NPM wave. NPM has undoubtedly helped boost the demand for evaluation in some of the countries that had not taken it up earlier (Furubo, Rist, and Sandahl 2002). At the same time, the NPM wave helped to push evaluation in certain directions. But it occurred only after many of the debates about evaluation had already taken place. It would therefore be reductionist to view the entire evaluation wave as merely an expression of NPM ideology.

The emergence and development of the wave of evaluation is generally best understood as growing reflexive modernization. As we have seen, evaluation is a child of the rationalism of modernity, but faith in progress is modified insofar as it is acknowledged that not all social initiatives and programs automatically succeed. Progress must therefore be "postponed" slightly, while experiments are carried out to discover what works. Later on, it is gradually acknowledged that politics and use of knowledge do not live up to the strict model of rationalism (Albæk 1988). Gradually, the ideas of progress are dissolved in a cacophony of objections, a multiplicity of views, and what corresponds to a virtual explosion of possible value positions, all of which make their claim to relevance. The early evaluation models thus were vulnerable to critical questioning of the modern faith in science, rationality, measurement, control, and progress, but recent evaluation approaches have focused on local, qualitative knowledge and on the plurality of criteria, viewpoints, and forms of experience. A clear division of labor between politics and knowledge under the banner of rationalism and technocracy is replaced by dialogue, inclusion, and negotiated reconstruction of social constructions (Guba and Lincoln 1989). "Empowerment evaluation" (Fetterman, Kaftarian, and Wandersman 1996, 139), which concerns "self-determination, defined as the ability to chart one's own course in life," must be said to be a preliminary high point in evaluation history with reference to copying self-development as a popular theme of reflexive modernity.

The growth of evaluation thus precisely reflects the gradual growth of reflexive modernization. If this thesis is correct, one could derive more specific hypotheses about the diffusion patterns of evaluation. Evaluation must follow the degree of reflexive modernization, which, however, is uneven over time and has an uneven impact on the various sectors of society as well.

Evaluations will be more frequent within the areas of society where reflexive modernity is most intense, such as the politics of life, health, and death; education; and social work (Beck, Giddens, and Lash 1994). Internationally, when reflexive modernity must make a theme out of its relationship to developing countries, evaluations are also extensive. On the other hand, evaluations must be rare or absent in those areas of society characterized by inherited traditions and symbols from earlier societal forms. To evaluate monarchies (in those European countries that still have them), for example, would be unlikely. The same applies to national languages and flags. The effectiveness of traditional national symbols is usually not evaluated, although it might lead to interesting findings if we also include, say, their side effects!

Evaluation would also be rarely used by those societal institutions with great concentrations of power, such as the judiciary or the military. In these sectors, it is more difficult to create a place for reflexive processes. Where tradition or strong power reigns, there is less room for contingency, without which evaluation cannot flourish.

On the other hand, where and when evaluation does take place, it creates further contingency. Several processes are initiated: comparison, benchmarking, standardization, quality assessment, critique from users, etc. These processes tend to reinforce contingency. The feeling that there is a need to change or readjust rises. Perhaps for this reason, consultants about to undertake a restructuring process in a resistant organization like to begin the process with an evaluation or two. The evaluation brings problems to the surface, promotes readiness for change, and lays the groundwork for reorganization. In other words, there is as a consequence a close and mutually reinforcing relationship between contingency and evaluation. They are signs, and carriers, of reflexive modernization.

The Easy and Uneasy Relation Between Reflexive Modernization and Evaluation

The close relation between reflexive modernization and evaluation is central to our theoretical argument. To fully understand this relation, we need to appreciate both its easy and uneasy sides. Let us first consider the easy side, or the nice cultural compatibility between them.

Evaluation is a ritual that fits with the demands and expectations of reflexive modernization. That evaluation has become a suitable, legitimate, expected, and demanded organizational formula helps to explain why it is sometimes introduced even though the specific purpose sometimes remains unclear. Why the evaluation wave has arisen in our time is no longer a mystery.

Evaluation may work as a ritual in line with its times even if the components of the evaluation are disconnected from one another, as we described using the institutional model of organization. As organizations attend to many pressures in reflexive modernization, it may be sensible to attend to the results of a given evaluation in a limited way. Organizations avoid doing evaluations in a way that makes it too liminal an experience, for example by adapting parts of the evaluation process to something well known, by detouring around uncomfortable topics, by formulating unclear objectives, or by generally not using the results. Instead, they can simply declare that they have done an evaluation and that reforms have been initiated that will contribute to improvements in the future (Meyer and Rowan 1977).

Organizations nevertheless retain faith in themselves and their evaluation by continuing to link evaluation to myths about organizational learning, improvement, and informed decision making. Although evaluation is explained on the basis of a logic of appropriateness rather than a logic of consequentiality, we get a fresh and perhaps provocative perspective on the function of evaluation. The myth of the always-improvement-oriented and learning-oriented evaluation is constantly promoted. But this myth remains credible only if terms such as *improvement* and *learning* mean different things in different situations, and sometimes perhaps almost nothing at all. And this is what happens under reflexive modernization. This sums up our analysis of the easy cultural appropriateness of evaluation after we combine the insights of the institutional model of organization with the sociological description of reflexive modernization as the contemporary social context in which evaluation unfolds.

But there are points this analysis overlooks, in what one might call the uneasy relation between evaluation and reflexive modernization. Problems do not just disappear because there is cultural compatibility between the two. We should remind ourselves of what the newer contributions to institutional theory say about the necessity of supplying an analysis of existing institutional and cultural norms with attention to conflict, contradiction, discussion, and change. We should also remind ourselves of a point made in the sociology of knowledge: that development of new forms of knowledge is contested and nonlinear.

More specifically, in evaluation under reflexive modernization, there continue to be problems to which evaluators, the users of evaluation, or researchers on evaluation attend. These issues are partly a product of evaluation's infiltration into reflexive modernization, but they are also potentially the motivation for new ways of conceiving and designing evaluation. In no era is evaluation free from problems. In no era so far has the social dynamic of evaluation stopped.

Just as evaluation, under the headline of modernity, gives rise to a critique that paved the way for subsequent forms, evaluation under conditions of reflexive modernization gives rise to revisions. It requires an analysis that goes deeper than what institutional organization theorists call a ritual. It must be an analysis that takes the social dynamic of the field of evaluation seriously. It must also include reactions to the limitations of evaluation and to social reactions on these limitations.

I now deal with five problems created by the reflexive modernization of evaluation or intensified by it: lack of enthusiasm, lack of utilization, unpredictable evaluation, lack of representation of society, and lack of reduction of complexity. Each inspires evaluators or users of evaluation to reform and update it so that it forms an active response and points toward the next phase in the development of evaluation, beyond reflexive modernity.

The five are all indicative of the perspectivity and fragmentation characteristic of reflexive modernity, but we shall look at them analytically one by one.

Lack of Enthusiasm

Modernity has legitimized itself through reduction of hunger and disease, and through tangible improvements such as income and longer life. Reflexive modernity does not benefit from the same kind of legitimacy because in reflexive modernity there is already too much progress. The consequences of modernity and progress are already questioned. The sources of legitimacy in reflexive modernization become insecure. Because evaluation is booming, it is possible that it will create some enthusiasm now that authorities can be critiqued and controversial issues discussed. However, if reflexive modernization is the era that has made evaluation possible and popular on an unprecedented scale, it is also the era that has paved the way for evaluation fatigue. People are not naïve; the marginal utility of their first evaluation may be great, but the 57th evaluation may not be carried out with enthusiasm. If authority is criticized, if tradition is questioned, and controversy created, what comes next?

Lise and Her Evaluation Fatigue

Remember Lise from the Introduction of this book? She is an ordinary person in contemporary society. Remember how much evaluation she is involved in during her daily life? Perhaps the same is true for her husband. Image that the two spouses meet in the evening, after a long day. Imagine one saying: "Let's evaluate our marriage! What do you think is a good marriage?" Perhaps the other is likely to answer, "The kind we had before you asked that question."

The drop in enthusiasm for evaluation may be a subjective reflection of four more objective and structural problems related to evaluation under reflexive modernization.

Lack of Utilization

Lack of instrumental use has been a classic problem in evaluation since its inception. But reflexive modernization intensifies it; evaluation looks at more complex evaluands with more capricious side effects. The social, political, and organizational structures that are supposed to deal with these problems become more complex as new forms of governance evolve. Social responsibility is distributed among many partners in many layers, and it becomes more difficult to see the societal responsibility for one's actions. Under reflexive modernization, it is more difficult to pinpoint one intended user of an evaluation correctly, which is why strategies for partnership and involvement flourish. But as the responsibility for use of evaluation is diffused, it does not become easier to secure utilization.

The entanglement of diverse problems also makes it more difficult to rationally solve them one by one.

Because of contingency, the speed of reforms accelerates. As management is expected to act swiftly, new actions are often set in motion without a proper evaluative conclusion for the previous policy or reform. The cognitive capacity to evaluate and the organizational capacity to learn are limited, and even if they grow they do not do so nearly as quickly as do the socially defined demands to perform evaluation.

On top of all this, reflexive modernization boosts the legitimacy of a procedure like evaluation, even if it is of limited instrumental use. There is among evaluators a growing belief in "process use," and in other good benefits of evaluation that are perhaps difficult to demonstrate in practice. Evaluation becomes fashionable on an unprecedented historical scale. Under reflexive modernization, evaluability assessment is suspended. Evaluation becomes an unqualified good.

As an organizational recipe, evaluation can be a ritual that is rather loosely linked to other aspects of organizational life. The evaluating organization attempts to meet the expectations of the environment, but only to the extent necessary. Evaluation becomes something that "we have to do." In this sense, evaluation is a ritual, but a ritual of the type that does not mobilize emotions or motivations. It is simply an organizational recipe that may or may not have meaning.

However, the idea of rationality continues to constitute an important motivation for advocates of evaluation. There is a desire to undertake initiatives that work. So something must be done.

As a result, initiatives are constantly undertaken to make evaluation more learning-oriented, more meaningful, more relevant, and more inclusive. Some recommend deeper and more intensified participation on the part of a number of stakeholders, with the purpose of incorporating them into systematic deliberative processes or learning processes. Internal evaluators are under special pressure to demonstrate that something comes out of evaluation (Mathison 1991), so they begin searching for more integrative organizational processes and more power for evaluation.

Evaluation that is typical of reflexive modernization therefore becomes ripe for change in the direction of something not typical of reflexive modernization as we have seen it so far. It creates a situation with a clearer need for a more systematic and controlled way of conducting evaluation and securing its use.

Unpredictable Evaluation

Under reflexive modernization, evaluation should be tailor-made, depending on the nature of a specific complex problem and the reflection it invites. It should relate in a specific way to an organizational, social, cultural, and political context. The spirit among those who seek to synthesize the development of evaluation theory is that now that we have so many models and approaches, each of them may have something good to offer, but they should each be applied in a contingency-oriented way and only after careful situational analysis (Shadish, Cook, and Leviton 1991).

But who can guarantee that even a good situational analysis deterministically leads to only one specific form of evaluation? Insightful observers note that evaluation design is an art, not just a science (Cronbach, cited in Shadish, Cook, and Leviton 1991, 349), and evaluation itself is a contested practice that embodies but does not eliminate value tensions (Schwandt 2002; Greene 1997).

When evaluation is executed ad hoc, and when the wave of evaluation as a whole exhibits considerable value pluralism, if not relativism, evaluation often becomes more or less tailor-made in a way that reflects the characteristics of the individual evaluator. Potential users of evaluation (clients and commissioners) are not always comfortable with the processes of evaluation, especially carried out by evaluators who were advocates of multiple values, constructivist dialogue, and empowerment.

The stakeholders in an evaluation have their own political interests in an evaluation, and this can lead to ongoing struggles in the various phases of the evaluation process when these interests are mobilized within some type of participatory evaluation. Last but not least, the entire evaluation process represents a knowledge-creation process that in essence reflects the general contingency of such processes under reflexive modernization. When one recognizes that knowledge is socially constructed, the tranquility in the process of creating knowledge is lost. Different parties have permanent possibilities to demand that the process could, or ought to, take another direction. The result is unpredictable evaluation. This phenomenon is a result of the general contingency in reflexive modernization, which hits evaluation specifically in terms of the contingency of the choice of evaluator and evaluation approach, of value orientations, and of the elements in the evaluation process.

Those who hire evaluators attempt to counteract this effect by exercising control over the evaluation process through selection of the evaluator, the terms of reference, establishment of a monitoring or steering committee, and continuing follow-up and guidelines for reporting. Many countries have established common guidelines, standards, and instructions for good evaluation, and these are occasionally desired by both the client seeking the evaluation and the evaluators themselves. Nevertheless, several large clients, such as the European Commission, continue to be less than totally satisfied with the low degree of predictability they experience when their evaluation tasks are conducted by the contracted evaluators, even if a number of bureaucratic control mechanisms are in place.

Evaluators themselves report on unpredictability as well. Radical, constructivist, deliberative, and fourth-generation evaluators, for example, report that their clients sometimes receive something completely different than they expected. Serious spokespersons for participatory evaluation speak of an inherent tension between pragmatic, action-oriented approaches and more explicit, politically transformative approaches (Greene 1997).

Advocates of involvement of users in evaluation of public services, as suggested by, for example, the UPQA evaluation (Krogstrup 1998), explain that this model has the intention of breaking with the established institutional order. Hence it must by definition entail unpredictability in the evaluation process. This tension is often felt in concrete evaluation processes in practice, not the least by commissioners of evaluation. Truly, reflexive modernization preaches the virtues of reflexivity and sometimes surprise. And evaluation carries the same norms. However, in practice, there is a limit to how much reflexivity and surprise specific authorities, organizations, managers, and other users of evaluation like.

What is extraordinarily uncomfortable for managers is unpredictable evaluation processes that happen in the name of management itself. Surprises that are sometimes unwelcome are one thing. More difficult are surprises for which one will be held responsible. For this reason, evaluation under reflexive modernization has paved the way for a desire among bureaucrats, managers, and others to ensure more predictability in evaluation processes.

We have already encountered the observation that the individual elements in the evaluation process have their institutionalized logics, which makes it difficult to summarize them in predictable, integrated processes. In practical terms, it is difficult to live with evaluations that take place within the existing management structure but do not conform with a minimum of managerial expectations. Over the years, unpredictable evaluation, together with other factors, has increased the need for some normalization, standardization, and bureaucratization of the evaluation processes.

The Lack of Perspective on Society: Pluralism and Anomie

The response of the evaluation field to reflexive modernization was not only to strengthen learning processes but also to develop several new approaches that enabled various stakeholders to enter the arena and be involved.

Many dimensions were revealed in the value landscape in which evaluation operates, and new models, schools, and directions established themselves on different value foundations. An ever-growing number of perspectives made themselves relevant, and numerous normative guidelines for fair and democratic evaluation were presented—without, however, any general acceptance of a particular normative framework.

Value pluralism spread in the evaluation field; it could well lead to relativism and subjectivism.

Truly, there were several approaches attempting to make the foundation for evaluation more solid and universally convincing. Included were perspectives on scientific generalization (Pawson and Tilley 1997), social betterment (Mark, Henry, and Julnes 2000), and a democratic evaluation process that could live up to universal principles for rational discourse (House and Howe 2000). However, altogether the many faces of the evaluation wave appeared as a supermarket of value dispositions rather than a synthesis and convergence.

In responsive evaluation, for example, the case study method is viewed as the best way of grasping the unique aspects of the individual local evaluand. Even though responsive evaluation can offer an interesting counterpoint to ideological standards-based school policy, the interest in the local appears to be a trap for responsive evaluators, if they seldom return to contribute to a larger societal debate.

In some forms of participatory, constructivist, or utilization-focused evaluation, there is a strong focus on selected stakeholders. Politicians are often too distant or seen simply as one group of stakeholders among others. The representative democratic dimension among stakeholders thereby becomes "neutralized" (Pollitt 2006). Viewed philosophically, however, even myriad stakeholders do not constitute a society. A similar conclusion has been reached after many years of work with user-oriented evaluation. Even though the involvement of users of services in evaluation can have considerable renewing effects and learning effects, it is impossible to lend it an independent and autonomous philosophical and democratic theoretical justification (Dahlberg and Vedung 2001; Fountain 2001). In fact, public authorities must invent techniques to evade, resist, or modify user-oriented evaluation, not because these authorities are sluggish and manipulative but because the idea of unlimited user influence through evaluation is a disingenuous philosophical and political idea—unless an effort is made to conceptually combine such an inclusive, participatory, and receptive evaluation approach with a larger democratic project or theory (for such an attempt, see Dahlberg and Vedung 2001).

Several recent evaluation approaches have entirely abandoned such ambitions. In empowerment evaluation, for example, the ideal is instead to enable others to gain control over their own lives. In some evaluation models, it is considered a great virtue in itself to give voice to those who are not normally heard. Even though this may be a laudable principle, it is difficult to place any kind of limit on who needs to be heard *more*. In fact, everybody does. No need should be ignored; all voices should be heard. Why should criminals not be regarded as a stakeholder group in an evaluation involving the whole local community?

In this way, some variations of evaluation may lead to a moral state of anomie. Its discovery of innumerable values and dimensions within values is a sign that the concept of value has practically exploded. It has become fragmented and can mean virtually anything at all (Boltanski and Chiapello 2007). Patients in hospitals who do not want small pieces of chocolate may have anti-chocolate values. If the term value is applied to such phenomena, it is no surprise that the value universe in society seems to be exploding.

The wave of evaluation has thereby brought itself into an anomic situation paralleling that which the humanist critic of capitalism brought upon itself, according to Boltanski and Chiapello (2007, 428). In their analyses, they use an argument from Durkheim: because people without a binding normative social framework are basically unsatisfied and unfulfilled, it is up to societies and communities to help establish a moral set of values and aspirations if anomie is to be avoided. Without a collective moral frame of reference, a wave of critique risks being dissolved into individual episodic outbreaks. The critique also risks (and here Boltanski and Chiapello 2007, 432, refer to Charles Taylor) losing its force of meaning if its ambitions are not linked together with a sense of society and construction of a community. In this light, one can imagine that the first user evaluations generated considerable excitement because they were refreshing and anti-authoritarian, but the effect gradually disappears without being replaced by anything else that can generate commitment and excitement. When several of the participatory evaluators report that participants find it difficult to make time for evaluation work, it is perhaps connected to the fact that they are not so excited by the prospect of evaluation. Someone simply reports that it is difficult to engage teachers in school-based evaluation (Monsen 2003). Scattered ideas about listening more, greater inclusion, and more dialogue may have a limited lifetime if they are not linked with ideas about interaction in a community or some larger moral framework. After a certain time with more dialogue, and more listening, the idea that more—even different—values should now be attended to may not create much enthusiasm. Evaluation fatigue may follow.

The field of evaluation, by virtue of its formation under reflexive modernization, has ended up without a well-defined idea of society or community. The many critics of society and the various sums of stakeholders involved in evaluation constituted, taken together, really only a fragmented set of voices, not a society. It was not possible for the many subjective points of view that came to expression by way of evaluation to produce a new societal agenda. Apparently, evaluation has not been the right instrument for this goal to be achieved.

I recognize that some evaluators are essentially subtler than others on this point and that evaluators have differing aspirations for society. Among the thoughtful ones are Schwandt (2002), Mark, Henry and Julnes (2000), and House and Howe (2000), but within the field of evaluation very few explicitly describe the lack of philosophically grounded societal perspective in evaluation as a shortcoming that needs attention.

Democratic accounts do form a constitutive part of the normative framework of democracy (March and Olsen 1995). And, as Nevo quite straightforwardly argues with teachers, "If you won't respect the authority and responsibility of the Ministry of Education and the right of parents to know about the schools their children go to, don't expect them to respect your right for autonomy and reflection and trust your judgment as a professional teacher" (2002, 15). From a societal perspective, it may not suffice to know that schools and other institutions are engaged in reflexive learning processes. Society, represented by official political and bureaucratic authorities, may define the need for accountability in different ways.

It cannot be assumed that the need for organizations to explain themselves to society through evaluation should wither away. Use of systematic data collection as a means of handling contingency is an appropriate way forward, and more adequate than appeals to, say, authoritarianism or tradition or endless "trust." But it may not be enough just to let the rest of society know that evaluation is being carried out and contingency is being dealt with. The rest of society may also want to know how contingency is dealt with, and how well. Evaluation results must be communicated, too.

This is especially true if the wider norms in society not only support soft and reflexive forms of learning, as the core scripts in reflexive modernization would suggest. The wider society as well as official authorities may insist on harder, more result-oriented forms of accountability.

For this reason and others, some advocates of learning-oriented evaluation seek new forms of cooperation with accountability-oriented, external evaluation. Although some of them insist that internal (self-)evaluation should come first (Ålvik 1996), the important point is the new and explicit search for cooperation between learning- and accountability-oriented approaches to evaluation as a way to counteract perspectives that are too subjective and solipsistic.

Nevo suggests a number of ways in which the two approaches can supplement each other. External evaluation can stimulate a self-evaluating, introspective process; expand its scope; and support its validity. In turn, internal evaluation (again, self-evaluation) can expand the scope of external evaluation, improve the interpretation of findings, and enhance utilization (Nevo 2002, 6–9). Internal evaluation can also be used to present the core values and beliefs of a school vis-à-vis external stakeholders. The internet affords new opportunities for combining such evaluation with external promotion.

In a survey, school teachers and professionals were asked to rate their ability to carry out a number of evaluation activities. Although they reported that many of these activities were an integral part of their daily routine, the two lowest-scoring items were doing evaluation in a methodologically competent way and explaining evaluation results to external partners (Dahler-Larsen 2006b). This suggests some of the difficulties with a greater external focus.

Internal and external perspectives may typically embody different views regarding how broad a spectrum of evaluation criteria should be included. For example, politicians, bureaucrats, and journalists tend to believe that school quality can be measured by indicators of pupil achievement, and that schools will work harder to improve their quality if they are measured along these lines (Nevo 2006, 454). Teachers (as well as many educational researchers) tend to believe in a more multidimensional description of school quality, including the mission of the school, its educational philosophy, characteristics of the students, the variety of programs, physical and economic resources, social climate, and sometimes the quality of teachers (Nevo 2006, 454).

Continued controversy is also likely as to who should hold control over which parts of the data (Monsen 2003), which data should be made public (Rowe 2000), and when such data are released, as well as who controls the kind of frameworks employed to interpret the data (Andersen and Dahler-Larsen 2008).

Forms of evaluation developed under reflexive modernization (with an emphasis on subjective viewpoints and formative, learning-oriented evaluation) run the risk of becoming functionally and symbolically inadequate if they do not attend to some form of feedback to society. In turn, the need to give such feedback depends on how one understands the role of evaluation incorporated into a vision of society. Without such a vision, evaluation under reflexive evaluation remains weak. Reflexively modern evaluation approaches may have to leave the scene to other plays able to furnish quantitative and hard-nosed evaluation results back to society without hesitation.

The Lack of Reduction of Complexity

From a management and control perspective, all these observations render evaluation that is typical of reflexive modernization a rather inadequate instrument. Evaluation—after reflexive modernization—appears to be fragmented into a large number of models with inconsistent perspectives, unpredictable processes, and limited utilization. One does not know what comes out of these many uneven and flexible feedback loops that characterize reflexive modernization and that the development of the evaluation wave so finely reflects. They do not have the capacity to report back in a manner that allows evaluation activities to be synthesized and summarized.

If, furthermore, we take into consideration how knowledge such as evaluation can be socially influential and productive in nonlinear ways (Stehr 2001), the dispersal of evaluation into innumerable fragmented processes must be disturbing when viewed from a control and management perspective.

From this perspective, there are complaints about lacking knowledge of how public-sector systems work. From the political side, there are complaints, for example, that we know precisely how much it costs to run the schools in a country, how many teachers are employed, and how much money is used on school books, but we know nothing systematically and generally about the outcomes of schooling and how things are going with children's learning. The former Norwegian minister of education, Kristin Clemet (2006), described the situation in this way when she assumed office.

The issue is often conceptualized as a question of knowledge about input, processes, outputs, and outcomes of public organizations. The idea is that over many years there has been too much focus on input and process. We know a lot about inputs and processes, but we know almost nothing about outcomes. Yet it is here that the focus of public policies and activities should lie.

This argument sounds attractive, and one can understand an education minister's anxiety at being held responsible for administration of an entire sector while knowing little about its outcome.

The argument, however, rests on two debatable assumptions. One is whether it is indeed correct that we know nearly nothing about school outcomes, simply because there does not exist much quantitative evaluation information about this topic.

The second is whether any system with quantitative evaluation information will ever be able to supply valid and adequate knowledge about a topic as broad as "the schools' outcomes."

The question, though, is what *valid* and *adequate* should mean in such a context. It depends on the perspective. From a leadership and management perspective, one can perhaps be satisfied with information that makes it possible to exercise leadership and management without other perspectives in society necessarily finding the information valid, convincing, and adequate. Here we can learn from some recent Luhmann-inspired analyses (Andersen 2004; Lindeberg 2007). Modern social systems are functionally specific self-referential. A system such as management operates with management tools on a world defined through managerial glasses. The task for management information is to make it possible to exercise management, and not much more than that.

Without reporting of evaluative information, management systems lack the sort of justification they need. With management information, management can act. The situation under reflexive modernization is therefore ripe for managers, leaders, and politicians to begin to demand their own evaluation information, information that they can use in their decision-making processes. The managerial perspective favors information that somehow cuts through complexity. It favors information that appears to be objective and is quantitative, comparable, standardized, and not difficult to digest.

From a management perspective, considerable demand arises for the kind of evaluation information that helps with an overview and reduces complexity. The evaluation wave, as we have described it in connection with reflexive modernization, has not in itself had the capacity to do this. It is too anomic, unpredictable, of too little use, and not able to provide the kind of overview of complexity that managers and politicians need.

Seeking Integration of Evaluation in Organizations: Evaluation Capacity and the Like

Based on this analysis of lacking utilization, lacking predictability, lacking societal perspectives, and lacking reduction of complexity, a need arises among managers to streamline and control evaluation processes and their results. But of course, the evaluation field itself has already responded to several of the same problems as it saw them.

Evaluators have known for some time that singular evaluations have little or no impact on the larger systems in which they take place. Learning-oriented evaluators took up the challenge of limited utilization of evaluation, only to find that to be successful, learning cycles themselves required close attention to a large number of organizational factors. One such factor is the technical competence to actually carry out evaluations, which is a critical factor in participatory evaluation (Cousins 2003). If an organization continues to carry out evaluations without an external evaluator, it should build up such competence in-house. However, it has often been found that the most important barrier to learning from evaluations is not related to the technical quality of the evaluation but to norms and values among decision makers and other stakeholders not favorable to evaluation. Increasing attention to the social context around evaluations and their utilization leads to a new focus on those structures and cultures that either hinder or promote evaluation as an idea and a practice.

As a consequence, evaluation capacity building and support of learning-oriented, evaluation-friendly organizational culture norms have become pivotal. For example, in developing countries a specific lesson was learned about what would later be termed evaluation capacity: if there is no local capacity for management and learning, then even large external injections of resources are of little help in the long run. Sustainability requires local capacity. Errors and side effects must be discovered locally if they are to be dealt with. This lesson obviously explains the need for local evaluation capacity building. The lessons learned about evaluation capacity in foreign aid seem to be generalized in the field of evaluation. Especially under reflexive modernization, the intensity and complexity of social change as a result of widespread social contingency put the capacity of organizations to evaluate under pressure. Quite logically, good evaluators interested in the survival (if not success) of evaluation thus identified the need to strengthen the evaluation capacity of organizations.

The building of evaluation capacity is generally defined as aiming at "a state of affairs in which quality program evaluation and its appropriate uses are ordinary and ongoing practices" (Baizerman, Compton, and Stockdill 2005, 38), but the emphasis is on the factors that undergird this potential state of affairs, not on the actual practice of evaluation.

On the structural side, evaluation hinges on the ability of an organi-

zation to insert it at an appropriate place in the horizontal and verti-
cal structure of the organization and to secure management support. It
also includes the ability of competent staff to carry out quality evaluation
within designated budgets and on the basis of organizational rules and
other formal and informal mechanisms of coordination.

On the cultural front, building an evaluation culture hinges on norms,
values, and habits favorable to evaluation, such as habits supporting written documentation of methods and objectives, ongoing measurement of
process and outcome indicators, support for experimentation, tolerance
for mistakes, knowledge sharing, forums for organizational learning, etc.

Evaluation Culture

After an OECD report recommended introduction of an "evaluation culture" in Danish schools, this became adopted as official
policy.

Until then, terms related to evaluation had, more often than, not
created tension between the government and teachers. At the outset,
however, the term *evaluation culture* did not. Perhaps because of
its vague definition and positive connotations, almost all relevant
stakeholders saw some potential in the term.

The meaning of evaluation culture, however, gradually began to
unfold. It meant mandatory testing, while test results were not to
be published. It meant annual quality reports from each school sent
to the municipal administrations who administer schools in Denmark. It also meant progress reports on every pupil to be compiled
by teachers and shared with parents regularly. Evaluation culture
also comprised a number of local and sometimes school-based projects seeking to promote the idea and practice of evaluation among
school teachers.

Evaluation culture and evaluation capacity are closely related concepts,
with capacity perhaps emphasizing structural aspects and culture being
the norms, values, and habits related to evaluation. In this understanding,
resistance or refusal to carry out evaluation activities among, say, teachers or administrators is interpreted as evidence of lack of an evaluation

culture in the given school or institution. However, this phenomenon can be repaired by means of a better evaluation culture. Since improving evaluation culture helps build capacity, there is overlap between the two concepts.

Evaluation systems cover the more specific guidelines, regimes, and procedures for how evaluative data should be collected, administered, analyzed, and used in organizational and political contexts. For a set of evaluative practices to constitute a system, there must be some level of explicitness and formality as well as institutionalization and mainstreaming. To constitute an evaluation system, there needs to be some understanding of the interaction between the elements of the system, both evaluative and organizational. More often than not, evaluation systems constitute an integrated view of how several evaluations or types of evaluation fit into a larger organizational picture.

More often than not, an evaluation system is thus—at least ideally—an integrated part of how an organizational system is managed, controlled, and legitimized. If it is also officially approved by political or managerial officials of a government or an organization, we may talk of an evaluation policy.

All these ideas aspire to become an integrated part of life in modern organizations. Without such integration, evaluation will continue to be circumstantial and improvisational, and its consequences too unpredictable.

Although tentative terminological distinctions can be made among the concepts of evaluation capacity, evaluation culture, evaluation systems, and evaluation policy, they all reflect the desire for an integrative and interactive view of evaluation and of the social contexts in which it operates. They all seek to compensate for or repair the inconsistent, fragmented, loosely coupled nature of evaluation processes and their use, which—if not attended to—would characterize organizational life under reflexive modernization.

The rise of these themes (evaluation capacity, evaluation culture, evaluation systems, and evaluation policy) opens at least three significant opportunities.

First, it stimulates a belief in the abstract norms, values, structures, and procedures promoting evaluation as such—abstract understood as above any specific evaluation. In this light, evaluation can continue its sociohistorical march toward becoming a general good rather than a situation-specific instrument.

Second, the rise of such terms as evaluation capacity, evaluation culture, etc., opens up great new areas of work for the so-called evaluation industry. Instead of facing a strictly rational set of entry criteria before selling one evaluation, such as those known from evaluability assessment, consultants are now in a position to sell not only one evaluation but a whole culture of evaluation. Undertaking an evaluation is a step toward promoting evaluation capacity, culture, systems, and policies as generally a good idea. The game of evaluation capacity building is "an infinite game of ongoing, emergent rules, procedures, practices and politics" (Baizerman, Compton, and Stockdill 2005, 38), compared to completion of a particular evaluation, which is by definition a finite game.

Power (1996) argues that it is possible for the audit industry to expand its market by moving from singular inquiries to a focus on systems. It should not surprise us that evaluators are interested in making exactly the same move. Instead of carrying out ad-hoc evaluations at the periphery of large-scale organizations on short-term contracts, evaluators now have offices closer to management and are paid nice monthly salaries. While enjoying these benefits, they argue that it is better for organizations to celebrate a more integrated view of the role of evaluation in organizational life. Mainstreaming of evaluation is generally good, and it happens to be good for evaluators, too. Evaluators are not alone in competing for managerial attention and privilege. Marketing specialists, communications consultants, and human relations experts also argue that their fields need to be seen in a more integrated organizational and managerial perspective. Logically, they all have good arguments, because all of them live a life in fragmented and partly uncoordinated organizations. Practically, all of them want systematic integration of their own function into management, and offices closer to management, as well as better salaries.

Third, integration of organization and evaluation in the broadest sense also defined a new way in which management could engage itself in evaluation, whether or not the specific term was used. Managers and evaluators could now find common ground and work together. They could agree that evaluation as such was a universal good, over and above how it performed in every individual situation. It is now the system, the culture, and the capacity to do evaluation that count. Managers were also invited to become familiar with evaluation and the like.

In this large-scale undertaking, evaluation as a field is not alone. Various techniques, approaches, and strategies that may not all have originated as "evaluation" are able to "generalize" themselves as broadly applicable social practices (Power 2005). For example, quality inspection has moved from a fairly technical domain (dominated by engineers) to a more general managerial domain (Power 1996, 300), first in the industrial sector, then in the service sector, and lastly more generally in society. Now, quality is the overarching headline for public reforms in several countries. In a similar vein, audit has moved from a strictly financial domain into broader organizational systems, partly blending with quality inspection, quality assurance, and the like (Power 2005, 333). And not surprisingly, accreditation is no longer a specific procedure used by insurance companies to check whether organizations can be insured, but rather a more general term for how external inspection leads to official, authoritative approval of an organization or institution. In other words, the field of evaluation as such is not a sociohistorical constant. It has managed to grow and expand through adoption and integration of a number of data-producing practices that have generalized themselves at the same time they have shifted their focus from looking at things to looking more abstractly at systems that do things, and building systems that look at systems that do things.

With this new focus, advocates of evaluation culture, capacity, and systems hold a more advanced view of the political and organizational context around an evaluand than did those who were interested in evaluability assessment. Recall that advocates of evaluability assessment viewed the social context around evaluation as a set of given contingency factors. If this and that factor were in place, evaluation was deemed appropriate; if not, then evaluation was seen as having little benefit and was not recommended. In contrast, advocates of evaluation culture, capacity, and systems view evaluation as a generally good fit for all circumstances. All that is needed in general installation of the proper structures, cultures, and processes. If this happens, no situation will be unfit for evaluation. The context around evaluation is no longer regarded as exogenously given. Instead it is now to be mainstreamed under the regimes of evaluation systems, cultures, and capacities. An era has been inaugurated in which the self-confidence of evaluation reaches new heights. Evaluation is now in an unprecedented alliance with managerial circles. The evaluation manager aspires to sit in the office adjoining that of the CEO. The aspiration is also to create forms of evaluation that are predictable, reliable, and managerially relevant.

If we are correct in our analysis, the need for such forms of evaluation springs out of genuine problems with evaluation in reflexive modernization. But if there is already evaluation fatigue, then no reform of evaluation and no evaluation system will be without problems.

To highlight the sociocultural significance where I think evaluation systems are, nevertheless, going today, I offer a conceptual construct to describe them in their ideal extreme form. I call this ideal type "evaluation machines."

We have come to the third part of our tripartite sociological journey after modernity and reflexive modernity. We call it the audit society, characterized by neorigorism. It is this latter social configuration and its social imaginary that evaluation machines fit into. The next chapter is devoted to how these phenomena are connected.

6   Audit Society, Neorigorism, and
Evaluation Machines

In the preceding chapters, we described the sociohistorical climate in which evaluation took place as a modern and reflexively modern phenomenon. The reactions of the evaluation field to the challenges in these eras were also accounted for. We followed the functions and dysfunctions of evaluation as a part of reflexive modernization, which leaves evaluation in need of reforms in the direction of something less subjective and more controlled and predictable. Still our main thesis is that to understand evaluation, we constantly need to attend to the changing social imaginary.

We have therefore come to our third sociological phase. It is called the audit society after Michael Power's diagnosis of a "society engaged in constant checking and verification, an audit society in which a particular style of formalized accountability is the ruling principle" (Power 1997a, 4).

The audit society has lost the courage characteristic of progress-oriented modernity and the flexibility and curiosity of reflexive modernization. Although it is still a type of modern society, it installs a new balance between the two guiding principles of the modern social imaginary: autonomy and rationality. In the audit society, rationality strikes back, with all its connotations of predictability, antisubjectivism, and focus on procedure. The audit society is connected with a military, political, managerial, and cultural neorigorism seeking to establish a number of values and principles as nonnegotiable, in stark contradiction to reflexive modernization, where the ideal was that everything could be debated. In this sense, the audit society and cultural neorigorism signify a turn away from the contingency, relativity, and perspectivism so characteristic of globalization and reflexive modernization. In the audit society, modernity is afraid of all these consequences of modernity, and it begins to defend itself against them. The audit society is preoccupied with security and safety and sees evaluation procedures as a way to manage risk and provide reassurance. In terms of evaluation, the audit society is thus antithetical to the subjectivism, contingency, and apparent arbitrariness of reflexively modern evaluation. Instead, it paves the way for new forms of evaluation of which its favorite is what I will call evaluation machines.

The machinery metaphor is completely intended. Evaluation machines are intended to work automatically, like little robots, without the intervention of human subjectivity, interpretation, and emotion. Evaluation machines are supposed to work predictably and reliably. They are an integrated ingredient in the type of rational, procedure-based organization that strikes back with full force in the audit society. One of the decisive logical moves in enhancing predictability is that the audit society bases its evaluation not on tailor-made, retrospectively designed evaluation processes (with all their complications) but on predesigned criteria, indicators, handbooks, manuals, and processes. When predesigned evaluation machines succeed, they not only (by definition) operate with well-defined indicators and procedures but also prestructure the reality they are intended to describe (Lawn 2007). This is how the predictability of rational organizations strikes back in a deep sense.

This chapter is devoted to how and why the audit society unfolds as a form of social order, with its characteristic cultural neorigorism, and how evaluation machines fit into its social imaginary.

Disaster and Risk

Worries about war, disaster, terror, and destruction of humanity by humans have been continuing themes in 20th-century philosophy and cultural criticism, as well as in the ordinary lives of many people. But after the tragic events of September 11, 2001, the fear of sudden and unexpected tragedy triggered by human beings upon human beings became an immediately manifest cultural theme, and the media did its best to expand this emotional state by endless repetition of the same horrifying pictures.

In the post-2001 social imaginary, the awareness of shock and disaster takes a central place (Hammerlin 2009; Klein 2008; Virillo 2005). In a statistical perspective, truly terrifying events happen fairly infrequently in our type of society. But we have an intense political and cultural preoccupation with them.

This social imaginary becomes a challenge to public authorities who must always act as if they are in control of things (Power 2004, 9). At the same time, political capital seems to flow from the willingness to fight back. It is a classic power mechanism to invent or exaggerate external threats. In this sense, if cleverly managed a culture of fear translates into political support and can be used to fundamentally transform the social order or solidify power bases by providing reassurance.

While a mentality of risk is spreading, a sort of risk management evolves, where an appearance of control is conveyed, but where one will not be held responsible if something goes wrong. In its advanced forms, risk management must go hand in hand with impression management. In a broader light, risks include negative reactions, bad public relations, and socially defined side effects. To convey responsibility and avoid it at the same time is therefore an important ingredient in risk management (whereas in reflexive modernity it is positively valued to take responsibility for coordination of side effects and complex social issues, even if this responsibility is not defined in formal terms).

Single risky events are amplified by mechanisms that are not under individual control. For example, media amplify risky themes (Power 2004; Thompson 1995). The focus of media on politicians who are held responsible for particular scandals seems to promote defensive mechanisms and systems that help manage risks. These systems become integrated into larger frameworks and machineries that define steering, governance, management, and administration in a post-2001 context (Power 2004).

Neorigorism

Neorigorism is my term for the social and cultural tendency to establish certain social arrangements that are not up for discussion. Although a certain form of rigorism is inherent in all social constructions that become institutional arrangements, neorigorism refers to a specific contemporary tendency to eliminate the sense of contingency and plurality of perspectives so characteristic of reflexive modernization. In other words, neorigorism is a contemporary form of avoidance of reflexivity. Neorigorism comes in different forms. Ethnic neorigorism is based on the idea that an indebatable history of origins can legitimize any form of defense of a particular ethnocentric view.

An Example of Ethnic Neorigorism

"We are Danes, and we have always driven on the right side of the road," say some Danes. "Immigrants, too, just have to drive on that side, without discussion," goes the argument. However, the argument is technically incorrect, because right-side driving was prescribed by decree in Copenhagen (the capital of Denmark) only in 1758. Furthermore, the argument overlooks that several European countries have skipped to the other side of the road at particular points in time. Austria did so, because it was occupied by Germany in 1939. Sweden and Iceland voluntarily changed their driving patterns in 1967 and 1968, respectively. The changes in these Nordic countries are particularly interesting, because there is no empirical evidence that driving on the right side of the road was inherently detrimental to the ethnic and cultural self-identity of the Swedes and the Icelanders. In other words, there is no inherent link between traffic patterns and the origins of ethnic groups. However, if such a link is assumed, it becomes impossible not only for immigrants but also for ethnic Danes to rationally discuss the institutional arrangement. The undergirding neorigoristic mentality suggests that social arrangements like it should also not be discussed. If reflexive modernization had dealt with the issue of which side of the road is good for driving, the conclusion would probably have been that the choice is absolutely arbitrary. This institutional choice can be made quite pragmatically without any ethnic argument behind it. But it is important that all car drivers do the same thing. It would also have been concluded that driving on the right side of the road continues to be a smart thing, because neighboring countries do the same, and there would be unnecessary transaction costs in making new cars and new traffic signs. This argument, however, would have been based on reason rather than on mythical, ethnic, and neorigoristic assumptions.

Military neorigorism is the idea that violence is the only effective form of solving particular political and cultural conflicts. Technical-managerial neorigorism is the idea that particular recipes for good management must be complied with, even if these recipes are not justified with reference to demonstrable technical superiority or democratic legitimacy.

In the spirit of neorigorism, there is joy and confidence in the strong belief in values and procedures that cannot be discussed, whereas the reflexive modernist finds pleasure in the critique and relativization of social norms.

The State Strikes Back

In a post-2001 situation, the state returns to the societal scene with renewed force. Although theory predicted its fall as a result of globalization, and as a result of its inability to govern under new complex realities, it has in fact invigorated its role, at least in some specific policy domains. One such domain is security issues. In the war against terror, the state has demonstrated a need for itself via new legislation, military initiatives, and monitoring of citizens and potential terrorists. Since the state is defined by its monopoly on legitimate use of force, issues that call for use of force are particularly fit for the mobilization of the state.

In addition to security issues, education is another area where the state seeks to prove its usefulness and ability to act (Novoa and Yariv-Mashal 2003). Education as a policy area gains new importance not only in relation to international comparisons reflecting the new international competition among globalized economies but also as—a reflection of it—a new policy area where the state can demonstrate its willingness to act and renew symbols of national identity. The former expresses itself in evaluations such as international PISA surveys, the latter in new definitions of national canons (mandatory materials that are seen as important for a particular language, literature, history, or national identity and that must be covered by schools in a country).

With respect to the ability of the state to actually govern, implementation research in recent years has led to a correction of earlier conclusions about the weakness of the state. Now it is admitted that legislation, large resources, and surveillance supply the state with unique and powerful policy instruments.

In a new sociopolitical situation, where most of the social critique comes from the right rather than the left (as it did during reflexive modernization), the state sees it as an important task to monitor threats against the security of the state itself. New status is given to police and military. Monitoring and surveillance of the state's own employees are also tantamount. In a cunning way, the critiques in reflexive modernity against authorities are now turned into an argument in favor of stricter control with school teachers and other professionals who play visible public roles. Steering models based on neorationalist economic thinking teach administrative leaders that all professionals are self-interested, and that the self-interest of professionals constitutes the most important impediment to effectiveness in the public sector. Without regimes to ensure predictability and control, the behavior of public professionals will be corrupt and egoistic, says the dominant neoliberal ideology, which becomes an argument in favor of bureaucratic control mechanisms.

In this way, the ground is prepared for a new and more rigorous evaluation imaginary, which I like to capture under the conceptual headlines of "evaluation systems" and "evaluation machines." But problems and issues in the very field of evaluation itself also contributed to the same development. We have already mentioned the limitations of learning-oriented and participatory evaluation with respect to how evaluation results are reported back to society. We have mentioned the problem among managers that evaluation under reflexive modernization did not contribute to a reduction of complexity and managerial oversight. Unpredictable and subjective evaluation as well as uncertainties about utilization of evaluation also contributed to making evaluation insufficient from a managerial perspective. Then came the idea that more systematic evaluation approaches (such as those under the names evaluation culture, evaluation systems, evaluation capacities, and evaluation policies) could be built up in cooperation between managers and evaluation specialists. Evaluation should no longer depend on local zealots with enthusiasm, nor on local propensities for reflexivity that come and go. There should be a system for evaluation and an official evaluation policy to secure it. Evaluation should not be left to change.

In the climate of these tendencies, managerial ideals about rationality, procedures, oversight, and predictability came back with new force. Bureaucratic organization had been asleep for too long.

Evaluation in the Audit Society

The audit society (Power 1997a) is a term for a cultural climate of regulatory anxiety in which audit and other control procedures institutionalize production of comfort (Power 1996, 291). Power's concept of audit is as broad as ours is of evaluation. It is not the exact boundaries that are important; it is the connections with a particular social imaginary.

Audit helps construct its own legitimacy, first by playing on the themes of fear and risk in society and next by demanding that public organizations make themselves "auditable" so that audit can be carried out. It is tacitly suggested that without checking, inspection, and other evaluation procedures, society would collapse.

When audit leads to production of comfort, it is not because substantial societal problems are being solved, but because audit and documentation facilitate a feeling that things are under control. This communication of the social and emotional state is especially useful for managers who must report back to other managers who must report back to other audiences in society. But citizens and journalists who have lost their perspective on terrible though rare catastrophes and scandals, and who find it difficult to tolerate uncertainty and complexity, are also partly responsible for the greater need for comfort production.

The ability of audit to become a widespread social procedure has to do with its focus not on quality but on quality assurance. Audit is not only control but control of control. This allows abstraction and generalization of the whole process. This logical move also introduces ways in which abstract control procedures can be compared and combined to give an overview of the control of control. Or the illusion of an overview of the control of control. It is nevertheless an illusion in high demand in society.

This is why Power speaks of the audit society instead of just audit:

> Not only can audits work, but they can be exported to a wide variety of organizational contexts which can be sold the benefits of system certification. In this way the management system is not only a technological construct; its elements have an essential public face (Power 1997a, 88).

It is the transformation of a specific control procedure into a larger social representation of a trustworthy social order that makes audit a significant sociological phenomenon. The flight from judgment and a culture of defensiveness may well create their own risks for organizations (Power 2004, 14), but we will come back to that in the final chapter.

In the social imaginary of the audit society, evaluation procedures are at the center of what is believed to hold society together.

The social vacuum, which evaluation under reflexive modernization had left for lack of a concept of society, gave way to a new evaluation imaginary that could express itself in a much clearer, shorter, and more rigid way. Steering, control, accountability, and predictability came back on the throne. The purpose of evaluation is no longer to stimulate endless discussions in society, but to prevent them. Instead of human subjectivity, a style of coolness, objectivity, and technocracy becomes the dominant ideal in evaluation.

There is a particular social investment in evaluation procedures that can be understood only if we try to keep together all the most significant theoretical elements of our various analyses so far: the organizational legitimacy that organizations enjoy only if they are in consistency with broader themes, norms, values, and expectations in society; the experiences with faulty, inconsistent, subjectivist, unpredictable, and overly complex evaluation processes in reflexive modernization; a new social imaginary that makes fear and risk management central cultural themes and celebrates a new rigorism concerning what cannot be up for critique and discussion; and a strong revival of rational, bureaucratic, management-oriented organization that is believed to guarantee predictability, nonsubjectivism, and order.

Evaluation Machines

To express the high point in the audit society's pursuit of eliminating arbitrariness and subjectivity in evaluation, the term *evaluation machines* is my best analytical metaphor, or ideal type, if you will.

Evaluation machines are mandatory procedures for automated and detailed surveillance that give an overview of organizational activities by means of documentation and intense data concentration.

To define evaluation machines more specifically, I shall build on some characteristics suggested by Leeuw and Furubo (2008: 159–160), who talk about "evaluation systems" based on the first four of the following points. But I offer my own interpretation of their definition and add further aspects that especially emphasize the automatic and desubjectivized character of machines.

Permanence. Evaluation machines are fairly permanent, repetitive, and routine-based. Permanence implies that a certain volume of evaluative activities should take place over time. Evaluation machines produce streams of information (Rist and Stame 2006) rather than stand-alone reports. The best way to secure the permanent operations of an evaluation machine is through some form of institutionalization. To support the institutionalization of evaluation machines, organizations promote such ideas as evaluation capacity building, evaluation culture, and evaluation policies. Evaluation machines operate repetitively or continuously so that evaluation data are automatically produced yearly, monthly, or weekly or are available online.

Organizational responsibility. Evaluation machines are embedded in organizational procedures of verification and relate to how organizations are held accountable to other organizations or the public. Evaluation machines are run by organizations because control *of* organizations makes control *in* organizations necessary. They are emblematic of organizations rather than individuals, and less dependent on the values and ideas and styles of individual evaluators. Evaluation machines are sanctioned by organizational and institutional rules and procedures such that their operation can rarely be stopped by individuals. To a great extent, evaluation machines are supported by power regulatory institutional pillars (Scott 1995); they perform not only an information function but also a resource allocation function (e.g., according to New Public Management prescriptions) and a legal function (as in some mandatory accreditation systems and many audit systems). Even in the absence of strong regulatory pillars, evaluation machines are often considered to be normatively legitimate and sensible recipes for good and modern management (Røvik 1998).

Focus on the prospective use of evaluation. The evaluative activities are planned in advance so they can be intentionally linked to decision and implementation processes (Leeuw and Furubo 2008: 160). As examples, periodic reporting is assumed to be linked to budget processes, or a positive outcome of an evaluation may be legally necessary for accreditation of a particular institution (Leeuw and Furubo 2008:160). For this reason, the evaluative information in evaluation machines is often fairly standardized not just in timing but also in form.

Distinctive epistemological perspective. Every evaluative machine is based on a particular set of cultural-cognitive assumptions, and it relies on a number of tools or scripts such as definitions, indicators, handbooks, procedures, guidelines, etc., to support fairly standardized operationalizations of the worldview inherent in the evaluation machine.

Abstract and generalized coverage. Evaluation machines cover phenomena that have broad scope in time and space. They describe extensive activities in a systematic and integrated way that permits comparison among areas of activity. To do so, they must generalize across many human beings, geographical areas, professional activities, or units of production. They produce data and statements that are based on high data concentration and are somewhat abstracted from the specific contextual or substantial activities that take place. This should not surprise us; it is a classic tenet of organizational documentation that it helps standardize and coordinate various activities across time and space. To do so, evaluation machines employ generalized and abstract formulas that can be used in a fairly standardized way. Evaluation machines promise to deliver a total overview of organizational activities and therefore represent in their data (for example) "the quality of organization X."

Evaluation machines operate on detailed documentation of organizational activities (or aspects of activities such as inputs, processes, outputs, and outcomes). This is why one of the first requirements of organizations under surveillance is creation of a paper trail that can be used as input or fuel for the evaluation machine.

Evaluation machines attribute evaluation data to units such as organizations, departments, branches, offices, institutions, teams, and individuals.

The operation of the evaluation machine is separated from the doing of the work under evaluation. The design of the evaluation machine is also separated from its actual operation. In other words, the "worker," the "evaluation machine engineer," and the "evaluation machine operator" all perform different roles. Through the eyes of each of these role players, there is no total overview and total responsibility for work and its evaluation, although the results of the evaluation machine are said to stand for quality as such.

Evaluation machines concentrate a large amount of data into results and conclusions with little complexity, often in terms of short statements, symbols, or figures, such as yes or no to accreditation, or a smiley face, or a placing on a ranking list.

This total picture of quality is adequate or fit for external reporting and can therefore easily function as input to another organizational or managerial process in other organizations.

For concrete examples of evaluation performed by evaluation machines, one might think of performance indicators, auditing, or accreditation (although there is no guarantee that each of these approaches to evaluation in all practical aspects corresponds to our ideal-typical evaluation machine). However, the common characteristics are striking. Performance indicators should support managerial oversight. They are produced regularly or online, and they describe activities of departments or individuals. They facilitate data concentration, as when all publications from a university in one year are expressed in a single figure. Changes in performance indicators can be coupled to managerial and organizational consequences, which happen when publication indicators are linked to a financial stream.

Auditing places emphasis on different subject matter, such as proper procedures, but it also operates with highly codified techniques describing how to check organizational activities. Auditing is based on an elaborate set of observations and documents; it results in a synthesizing report. It can lead to recommendations that management must act on.

Accreditation can also have quite its own thematic emphasis, criteria, and procedures, although it shares numerous characteristics with our ideal type. It is based on review of a number of documents describing criteria for inputs, structures, activities, or results; it is performed regularly. The final result can be one of three (unconditional, conditional, or no accreditation). Accreditation is often mandatory; without it, an institution can lose the right to offer a program or even the right to exist.

There are strong similarities between differing evaluations regardless of whether they are internal or external to the organization under evaluation. An external evaluation machine often requires an internal one to support it. Relations of power may differ from one situation to another. Still, our metaphor captures the mechanical, procedural, and objectified essence of evaluation machines.

Because of their codification of the evaluation process, evaluation machines offer great advantages for managers. Results appear to be technical and objective, and even if exact results are not known in advance the dimensions along which evaluation results may fall are clearly defined by the indicators, standards, procedures, and checklists inherent in the machine itself. The reduction of complexity offered by evaluation machines allows them to cover large areas of time and space as well as substantially different activities. Thus evaluation machines facilitate interoperationability (Lawn 2007), meaning coordinated handling of quite diverse elements or activities by way of the same abstract organizational procedures. So even if evaluation machines seem to demand considerable resources and manpower, they are efficient because of their ability to cover an enormous amount of ground with machinery of fairly low complexity. If an evaluation machine runs into capacity problems, it will just require more evaluation machines to help. In this way, a controlling organization with an evaluation machine can require so much documentation from evaluated organizations that only internal evaluation machines in those organizations will be able to do the job. Lindeberg (2007) has documented how chains of evaluation machines delivering data to other evaluation machines are established. In a Luhmann-inspired theoretical universe, one might then describe the system of evaluation machines feeding and sanctioning evaluation machines as a self-referencing and functionally differentiated system in society.

Through the automated character of their operation, the procedures of evaluation machines become less person-dependent, and more predictable. Formalization of evaluation also makes daily operation of evaluation machines less dependent on specialized expertise. Evaluation machines thus do to evaluation what McDonald's has done to cooking. I use this example only because Ritzer (1996, 579) coined the term "McDonaldization" to capture the larger trends toward rationalization of society, based on such keywords as efficiency, predictability, and substitution of nonhuman for human technologies. One of the benefits of McDonaldization, in evaluation as well as in society in general, is that it helps reduce the need for expertise, wisdom, and educated staff. In a similar vein, evaluation expertise is less in demand if only evaluation machines are in operation.

Predictability in and around the evaluation machine is facilitated not only by internal logic of operations but also by continuous and repetitive use. People under evaluation know they are under evaluation and will be again shortly, if they have not already internalized the idea that everything they do will instantaneously be an object of evaluation. For an academic, an upcoming publication may no longer be one that contributes to a career or a subsequent committee's evaluation of one's work. It is instantaneously defined as a contribution to this year's score, on an indicator of productivity in the performance indicator system.

In this light, the future is already under measurement. This preemptive function of evaluation machines makes it possible for the risk- and responsibility-averse manager to claim that any potential problem is already under control because indicators are in place to describe it. Performance management systems thus, in a sense, really "manage" performance. Evaluation machines can already contain future damage, in contradistinction to evaluation under reflexive modernization, which sought to learn from experience through reflexivity. However, the two are closer to each other than one might think. Reflexive modernity soon led to a preventive mentality in areas as diverse as child care, insurance, public health, the environment, management—and evaluation.

To be truly preventive, evaluation machines must be comprehensive. No important area of activity should be exempt from evaluation. Altogether these tendencies pave the way for a much tougher role played by evaluation in society. Evaluation should leave nothing to chance. It should give a total picture of quality, and it should be tightly integrated with managerial procedures and decision making.

We have described evaluation machines and their ramifications clearly enough to see their striking similarities with Weberian bureaucracy. Evaluation machines usher in a comeback for rational bureaucratic organization. Evaluation machinery is how rational bureaucratic organization responds to the excesses of the subjectivism, unpredictability, inconsistency, lack of synthesis, and inadequate use characteristic of evaluation in reflexive modernization. In evaluation machines, the ideals of predictability and control triumph again. The tools are surprisingly similar to those of classical bureaucracy: formalized procedure. Separation of work and surveillance. Division of labor into detailed operations. Attribution of responsibility to every part of the organization, horizontally as well as vertically. Elimination of human judgment as human activities are substituted for nonhuman technologies. Written documentation. Abstraction of cases and situations, as a variety of phenomena are classified and operated on by means of general categories and indicators. Concentration of data and reduction of complexity as information moves upward.

Rational organization strikes back. It is deeply rooted in modern society, reflexive or not.

Sociologically speaking, three observations stand out as significant aspects of evaluation machines. First, evaluation machines embody a set of cultural values emphasizing risk management, quantification, standards, and a preemptive or prospective approach to quality control.

Second, evaluation machines are comprehensive and general in coverage. They come with a suspension of evaluability assessment. Evaluability assessment represents a view where evaluation is a situational good, the value of which depends on careful analysis of the social and organizational situation prior to evaluation. In contradistinction, evaluation machines are installed according to the view that evaluation is a general good. They operate on a continuous and mandatory basis. There is no longer any situation unfit for evaluation. Reality must now become generally evaluable and thereby fit the demands of the evaluation machine, not the other way around.

Third, evaluation machines seek to substitute subjective judgment for some objective evaluation based on standards, manuals, handbooks, procedures, or indicators. They are to function reliably and predictably, regardless of the individual persons who operate them.

In all three aspects, evaluation machines remind us of rational and bureaucratic organizations. All three have serious ramifications for democracy.

Fortunately, what we have described is not reality, but an ideal for evaluation that seeks to embody itself in reality. In the final chapter, we discuss the meaningfulness and appropriateness of evaluation machines in society, taking into account actual functioning, which may differ from their ideal as well as their democratic implications.

7   The Critique of Evaluation Machines

During the era of reflexive modernization, it was possible to dream of more evaluation. The spirit of that time supported the idea that authority should be questioned, side effects discovered, and a climate of discussion and self-reflection promoted. As is often said, you should be careful what you wish for, because you might get it. In the era of evaluation machines, our dreams have been fulfilled: we now have so much evaluation that we cannot hope for more.

The dream has become, for some, a nightmare. The problematic aspects of evaluation machines are increasingly visible. The discussion about them has already begun in society, among such practitioners as teachers, nurses, and public agencies.

For example, a survey in Denmark (FTF 2007) among directors of institutions within health care, pedagogy, and education revealed that even though more than 80 percent of the respondents felt a lot of work had to do with documentation, and many felt that documentation demands had increased during the last two years, only 10–20 percent of them (depending on the sector) felt that time was generally well spent on documentation. To varying degrees, it took time that could otherwise be spent on clients, it was not conducive to quality improvements, and it was not professionally meaningful. The most negative views on documentation were found in the educational sector.

These views represent a form of dissatisfaction that is not very articulate and lacks a precise target. Documentation practices take many forms and are not necessarily related to evaluation machines. Academically oriented critique of present evaluation, documentation, and audit practices is also multiplex (de Bruijn 2002; Pollitt 2006; Power 1997a; Schwandt 2002). The discussion is indeed nuanced, covering many items and aiming at many targets.

The purpose of this final chapter is not to give an account of the existing critique of evaluation machines, which is obvious since the very term *evaluation machine* is just one of many (constructed) analytical terms for problematic contemporary evaluation phenomena. Instead, our purpose is to pinpoint aspects of the debate that correspond to weak aspects of evaluation machines that may (or may not) be decisive for critical discussion and development of evaluation practices in the future.

From its beginning, and through the current phase of reflexive modernization, to our era of evaluation machines, evaluation has delivered various forms of social critique, and it has been the object of critique (including from evaluators). The balance between being constructive and being critical has always been delicate in evaluation, and it continues to be so in the era of evaluation machines. We now look at each point in turn in this analytical discussion of evaluation machines.

It is possible to agree with some aspects of the critique and dismiss others as exaggerated or uninformed. Several theoretical positions are possible in the debate, depending among other things on the underlying understanding of the socially productive role of knowledge in organizations and society. For example, evaluation machines are seen by some as problematic because they do not work and by others because they *do* work.

We have to turn the theoretical kaleidoscope here and there under each point in the discussion if we want to get to the depth of the issues.

The Costs of Evaluation Machines

Evaluations are costly, and it is most likely that they incur costs for which no one is held accountable. Evaluation machines may make this problem worse. In this section, I unpack the argument.

In some situations, 10 percent of project budgets are allocated to evaluation. The World Bank claims to spend about 3 percent of its budget on evaluation (in addition to the costs of knowledge management).

A study of 452 stand-alone evaluation reports in Denmark documented that more than 98 percent of them did not describe how much they cost (Hansen 2003). But the Danish National Audit Office (Rigsrevisionen 2005) found that every evaluation cost a little more than 1 million Danish kroner (a bit more than U.S. $200,000) on average, and that the salary to evaluators varies a lot. It also found that ministries are not expected to report how much they spend on evaluation—and most of them do not.

The costs of evaluation are both direct and indirect. The former include data collection costs, salaries to evaluators, and practical costs. The latter include the time that evaluees and other stakeholders spend on providing documentation, sitting in meetings, filling in survey questionnaires, or otherwise participating in the evaluation. A measurement of the time devoted to documentation is complicated because many modern professions include some documentation as a natural part of their knowledge-based practice. The very essence of several professional practices is to keep a careful log of activities and on that basis encourage reflexivity about practice. For this reason, the time devoted to documentation is often seen as a necessary aspect of professional practice, not a cost connected to evaluation. Evaluation systems that operate intelligently seek to incorporate as much as possible of existing documentary practices into the functioning of the evaluation machines; they also seek to use modern information technology to make their operations as efficient as possible.

However, just because indirect costs of evaluation may not be visible or counted, this does not mean they do not exist. Persons interviewed by the National Audit Office said that in some cases the indirect costs exceeded the direct costs. The office recommended that commissioners be more attentive to the indirect costs they incur, for employees and others who cannot refuse to participate.

The indirect costs may be problematic because they are often invisible, and because there is more than one way to count their monetary value if one wishes to do so. Alkin and Ruskus therefore warned the evaluation field as far back as 1984 that indirect costs are often overlooked or underestimated. The indirect costs can multiply if we count unintended side effects of evaluation as additional indirect costs. Even if we don't, the costs of evaluation constitute a somewhat neglected topic. Books on evaluation that are otherwise good and well respected often do not devote much attention to this topic (Fitzpatrick, Sanders, and Worthen 2004; Mathison 2005; Shaw, Greene, and Mark 2006; Ryan and Cousins 2009; Vedung 1997).

Without some more or less precise estimation of the costs of evaluations, we are not in a position to rationally weigh the costs and benefits. The lack of cost concerns may be indicative of a ritualistic or dogmatic faith in evaluation as an unqualified good. The evaluation industry may, of course, have an interest in not being too explicit about the costs of evaluation. In a larger societal perspective, the more the establishment of evaluation systems is taken as a sign of acceptability and legitimacy, the less interest there is in finding out exactly what evaluation systems cost.

In this perspective, it is a shame that evaluability assessment is no longer fashionable. With assessment, one might initially get a clearer picture of the costs and benefits, or at least of the likelihood that evaluation would make a positive difference in a particular situation.

We can now move to hypotheses about the costs related to evaluation machines specifically. There is no overwhelming evidence showing that organizations with evaluation machinery in operation are performing better than those without it. The general emphasis on creating a climate favorable to evaluation or the practice of installing mandatory evaluation machines may in practice imply that recommendations of modest use that would otherwise be suggested by evaluability assessment will be overruled. In a generally evaluation-friendly culture, evaluation may thus be carried out in situations where it would not be recommended, were the decision to evaluate based on strictly rational analysis of each situation. As a mentality that supports differentiated and situational use of evaluation—signified in a preference for evaluability assessment—is replaced by a preference for general and mandatory establishment of evaluation machines, the result may be heightened evaluation activities even in situations where the cost-benefit ratio is unfavorable.

Furthermore, evaluation machines may be especially blind to their own costs. They are not primarily there to help professionals improve their performance; evaluation machines are promoted because of the ease with which they reduce the complexity of control and inspection *in the eyes of the inspecting system.* The costs of evaluation systems, especially the indirect costs, are often made invisible or irrelevant in the eyes of evaluation systems themselves (Power 2005, 340).

This does not mean that the total social costs of evaluation systems are also diminishing. There is no reason to believe that the general evaluability of public interventions has automatically risen over time. In many situations, the opposite case can be made. If public interventions are becoming more complex, more multilevel, and consisting of packages of policy instruments, they do not become easier to evaluate (at least not without a corresponding extraordinary effort to clarify the intervention, program theory, objectives, data requirements, and options for program improvements).

Evaluation machines may, of course, reduce the costs of evaluation because of their standardized, streamlined, and robotlike modes of operation. Or they may increase costs because the present evaluation ideology insists that they be installed everywhere, regardless of evaluability assessment. We have few reliable estimates of the real costs and benefits of evaluation machines. One reason is the very ideology of evaluation machines, which rarely insists that they should be subject to the same criteria as the programs they themselves evaluate. As evaluation becomes a generalized norm, the average contribution of each instance is likely to be diminished, as evaluation is applied to a wider range of situations regardless of whether an evaluability assessment would have recommended it at all.

The evaluation imaginary inherent in evaluation machines tends to increase the costs through steady expansion of the machines, but it also tends to keep the costs out of sight and discussion.

These observations about the lack of attention to the costs of evaluation machines are consistent with Pollitt's noting the lack of evaluation of New Public Management initiatives. The pros and cons of evaluation ideology and machinery are, paradoxically, not scrutinized nearly as coolly and systematically as they claim other practices in society should be.

Among the *qualitative* costs of evaluation machines, we might count how these machines affect our view of problems in society and our ability to solve them.

The Downside of Risk Management and Defensive Quality

In Power's 1996 analysis, this self-congratulatory process of evaluation checking evaluation fits into a larger social project of "producing comfort." However, it may be a false sense of comfort. In fact, control and inspection of an evaluation system easily become an institutionalized mechanism for acting as if we know the risks we face (Power 2004).

Hood (2002) argues that risk is managed and blame shifted because politicians seek to install "quality assurance systems" that, in the name of accountability, often tend to be used by the politicians themselves as mechanisms of assigning risk, placing blame, and avoiding responsibility. With intense media focus on potential scandals, the motivation of politicians to install self-protecting mechanisms is only further enhanced.

"More monitoring of various kinds is an easy and politically acceptable solution to perceived problems and scandals in society," says Power (2005, 341).

However, risk does not disappear just because evaluation machines are installed. New complications are transferred to mediators and translators somewhere in the bureaucratic chain of control, as abstract demands on measuring quality in a limited set of indicators must be translated into specific activities that, say, teachers and pupils need to do (de Bruijn 2002). Somebody must translate what the school teaches into manageable systems that test what has been learned. This is presented as a nonpolitical and technical issue, but it is controversial nevertheless, because the substantial logic of teaching and learning on the one side and the formal logic of bureaucratic control on the other are fundamentally different.

There is of course also a risk of being exposed as an underperformer in eyes of the evaluation system, which defines criteria for performance that the evaluees are not in control of and which also amplifies the phenomenon of underperformance through statistics, as well as the transport of evaluative information through time and space, perhaps including publication.

Institutions such as schools hesitate to take on the new risks installed by indicators, quality control regimes, etc. No one wants to be placed in the bottom of a ranking list, regardless of whether the indicator system leading to this ranking is based on valid or invalid measurement. In other words, ranking systems incur their own new risks (Hood 2002; Rothstein, Huber, and Gaskell 2006).

Institutions at the bottom of the list seek to avoid, or push back, the risk imposed on them by evaluation machines installed from the top of the administrative and political pyramid in society. As a result, risk is not reduced but instead dynamically managed and pushed back and forth by the various parts of the governmental structure in society (Rothstein, Huber, and Gaskell 2006).

The critique of formalized and bureaucratic risk management comes from several sides. Some organization theorists argue that in complex systems accidents and catastrophe are better prevented through mindfulness, attention, and cooperation (Weick 1991, 2009; Weick and Roberts 1993; Weick and Sutcliffe 2006) than through formal control and reporting. The dehumanization and mechanization of control mechanisms in fact tends to numb the richness of human interpretation necessary to detect early warnings in complex interactive systems. Formal and mechanistic control systems are in many situations less effective than abundant human attention when it comes to preventing disasters and accidents.

The emphasis on risk, some would argue, may negatively affect the problem-solving ability of institutions in society (Hood 2002, 34). Evaluation machines attribute results to particular units in society, such as counties, schools, teachers, and the like. In the utopian vision of performance management system architects, each administrative unit should be held accountable for a small and exclusive set of indicators. Although the responsibility in that unit for exactly those results may increase, its willingness to contribute to the results of other units is undermined. Instead, the unit under evaluation may seek to pass on complicated cases or cross-sectional problems to other units. In other words, *microquality is enhanced at the expense of macroquality.*

Macroquality has to do with how policies, activities, and services fit into larger social patterns (e.g., have we underinvested in public transportation?). Microquality has to do with how well organizations live up to standards and procedures and criteria (e.g., how long are these passengers waiting on the platform for the train?).

In a complex society, a large number of social problems are complicated, cross-sectional, wicked, and dynamic, and thus genuinely macro-sociological. Solving such problems requires cooperation. Just because bureaucratic organization is supported by evaluation machinery that confirms fundamental bureaucratic ideas of graded authority and strict division of labor, it does not follow that the complex social problems emerging under reflexive modernization have disappeared. These were problems that required attention to systemic interactions, side effects, complex social cooperation, and multiple perspectives. Instead, evaluation machines impose an atomistic view of the social world and seek to control it accordingly.

It is possible for a society to invest an enormous amount of energy in collecting extensive amounts of evaluative data in micro-oriented evaluation and still have insufficient data to support macropolitical choices. Large amounts of micro-oriented data from evaluation machines in no way guarantee that policies on the macro level are in fact based on evaluation data. This is because evaluation machines are designed to focus on the performance of atomized social and organizational units, not to give feedback on policies or policy instruments, or the handling of large-scale, cross-cutting problems in society. An effect of evaluation machines may be to keep evaluees locked in a cage of accountability for microquality-based criteria. Exactly as modern technocratic organization tends to leave the atomized individual employee without a sense of the total product of the whole organization (Berger 1964), the modern evaluation machine tends to tie evaluees to specific indicators, but not give them any motivation to engage in a broader understanding of how they can contribute to problem solving in society beyond what they are held accountable for. Academics, for example, should produce publications in good journals, and not care about the role of the academic in society. If an acceptable score in a performance measurement system requires all the energy and resources of the academic, he or she is effectively locked in.

This problem is felt with particular intensity by academics and students, because one of their important missions is to contribute to knowledge making for the future. The distortion in proxy variables is therefore likely to be considerable. What happens in the future is inherently impossible to measure. For example, how do we educate young children to be competent, democratic, and competitive in a future global economy? This problem is genuinely complicated, partly because we do not have the capacity to sketch or foresee the contours of that new reality-to-be. However, the argument against evaluation machines is that putting pupils today under the regime of strict and continuous testing is not the best way to prepare them for an unknown future. Conformity to standards is, both practically and philosophically, a poor approach to complex problems that require independence, risk taking, and intelligence. Evaluation machines that test children according to standards reproduce the values of an earlier industrial mass society but have nothing interesting to offer with respect to the complexities and challenges of the future society.

This type of critique comes not only from left-wing radicals but also from innovators in the business world who think that evaluation machines represent a conventional and obsolete bureaucratic and industrial approach, a 20th-century approach for solving 21st-century problems.

Evaluation machines represent overemphasis on a defensive view of quality: risk should be avoided and nothing should fall below standards. At the same time, *an offensive view of quality is sacrificed*. This view of quality emphasizes innovation, risk taking, learning, and a courageous approach to unconventional, cross-cutting, dynamic, challenging, and complex problems. The balance between risk taking and risk avoidance, between offensive and defensive quality, is of course an issue in any society. The issue is not whether a defensive view of quality has an important role to play in managing, say, air traffic or heart surgery. However, with evaluation machines a rigorous belief in mechanistic risk management is institutionalized. The problem is that defensive quality has established itself as a general code for proper management of the social order in the wider social imaginary. Public attention to scandal tilts this balance further in the direction of defensive assurance.

In conclusion, the paradox is that in spite of—or one might even say because of—the societal investment in evaluation machines, with their atomistic and defensive focus on the steering of microquality, society's capacity to handle complex macro-oriented problems may not have increased at all.

The Mechanization of Control and the Degradation of Work

To achieve maximum efficiency of the control carried out by evaluation machines, they tend to rationalize control procedures. In practice this amounts to mechanization of control. When control procedures are made easier, life will be easier from the perspective of the evaluating system. The resources saved must not necessarily be spent to cut down the costs of evaluation. As we have seen, evaluation machines are not always interested in not being costly. Instead, rationalization of the control procedure goes hand in hand with expansion in time and space of the social domain covered by evaluation machines.

In evaluated organizations, a typical response to documentation demands made by evaluation machines is the corresponding mechanization of necessary documentation. Computer systems may help rationalize production of documentation. Consider an example. In a hospital system, financial incentives were offered to hospitals that allocated a contact person to any patient treated at the hospital. The arrangement with contact persons is known to reduce confusion, disorientation, and anxiety among some patients who feel that they are being sent from one specialist to another through the whole health care system. The hospitals then organized the keeping of electronic journals in such a way that the person filling in data could progress through the computer program only if the box describing the existence of a contact person for that patient was ticked. As a corollary, all patients were given a contact person in the digital file, and in the eyes of the external person who asked for documentation. In the eyes of the controller, control of the control system was sufficient, since the computerized system did not allow a journal for any patient not to be filled in affirmatively.

Only health care staff knew that the coupling between the electronic data and reality might be loose or nonexistent. For example, in emergencies where care was immediately needed, allocation of a contact person was handled administratively after the fact. The contact person was then later connected to the patient in the documentation system, perhaps after treatment was completed. Or perhaps there never was a contact person, except in the computer file. The control system acquires a life of its own. The evaluation machine in this situation is instrumental in creating a fiction that makes little sense for the professionals who must live with it.

Some professionals feel that evaluation machines are not only producing fictions but in fact undermining their professional discretion. This is the ability to exercise judgment and apply complex theoretical or practical knowledge to various situations on the basis of careful analysis of a situation. Evaluation machines may restrict this discretion by imposing narrowly defined criteria. In some ideologies of steering, such as New Public Management, the evaluation machines focus on outcome criteria, such that organizations and their professionals are given the freedom to determine the best practical ways to achieve the desired outcomes.

Still in the ideal world, traditional rule-oriented bureaucratic control is therefore replaced by outcome-oriented evaluation. Evaluation systems should liberate professionals from procedural routines, while enhancing the focus on outcomes. But this is often not how professionals experience the practical functioning of evaluation machines. One reason for the lack of optimal implementation of evaluation machines is that they are driven more by a motivation to avoid risk among those carrying out control and supervision than they are driven by a desire to increase the quality of services.

Another reason the focus on outcome criteria allegedly promoted by evaluation machines does not lead to emancipation of professionals from routine is that the term *outcome* permits very flexible use for control purposes. Outcomes are defined relative to some system or process. There is no God-given definition of outcome. In evaluation vocabulary, an outcome is a causal effect of a professional intervention. In fact, it is often methodologically difficult to pinpoint such causal effects. For example, to determine the outcome of an educational program, such as average grades, one has to control for the socioeconomic background of the parents (and perhaps other background variables). In practice, it is often difficult, if not impossible, to control for all these factors.

Although there is a stark methodological difference between a change in an outcome variable and a true intervention effect, outcome and effect are often confused in practice. It may be in the interest of the evaluation industry to keep this confusion in place, because it supports more flexible criteria for many evaluation machines. If outcomes, outputs, and processes are renamed in this way, evaluation machines can operate more freely in a wider social space.

Since both outcomes and intervention effects may be difficult to measure, what counts as outcomes is often measured in purely pragmatic and circumstantial terms. Sometimes an "immediate outcome" is measured instead of a "final outcome." Sometimes an output measure is used to replace an immediate outcome. On a bad day, process measure can substitute for an output indicator. When we need it rhetorically, we need to go to the end of the chain: the final outcome. If that strategy brings trouble because of statistical problems, resource problems, or politics, it is also possible to measure another earlier point in the chain of events. After all, we know that processes, outputs, and outcomes are links in the same chain. So, when we rhetorically need it, we can measure more or less what we like, if only we appear to promote efficiency, effectiveness, and control.

For example, in assessing the effectiveness of employment bureaus, the evaluation machinery might focus on the number of consultative dialogues that an employment agency has with unemployed persons. Performance indicators often focus on managerially defined aspects of quality rather than client outcomes (Tilbury 2004). The Danish National Audit office found that indicators in contracts with public managers almost never focused on effects or outcomes, but instead on process criteria or outputs (Rigsrevisionen 2009).

Evaluation machines function as they do even if evaluation criteria are process indicators called outcomes. Sociologically speaking, there is no institutional authority that can prevent outcome measures from being confused with all sorts of other variables. In practice, a lot of so-called outcome measures and evaluation criteria institutionalized in the name of a "results orientation" are in fact measures of conformity to standards, or productivity measured through processes or outputs. In this respect, evaluation machines, though presented as antibureaucratic and outcome-oriented, in fact reinstall classic bureaucratic forms of control. Procedures should be followed; standards should be met. Productivity indicators should be measured, and written documents produced. Reports should be sent in. Everything should be documented. The amount of paperwork required in documenting work in minutiae is close to what we otherwise know from excessive bureaucracy.

This bureaucratic element in evaluation machines helps explain why many professionals see evaluation machines as more detrimental to their professional practice than the ideology of New Public Management would suggest.

The Audit Commission in the UK (2002) found a number of factors helped explain why staff in social work wanted to leave their jobs: the sense of being overwhelmed by bureaucracy, paperwork, and targets; unmanageable workload; a change agenda that seems imposed and irrelevant; and feeling undervalued by government, managers, and the public.

The last one is especially important. It is necessary to understand how the self-understanding of professionals is affected by evaluation machines. In a recent survey among teachers in Finland, the UK, Sweden, and Denmark, it was found that the best explanatory factor behind teachers' perception of whether evaluation machines had made it less attractive to be a teacher was not that evaluation machines negatively affected the actual teaching but that they generally signified lack of trust in teachers (Pedersen and Dahler-Larsen 2009).

To understand the depth of these findings, we can turn to Hannah Arendt's distinction (1950) among labor, work, and action. Labor is what we have to do out of functional and biological necessity. Work is what we do instrumentally to achieve certain goals. Action is what we do as human beings when we realize our full creative potential, working collectively in the light of recognition of others. One of the most serious effects of evaluation machines is that they reduce human activity, in Arendt's terms, to labor and work. What is socially meaningful becomes reduced to what the system—represented by a bureaucracy and an evaluation machine—requires.

If we acknowledge that evaluation machines in many respects resemble what we historically know from bureaucratic and rational organization—more specifically productivity measurement in early industrialism and socialist-style Stakhanovism, which have more in common with contemporary evaluation than we usually think (Hood 2007)—it is not difficult to hypothesize about the detrimental effects of work itself and of the self-understanding of those who actually perform the work.

In managerial circles, there is often little interest in the value of work as seen from a street-level perspective. After all, "we are concerned with steering, not with rowing," goes the saying among some consultants. The underlying mentality may support establishment of evaluation machines to control staff who are regarded as lazy or unreliable. Paradoxically, evaluation machines may also overlook or reduce a sense of pride in work, if not the very meaning of work, among professionals and service providers. From a steering perspective, steering is thus needed. From a larger sociological perspective, however, it is striking how dependent steering is on rowing. A boat that is not rowed does not move and cannot be steered. This dependency may become more obvious when important functions in modern welfare states—such as teaching, nursing, and research—are defined by the productivity criteria inherent in evaluation machines. Inquiry into recruitment problems in teaching, nursing, research, etc., may reveal that evaluation machines make it more difficult to recruit new candidates to jobs in these areas and make jobs less attractive for those who work there. Decreasing attractiveness of jobs may lead to recruitment problems that are detrimental to the quality evaluation machines were originally installed to assure.

Of course, the tendency to degrade work described in this section cannot be entirely attributed to evaluation machines alone. But we have illustrated mechanisms that make it likely evaluation machines do contribute to the degradation of work. If we take this contribution seriously, it will be necessary in the future to combine the thinking of staff policy (HR and the like) and the thinking of evaluation (quality management and so on) into a single framework that reassesses the meaning of work in a new light. Indeed, there is in our time an interest in restoring the idea of pride in work and a sense of craftsmanship (Sennett 2008). This interest should not be separated from how we evaluate the work that is carried out.

The Utilization Problem Has Changed

We must now consider in depth how the nature or content of work in public organizations changes as a result of evaluation machines.

One type of critique is inspired by neo-institutional organizational theory. Organizations adopt the ideas of evaluation machines because these ideas largely reflect current myths and mentalities in society, not because this is the best way to use evaluation results. The field of evaluation largely reflects exactly the same mythology, because it views establishment of evaluation capacity in general as a good in itself. The present evaluation imaginary cares less about the value of each individual instance of evaluation and whether the actual evaluation in fact makes a difference. The evaluation industry has very little interest in any empirical demonstration of the substantial difference that evaluation capacity, culture, and systems may make. Evaluation has always been a ritual, says the critique, and evaluation machines are but a mega-ritual. The spirit in this critique is that evaluation machines may be costly and irritating, but their main impact on real life is not substantial, only symbolic.

However, the shift in ideas of utilization and evaluation's responses to them should make a difference for our conception of evaluation as a ritual. If it ever meant "purely symbolic," which is not what a constructivist or discursive institutionalist would think (Tompkins 1987), historical changes have made it likely now that evaluation interferes more directly in social reality. Evaluation machinery has become invasive.

The main problem, at least from the 1970s onward, was that evaluations were not being used for their intended purpose. We have already seen how the field responded to this uncomfortable utilization problem through evaluability assessment, utilization-oriented evaluation, participatory strategies, and the like. At that time, the focus was still on the use of stand-alone evaluations.

In situations where evaluation machines are mandatory, and where evaluation culture, systems, and policies are the order of the day, the corresponding use of evaluation may be "imposed use" (Weiss, Murphy-Graham, and Birkeland 2005). If evaluation machines are systematic, mandatory, repetitive, comprehensive, and integrated into organizational structures, cultures, and processes, they are much more likely to be invasive in practice.

The utilization problem changes its nature when it moves to the systemic level of analysis and when evaluation becomes more integrated in organizational machinery and infused with more regulatory power.

Hypocrisy in organizations—and thus evaluation as institutional window dressing—may have been an option in the past, but the demands for evaluation today are manifest and supported by powerful institutional structures. It is now the regulatory pillar in institutions that requires evaluation, not only the normative or cognitive pillars. The term *ritual* may thus be misleading if it causes some to believe that evaluation is a voluntary symbolic activity. It is rather an imposed ritual undergirded by power structures.

Evaluation is no longer just a fashionable thing to do that fits with the culture of reflexive modernization. According to Power (1997b, 8), advocates of reflexive modernization underestimate the rigidity of authoritative organizational practices and controlling regimes such as auditing, accounting, quality inspection, etc. In fact, organizational evaluation capacity, culture, and systems are themselves subsumed under strict regimes for auditing and inspection. Agencies that control organizations sometimes focus on the "evaluation culture and capacity" of the organization under control rather than on the use of actual evaluations.

Evaluation systems must be in place in organizations so as to render them auditable, evaluable, inspectable, and certifiable. The primary function of an evaluation system may not be to monitor quality but to be externally auditable (Power 1996, 300). The institutional advantages (or potential disadvantages) of evaluation systems depend to a large extent on demonstrability, auditability, and verifiability (Power 1996, 302). Evaluation machines are not left to chance, because they are themselves under the surveillance of evaluation machines.

In the present era, the control of control is supported by strong, regulatory, institutional forces. This is a long and comprehensive development that evaluators themselves have contributed to as they took part in formulating evaluation capacities, evaluation cultures, evaluation systems, and evaluation policies. All of these are, on an ongoing basis, likely to be anchored in strongholds more tightly connected to organizational power structures than the average stand-alone evaluation.

In order words, whereas the first critique looks at the fashionable and the ritualistic in evaluation systems (i.e., the mimetic and normative aspects of organizational isomorphism), a more contemporary critique would emphasize the regulatory pillar in the institutionalization of evaluation capacity, culture, and systems. In the latter view, what organizations do in order to construct evaluation systems cannot be understood without reference to how external agencies control, audit, and certify them. With the emergence of the idea of evaluation culture and capacity, the increased self-confidence of the field of evaluation, and the regulatory control of control, the fundamental problem with regard to utilization is not ritualism, symbolism, and nonutilization. If there were a power balance in the days of stand-alone evaluations, some would be advocates of evaluation, and others would resist it. Each would have some power base. The same continues to be true in the case of evaluation machines, but the power balance is shifted in favor of evaluation machines because of the sometimes heavy investment of manpower, time, resources, and institutional regulatory in them. Now, those who would like to resist evaluation can have their energy tied up in mandatory documentation tasks. They will be outnumbered by the massive staff in evaluation centers, quality assurance offices, and accreditation agencies. The resources of the critical views will run out long before those of the owners of evaluation machines.

The whole character of the utilization problem in evaluation has changed. The problem is no longer that evaluation is not being used. The problem is that evaluation machines may now have a power base and a degree of institutionalization that leads to a potentially enormous impact far beyond their official purposes. To analyze the nature of this impact, the concept of "constitutive effects" is useful (Dahler-Larsen 2007).

The Constitutive Effects of Evaluation

So far, we have not fully attempted to understand the effects of evaluation machines on the very content of work. Observations have been made that are relevant for such analysis; for example, in the era of evaluation machines, much regulatory power is invested in indicators, standards, and so forth. At the same time, because of the intense expansion of evaluation machines into a number of activities in society, and the suspension of evaluability assessment, much evaluation is put in place where good criteria are not easy to establish. Because of the intense institutional pressure to establish evaluation machines, methodological reasons for choosing criteria may be relegated to a minor role.

What are the effects of evaluation machines under such circumstances? Consider, as a beginning, these examples:

Example 1. Waiting times are long for incoming patients in emergency rooms. An indicator system is set up to monitor the time from when a patient enters the emergency room until he or she first meets a member of the staff. As a result, the hospitals hire "hello nurses" who immediately approach incoming patients with a greeting and say, "Hello, my name is Elizabeth." The time until first contact is reduced, but the actual time interval for treatment remains unchanged

Example 2. Hospitals make a contract with top administrators according to which waiting lists will be reduced in return for increased budgets. An indicator for waiting lists is constructed, measuring the number of days patients wait from their first consultation at the hospital to their actual hospitalization. Hospitals manage to reduce waiting lists dramatically. They do so by reducing the number of patients accepted for first consultation.

Example 3. Schools are ranked according to quality using average grades, but without statistical control for socioeconomic and other differences between pupils. This indicator of school quality is criticized by school professionals and statistical experts for low validity. Nevertheless, one of its effects may be to make it easier for some parents to identify and choose schools where well-scoring pupils attend, regardless of whether the schools are statistically responsible for the good grades. Publication of these data may thus lead to increased social segmentation among schools.

On the basis of observations like these, evaluation machines are not only a way of measuring and seeing; they should be fundamentally understood as a way of defining something and doing something. In this sense we can talk about the *constitutive effects* of evaluation machines. (Both theoretically and empirically, constitutive effects extend beyond conventional types of use such as accountability, learning, enlightenment, strategic use, etc.) Constitutive effects exemplify what researchers are beginning to identify as a "performance paradox" (van Thiel and Leeuw 2002), an umbrella term for situations where more measurement of quality may lead to everything else but "better quality." Constitutive effects cover the many subtle and not-so-subtle ways in which evaluation machines steer certain values, orientations, interpretations, and practices in the direction of a particular construction of social reality. Constitutive effects include reactions to reactions to evaluation.

The Limitations of Conventional Critiques

Because of the centrality of "use" to the definition of evaluation (Vedung 1997), the quantitative and qualitative variations of use are of immense interest to evaluators. Controversy over use has been the most important driving force behind development of the field (Hellstern 1986). However, the repertoire of concepts describing use remains unclear, if not paradoxical (Mark and Henry 2002).

There are a growing number of categories of use, among them accountability, learning, conceptual, strategic, tactical, symbolic, and process use. But they are rarely strictly defined. They relate to aspects of evaluation and to outcomes, and they partially overlap, though unclearly (Mark and Henry 2002). Despite this overgrown typology, many evaluators still have a blind spot concerning the many uses of evaluation that are not planned, and not instrumental, because the very definition of evaluation often promises "use" or "good use" (Mark and Henry 2002). This dependence on a tacit normative framework is not analytically satisfactory, especially if it inhibits fuller understanding of the actual rather than promised effects of evaluation.

What I have to say in the rest of this chapter can be understood only if one suspends the immediate normative distinction between good uses and bad uses. In a sociological perspective, however, it is quite normal to seek to suspend, or at least delay, normative judgment in order to pave the way for analytical understanding. Only in evaluation is a normative standpoint commonplace.

When evaluators take a position in relation to potentially unconventional, unforeseen, and perhaps complex effects of evaluation machines, they sometimes unthinkingly categorize new phenomena into old categorical boxes. I shall therefore deal, at some length, with the inadequacies of conventional typification of such effects.

For example, Bouckaert and Balk (1991) suggest that there are "diseases" in indicator systems. This terminology assumes, alternatively, "healthy" ways of measuring quality. This medical/biological metaphor is analytically inadequate; it is not evident what a healthy evaluation might mean. A similar argument can be made about "dysfunctional consequences of performance measurements," which is also the contrary of a functionalist utopia where uncontroversial "goals of the organization" (Ridgway 1956) are assumed without reflection. The distinction between destructive and constructive uses of performance indicators (Munro 2004) is also based on a similarly opposite, taken-for-granted, and truly implicit positive norm. The same is true for "perverse effects" (de Bruijn 2002; Munro 2004).

Others argue that performance indicators can be "misused" (Perrin 1998). Again, the distinction between use and misuse is based on a subjective, normative framework that is often not made clear. In strict analysis, however, one person's use can be another person's misuse (Shulha and Cousins 1997). Furthermore, applying derogatory terms to certain consequences does not help us understand them; nor does it explain their causes and the mechanisms through which they work.

In the same family of judgmental thinking, there is a critique suggesting that evaluation machines, performance indicators, and the like are expressions of a particular neoliberal ideology that corresponds to the interests or hidden agendas of powerful decision makers. Of course, there are ideological overtones and power differentials in evaluation, and hidden agendas certainly exist. However, it is one thing to identify these phenomena and another thing to empirically demonstrate that all outcomes of particular forms of evaluation can be explained with reference to hidden agendas. Such an explanation would assume a uniformity and linearity in social and political processes that is inconsistent with the more complex explanations given by those who actually study such processes (Beck 1997; March and Olsen 1976; Rothstein, Huber, and Gaskell 2006).

Perhaps the most frequent critique of evaluation machines is that these systems have many *unintended* effects (Courtney, Needell, and Wulczyn 2004; Espeland and Sauder 2007; McBriarty 1988; Osterloh and Frey 2010; Smith 1995; Weingart 2005)—a logic almost the opposite of the ideological stance previously mentioned.

Unintended consequences may in fact be positive or negative. Evaluation machines have ramifications that are not, and often cannot be, foreseen by their architects. Unintended consequences are a classic theme in sociology and organization (Flap 2001), and given the complex nature of the contemporary social, organizational, and political contexts in which evaluation machines operate, their unintended consequences are likely to be many and diverse.

Although this hypothesis is charming and seems to be consistent with practical experiences, it might be built on conceptual quicksand. Does unintended simply mean "not intended," or "counterintentional"? If unintended is the logical opposite of intended, then which is exactly the set of intentions an observer applies as an analytical standard?

Assume the analyst identifies with the architect of a particular indicator system, or with the principal in a principal-agent model of public management (Smith 1995, 283). Do the intentions of that architect only at a set point in time (prior to implementation of the indicator system) count? If yes, are these intentions empirically mapped, or simply assumed? If empirically verified, how are unofficial, strategic, or underlying political intentions registered? If assumed, what are the theoretical assumptions about the intentions of the policy architect and his or her degree of rationality? How clearly do we expect the architect to omnisciently predict all effects of his or her construction in order to conclude that the effects are intended?

If we lift the restriction in time, do we allow the architect of an evaluation machine to learn over time and develop new preferences as his or her experiences with the indicator system evolve? If we lift the restriction on who holds intentions, whose intentions count? Do intentions held by stakeholders other than the policy architect count? If the architect is a complex political-organizational machinery with many actors in it rather than a specific person, do the same assumptions hold?

Perhaps the most fundamental problem with the idea of unintended consequences, however, is that it is practically impossible to empirically determine a certain effect as unintended. This would require knowledge about intentions that is out of reach. Consider example 3 in the opening of the section on constitutive effects. Suppose parents use data with poor validity to choose a school for their children. Suppose the indicators make it easier for parents to make this choice. Perhaps it is consistent with the preferences of socioeconomically privileged people to be able to identify those schools where other socioeconomically privileged people send their children. Can an analyst guarantee that this effect was intended? Or unintended? Why should an analytical observer remove the tension, the controversy, and the reality from this situation solely to classify it as either intended or unintended? Why is this distinction seen as so fundamental to a critical discussion of the effects of evaluation?

The distinction between intended and unintended consequences assumes a distinction between planning and outcome where ideas and actions are clearly separated. This may not be how the world works.

Let me illustrate the point with reference to what van Thiel and Leeuw

(2002) call "measure fixation." This occurs when practitioners focus on exactly what is being measured as an indicator of quality, often at the expense of genuine quality. This may be termed a trivial form of measure fixation because it still operates with a sense of "genuine quality" from which the measure fixation deviates. In this sense, measure fixation is unintended. In contradistinction, under advanced measure fixation the indicator constitutes a definition of quality along with a way to measure quality. For example: "Intelligence is what we measure in an intelligence test." Or: "Nobody knows what school quality is, but in our municipality we think that good average grades constitute an important aspect of school quality." Consider the latter example. Some educational researchers argue that the indicator is invalid, either because grades do not reflect all aspects of life in the school or because the grades are published in raw form without controlling for the socioeconomic background of parents, such that the genuine contribution of the school is not measured. Educational researchers might also argue that publication of the grades (and of raw grades in particular) may have unintended effects; for example, there could be further social segregation between schools because privileged parents may move their children to schools where grades are higher. Some parents may think, however, that average grades constitute a fine indicator of school quality; they want their children to be together with other children who get good grades. And the better the grades, parents might think, the better the chances that their children will also get good grades. For this reason, some parents may move their children from low-ranking to high-ranking schools, where the average grades are higher. To simply call this effect unintended may be to misunderstand how consistent the data are with the actions that these parents find relevant, useful, and appropriate. For the sake of the argument, the architect of the indicator system may care or not care about these effects.

To understand the actual effects of parental action, the potential "intentions" behind the ranking lists are not a useful analytical tool, neither in their positive nor their negative sense.

To understand the meanings that actual actors attach to such phenomena as average grades, and the consequential social constructions, the original intentions (if they exist at all) are of very limited analytical relevance.

With advanced measure fixation, it is not possible to demonstrate a cleavage between genuine quality and quality measured by an indicator, since the latter helps define the former. This is a constitutive effect that should be taken seriously and that is not properly understood when categorized as pathological or unintended. This is because both the indicator and the phenomenon it is supposed to measure—school quality—are socially constructed. A critique of the measure, which holds the phenomenon constant as something we all know and agree on, or rationally intend to achieve, is therefore insufficient. In a similar vein, when the term *gaming* is used to describe the inappropriate and manipulative ways in which some practitioners cheat with procedures in order to achieve good scores, it is assumed that their practice is a deviation from a good and correct way to measure things. The measure fixation to which they are victims is a trivial one. However, if the definition of what should be measured changes along with the indicator that seeks to measure the same thing, it is analytically insufficient to blame practitioners of gaming. Instead, as suggested in the term *constitutive effects*, a new reality emerges out of the indicator because of the reactive behavior it triggers.

It is generally inadequate to grasp interesting phenomena such as constitutive effects only in terms of what they are not. Constitutive effects deserve to be studied in their own right in terms of what they are.

Manifestations of Constitutive Effects

HOW CONSTITUTIVE EFFECTS EMERGE

In a fundamental sense, evaluation machines, like evaluation in general, are a form of "assisted sensemaking" (Mark, Henry, and Julnes 2000). They offer interpretive keys that draw attention, define discourse, and orient actions in certain directions. Their most basic function is not to verify what goes on in a particular area of activity but to construct a definition of the activity so it can be evaluated (Power 1996, 293). There are several social mechanisms that help us understand how this goes on. Reflexivity is fundamental to social life, and for this reason reactivity is commonplace, as people simply react to being measured (Espeland and Sauder 2007). When certain measurements are institutionalized, they help create a lock-in effect that keeps people in place (Osterloh and Frey 2010). For example, people who oppose the measures are accused of being afraid of competition or objective measurement, or it is tacitly assumed they are not clever or productive enough to score well on the indicators.

Regulatory sanctions and economic incentives may help stabilize the lock-in. But the cognitive aspect of institutional life also helps. The more naturalized the evaluation criteria become, the less visible and less "real" the things that are hard to express in this form become (Espeland and Sauder 2007, 18). After some time, self-fulfilling prophecies emerge, for example if ranking is based on reputation and reputation becomes defined by ranking. In the long run, those who are ranked may behave according to the criteria that lead to the ranking. Evaluation criteria are magic mirrors in which people can see themselves and their realities anew.

EVALUATION MACHINES DEFINE INTERPRETIVE FRAMES AND WORLDVIEWS

An illustrative example is a survey instrument to help managers check how their families evaluate their participation in daily family activities (Hochschild 2004). Although presented as a progressive tool to remind managers of the importance of family life, the survey also helps constitute family life as something reduced to a limited number of rationalized, quantifiable, and manageable dimensions. Further, it introduces the idea that the focal person can, will, or should change his or her family behavior with the intention of influencing survey scores. It also constructs the idea that poor survey scores on the family survey may affect the manager's career in the workplace, thus adding an additional factor that the manager has to worry about in terms of performance.

Evaluative knowledge may thus colonize areas of social life that were otherwise not prone to such explicit discursive specification and quantification of inherent value. A similar constitutive, transformative (and thus threatening) effect of evaluative knowledge on the idea and self-understanding of communities is discussed by Schwandt and Dahler-Larsen (2006). When any social community looks at itself through evaluative eyes, its members may take a new look at who they are and what constitutes their community. The very core of the community may be based on something that cannot be said explicitly, but evaluation makes things explicit. Evaluation may thus fundamentally disturb the idea that the community holds of itself (unless, of course, the community takes steps to defend itself against such threats, which many communities do; churches do not evaluate their gods).

For an example of how evaluation reconfigures fundamental social ideas, look at testing of academic knowledge. Because a test of a student may be based on the idea that it is the student's knowledge being tested, the broader relation between the student and the academic community that produces knowledge collectively may be disturbed. In classic academic life, the ideal is that each individual borrows something from a large, historically accumulated pool of knowledge but also contributes to further development of that knowledge. This is why we call a presentation, a book chapter, or an academic article a "contribution." The academic is thus constantly connected to and in interaction with a community of scholars. Testing, however, suggests otherwise. Testing suggests that an individual's knowledge can be appropriated, owned, and measured (Willinsky 2009). In other words, fundamental understandings of the world are sometimes at play when evaluation moves forward. More specifically, we can talk about constitutive effects in the domains of the content of work, the timing of work, and social identities and relations.

EVALUATION MACHINES ARE CONSTITUTIVE OF "CONTENT"

Evaluation machines define what is central in work. Evaluation criteria help determine what actors should strive to accomplish in a given activity. Evaluation sometimes forces otherwise more intuitive and implicit forms of practice to formulate explicit criteria of success (Munro 2004, 1082). Evaluation is the occasion to do this for the first time in many areas of activity, so it has a constitutive effect on defining the central explicit dimensions of work activities.

For example, if testing becomes a widespread social practice, it may trigger unexpected reactions. In schools, it may stimulate teachers and pupils to redefine what counts as successful teaching. A concept such as "teaching to the test" describes some of these reactions. As an example, a pretest is given in which the teacher places many of the questions he or she knows will be on the real test. After the pretest, the pupils have the possibility of seeing the correct answers. In the real test, the students' ability to remember the answers to the questions given in the pretest is then rewarded. Thus teaching is focused not on learning a body of knowledge or skills but on teaching the pupils how to pass the test.

Explicit criteria sometimes invite short cuts and gambling in order to score better with regard to established indicators (Courtney, Needell, and Wulczyn 2004; see also the earlier example 2). In fact, the more political and organizational importance is invested in a particular performance indicator, the more the indicator is prone to be the object of complex social processes that sometimes threaten the indicator's validity and reliability, making it more difficult to understand what the indicator actually measures (Vulliamy and Webb 2001). The political and organizational interests invested in the indicator may even make it more difficult to openly discuss alternative interpretations, much less call the indicator into question. This may be the case when it is politically defined that a particular indicator stands for quality or effectiveness as such. Those who wish to discuss the validity of the indicator may then be portrayed as opponents of quality or effectiveness.

Because of their political and organizational significance, evaluation machines may produce a range of activities aimed solely at affecting the scores on indicators, such as skimming or creaming (Fountain 2001, 66), but not at the quality in the performance itself. However, it is only if we know what constitutes quality that we can criticize particular indicators for low validity, or "corruption" of practice. In an earlier section, this was referred to as trivial measure fixation. On the other hand, with "advanced measure fixation," test scores become a socially privileged form of knowledge and help establish socially dominating definitions of quality. Insofar as school quality is equated with higher test scores, distributing pretests with incorporated test questions along with efforts to teach pupils how to pass tests become a strategically meaningful way to improve school quality (why and how school quality came to be defined as high test scores is another question altogether).

If reducing a waiting list is defined exactly as in example 2 above, then actors in the evaluated system were not corrupt. Rather, they took this specific evaluation criterion seriously. In this light, evaluation criteria are templates for knowledge and count as political communication about what is desirable within an area of work. These templates are quite socially productive. Perhaps politicians, managers, consultants, and administrators do not comprehend the full political implications of their sometimes careless definition of certain performance indicators. They may get what they want—objective, easily digestible measures—without understanding the ramifications of the evaluation machines they have set in motion.

In fact, evaluation criteria may become goals in themselves. They may attract all the attention to their own icons or symbols of quality, so that what is not (or cannot be) measured is simply nonexistent—so-called tunnel vision (van Thiel and Leeuw 2002). Quality is perhaps an "essentially contested concept" (Gallie 1955) open to ongoing social construction, but when a given indicator system defines quality measurably this operationalization itself takes the place of a socially valid definition.

For example, in Denmark many schools now focus on what are called "soft qualifications" and "social competence"; but these new concepts are loosely defined and difficult to grasp. As strategies and techniques for operationalizing and measuring soft qualifications emerge, practical definitions of this phenomenon become available and circulate in the field. An apparently methodical or technical operationalization (i.e., the choice of an indicator) is thus an essentially interpretive action with socially productive implications. It cannot be criticized for low validity to the extent that it co-defines the conceptual definition of what it intends to measure while measuring it.

Some indicators have more cultural and institutional support than others. Indicators that redefine the value of public activities in the light of customer satisfaction seem to be in line with contemporary expectations. In fact, evaluation machines emphasizing consumer values may be one of the most important mechanisms for importing market discourse into public organizations, despite the market's undermining effect on civic virtues (Fountain 2001, 71).

In medicine and public health, initiatives proven to have good results in randomized controlled trials may have a higher survival rate in society than other initiatives do. This may be good or not good in itself. However, if we recognize that the ability to finance and carry out randomized control trials is not evenly distributed among various institutions and companies, this constitutive effect may help explain why some initiatives that would otherwise be good are not promoted, if there is no institution to support the kind of testing where they would come out positively. This is why, some say, interventions financed by the medical industry are oversold, and more structural preventive initiatives in society may be undersold.

EVALUATION MACHINES ARE CONSTITUTIVE OF SOCIAL IDENTITIES AND RELATIONS

Evaluation machines stipulate social identities and their mutual relations. For each social category defined by indicator systems, norms are often set in a standardized way. A simple but powerful constitutive effect flows from comparison of indicators across social units such as institutions, groups, or individuals. Good standards are sometimes inherently difficult to set on the basis of logical argument (Stake 2004), but some indicator systems simply allow the mathematical average to set the norm against which individual units are compared. Although mathematically simple and philosophically unsophisticated, this approach has significant social repercussions. Rankings and league tables imply not only that the identities of the different units are of the same nature but also that they stand in a competitive relationship with each other. The competition suggested between the listed units may extend so far as to instill in each of them an objective interest in lowering the scores of the competitors because the average defines the standard.

In a performance appraisal of personnel, a forced distribution of ratings had severe motivational effects on the half of the staff who were categorized as average or below (McBriarty 1988). There are thus interesting constitutive links between the properties of measurement scales and social identities and relations. We know from theories of labeling and stigma that individuals are affected by the labels put on them by others. Evaluation is also a form of labeling.

When a quantitative comparison is made, differences in scores emerge depending on the nature of the measurement. From the mathematician Mandelbrot, it is known that by increasing the sensitivity of measurement systems, more fine-grained differences will be found (Bouckaert and Balk 1991; van Thiel and Leeuw 2002). Such differences often command political, managerial, and professional attention. In this way, evaluation machines help constitute the very problem or risk they are supposed to be measuring (Rothstein, Huber, and Gaskell 2006). They also reconfigure the relations between the social actors involved.

Indicator systems are often followed by recommendations about steps each unit can take to improve quality, thus paving the way for installing a set of common steering techniques among the units (Rose 2003). As Foucault (1991) suggests, evaluative discourse paves the way for strategies and techniques that are instrumental in the self-definition and self-regulation of subjects.

Evaluation machines help constitute the involved actors in particular capacities: patients, clients, consumers, and so on. Indicators of consumer satisfaction may tacitly promote the identity of a "consumer" in higher education, at the expense of other identities such as student (Cheney, Mc-

Millan, and Schwartzman 1997). The apparent freedom of the consumer is bought, but at a price. The consumer does not have any responsibility for the formation of policies. The consumer is also the object of a range of control, socialization, and normalizing mechanisms (Bauman 1983), and an individual's preferences are often kept under strict quantitative control in evaluation machines.

For example, in an emergency room incoming patients are immediately categorized into groups according to the severity of their injury or problem. Patients in, say, category 4 are informed that they can expect to be called in from the waiting room after a maximum of three hours of waiting. They are also informed that treatment begins when they are called in from waiting. If additional waiting time occurs between different phases of the treatment, this extraordinary waiting time will not be counted in the evaluation machine describing the performance of the emergency room. Presumably, this whole system is built to allow the staff to make priorities so that severely hurt patients will be treated even if others have been waiting for a longer time. At the same time, the evaluation machine defines which parts of a patient's time are counted and not counted as waiting time, and as a corollary the evaluation machine defines what the emergency room will be held accountable for. Categorization of patients and definition of their waiting time are thus constituted according to how emergency room accountability is defined. The question is, however, whether patients would be unable to understand the fact that they are called in not according to their waiting time but according to the severity of their problems. Instead of seeking to explain the difficulties of medical priorities to the patients, an evaluation machine is put in place that in fact regulates the relation between the emergency room and the patients. The patients thus become defined—and so does their waiting time!—by the evaluation machine.

Perhaps as a reciprocal role to the consumer, evaluation machines also influence the very definition of a professional, if not reduction of the role of professional. The staff in the emergency room may base their work on how the evaluation machine counts waiting time, thus creating a set of constitutive effects. However, in this way the evaluation machine also helps redefine what it means to act professionally.

The balance between professionals and managers may shift, as many evaluation machines emphasize how organizations internally control themselves rather than make direct examination of the practice itself (Munro 2004, 1079). In fact, indicators based on customer satisfaction are not chosen because they offer much insight into the characteristics of activities; rather, they are expressions of a new strategic alliance between managers and customers at the expense of professionals.

The collegial relations between professionals, such as teachers, are affected to the extent that the evaluation machine clusters some teachers (in schools or groups) and pits the clusters against one another. The effect of performance indicators on professional self-understanding, commitment, and morale is perhaps one of the most critical issues.

EVALUATION MACHINES ARE CONSTITUTIVE OF TIME FRAMES

The constitutive effect of an evaluation machine reveals itself not only in the definition of the content of work and in social relations. It also restructures the work process and establishes time frames for completion of activities.

Time is often a privileged dimension to measure, because, like money, it is generalized and abstract. For this reason, evaluation machines may transform more substantive dimensions of quality into measures of the speed of delivery (Munro 2004, 1080).

Indicators with narrow time frames may privilege some activities at the expense of others. Achieving testable qualifications may be prioritized over more qualitative, long-term, democratic and enlightened formation of character through education ("*Bildung*"). In a similar way, a rapid cure may take priority over long-term prevention.

In a stage drama, the plot, the timing, and the characters are related. The same is true for the corresponding types of constitutive effects of evaluation machines. Højlund and la Cour (2001) demonstrate how digital time measurement of care for the elderly fundamentally changes both the content of the services and the relations between the caretaker and the recipient. In a similar vein, establishing time frames defining what the "normal child" is supposed to achieve at a certain age produces a distinction between normal and "underachieving" children.

When consumer satisfaction is introduced as an evaluation criterion in higher education, the idea of instant gratification often comes with it, and together these factors tend to redefine the role of the teacher toward students.

CONSTITUTIVE EFFECTS MAY BE DISPLACED OVER TIME AND
ACROSS LEVELS OF ANALYSIS

Testing in educational institutions may have broad and large-scale effects, reverberating through society and personal attitudes. An interesting study of examination systems in China demonstrated centurylong effects on culture and social structure. Particular examination criteria also trapped the whole country in a particular educational strategy that over the years proved to be competitively unproductive (Suen 2003). Test systems and indicator regimes have "washback effects" (Bailey 1996) on curricula, educational planning, and teaching practices. Among these effects one might also count new political and institutional arrangements. In Denmark, for example, an international wave of educational tests paved the way for establishment of a national evaluation center. Over the years, this center expanded its tasks and became a significant player in the field of education as such. Regulations for publication of school data have now been introduced, as have proposals by a think tank to measure the quality of individual teachers.

The effects of evaluation machines may thus wander across time and space and across levels of analysis.

A New Performance Indicator System at the University

The government demanded a new system concerning how resources were allocated to universities. Publications were to be counted in a new bibliographic indicator system, and the scores were to be inputs into a mathematical algorithm determining redistribution of resources among universities. Some frustration followed, among academic staff. At what organizational level should the publications be counted? The dean of the school of social sciences claimed that he would just let his school contribute generally to the university's score, but no comparisons would be made between departments, not to mention between individuals in the staff. After some time, however, departments that contribute a lot to the score of the school of social science and to the overall university score may see an interest in interdepartmental comparison. Since publications are by definition public, the comparison is not difficult to make. How can the dean guarantee that no such comparisons will be made in the future? The effects of indicator systems may spread in complex organizational systems in a way that is not intended or controlled from the top.

Do Constitutive Effects Occur Deterministically?

At a presentation I gave to a group of medical doctors, some participants said that publication of indicators for the performance of individual doctors would lead the profession to cheat on the reporting of data. I replied that cheating could not be assumed to happen automatically; it had to depend on the values and ethics of the profession and its members. They could not disagree.

Some critics of evaluation machines assume that these systems have deterministic negative effects. Their underlying ontology is surprisingly similar to that of gurus of performance indicators, who promise automatic positive effects from these systems. None of these assumptions, however, are consistent with the socially constructivist view on knowledge advocated in this book. According to this view, the effects of indicator systems are complex and depend on interpretations, relations, and contexts. From a Foucauldian perspective, discourses, strategies, and techniques definitely pave the way for certain social constructions, but they are not fully imposed and implemented on the social body as a whole. Techniques and their effects are of different orders (Gordon 1980, 246). Or as Koselleck reminds us: instruments, measurements, and numbers—like concepts, hopes, and aspirations—are in constant tension with the reality they seek to describe. They are "more-or-less realities," depending on time, place, and context.

Why do constitutive effects occur more strongly in some contexts than in others? Here is a laundry list of factors one might subject to further study. First, evaluation machines are backed up by varying degrees of institutionalization. Some are only normatively recommended, while others are supported by legal frameworks or financial incentives. Voluntary innovations are adopted with more enthusiasm in organizations (Scott 1987), but compulsory institutional ones are backed by tougher sanctions. Binding mechanisms without normative support may lead to organizational hypocrisy, that is, a discrepancy between talk and action, between external procedures and internal practices. Each organization in each context may strike a particular negotiated compromise between the official rhetoric about evaluation machines and the colonization, on the part of these machines, of organizational practices.

Second, evaluation machines operate at different levels of analysis. Some studies suggest that indicators focusing on individuals rather than groups or organizations have a stronger behavioral impact, perhaps at least in individualistic cultures. On the other hand, evaluation machines operating at a high level of generality may have a wider societal influence. It cannot be concluded, however, that a general evaluation machine will have deterministic impacts all the way down to the individual level. For example, indicators of research productivity can be measured at the institutional level, while a department or a group of researchers may or may not collectively decide to break down the results to the individual level.

Third, publication of data may reinforce the constitutive effects of evaluation machines. However, it makes a difference in what form the data are published and in whose name (Andersen and Dahler-Larsen 2008). Furthermore, the nature and quality of a public debate about the data and their implications can make a difference for future policy making.

Fourth, no evaluation machine stands alone. Many public agencies seek to promote documentation and transparency through evaluation, each from its own perspective (Sahlin-Andersson 2004). Control of public institutions is often redundant, overlapping, and partly confusing. Sometimes evaluation regimes and their corresponding evaluation machines are reformed or revised, so that on occasion the evaluees cannot predict when and how they will be evaluated. Along with formal systems, a number of informal norms, professional values, conscience, and trust regulate public institutions, to varying degrees in various contexts.

Paradoxically, what from the perspective of New Public Management is an optimal mix of these factors (strong incentives, individual data, publication, and an exclusive focus on indicators) might comprise precisely those conditions that produce the most intensive constitutive effects of evaluation machines. Alternatively, the reason some evaluation machines may not create strong constitutive effects is that some of the conditions are relaxed compared to what is prescribed by NPM. In some countries, NPM regimes are introduced with a weak or missing link to financial incentives. Professional ethics, conscience, and traditions may prevent NPM regimes from having far-reaching constitutive effects. However, paradoxically, the ideology does not recognize the importance of such soft values.

A fifth factor should be taken into account that is fairly obvious but often forgotten, as the contemporary evaluation imaginary spreads to a broader set of social domains. This is the substantive area of activity. In some areas of activity, it may be easier to identify fairly obvious, relevant, and measurable criteria of success. The problem is thus not evaluation but an evaluation ideology recommending colonization of all areas of activity under evaluation regimes.

A Counterargument: There Are Not Always Negative Constitutive Effects

Kelman and Friedman (2009) argue that it is a popular notion among academics that performance measurement in the public sector often has negative and dysfunctional side effects. However, this notion is often empirically unwarranted, they say. They report on a case study of a new scheme in English hospitals for reduction of waiting time. They empirically test for a number of potential side effects, such as effort substitution and gaming, but they find none of these effects. In fact, people just generally wait for shorter periods, and that is it.

Their explanation is that sometimes a good indicator is simply related to other good things in organizations. Importance and measurability are not always negatively correlated! In the terminology offered earlier in this chapter, measure fixation thus does not imply sacrificing other valuable deeds that are not measured. This has to be determined empirically in each situation (Kelman and Friedman 2009). Even if an interaction between subunits is involved, a subunit may not push problems over to other subunits, if they object. Then a more functional organizational solution to the overall problem may be found.

One reason Kelman and Friedman find no serious negative side effects of the indicators of waiting time is that perhaps in this situation the focus was on a fairly good indicator (although we have seen examples earlier in this chapter of many tricks played with this very phenomenon of waiting time). Perhaps they just focused on hospitals where a lot of improvement could be made. This does not mean the same thing can happen in other hospitals around the world. Another reason is that perhaps they did not look for the cleverest ways in which the measurement might have been circumvented (such as ambulances waiting outside until hospitals were ready; Kelman and Friedman 2009) or other tricks that are difficult to imagine.

What we can learn from Kelman and Friedman is that there may not always be negative or unintended side effects. Sometimes indicator systems simply lead to improvement. It depends on the situation, the nature of the substance area under measurement, and the nature of the indicators.

This observation is, however, consistent with the line of reasoning in this chapter, not detrimental to it. The point about constitutive effects of evaluation machines is not that constitutive effects are always negative. In fact, the problematic character of terms such as negative, unintended, and dysfunctional from an analytical perspective has been pointed out.

The interesting analytical point about constitutive effects is not their negativity, but their very constitutive character. What Kelman and Friedman capture is the (apparent) absence of trivial measure fixation. They do not discuss whether indicators help define goals in deeper sociological or philosophical ways. They do not say much about what in this chapter has been called advanced measure fixation.

As a final, peculiar point, Kelman and Friedman (2009) mention that so-called dysfunctional effects of indicators may be moderated through new and improved measures, or through cultivating public service motivation among employees. A good professional culture may prevent too much gaming with the indicators. Even those who are fairly optimistic about performance measurement do recognize that its value depends on the interaction with culture and interpretations.

Effects over Time and the Second-Order Construction of Indicators

The main idea in constitutive effects is that the world changes as it is being measured. As a consequence, the meaning of the indicator changes; we may call this a "second-order change" or "second-order construction" of the indicator. In first-order construction, we methodologically select an indicator in a world assumed to be stable. We often select the indicator in textbook fashion, aiming for reliability and validity. As the world changes, however, the phenomenon we intend to measure also changes, such as the concept of school quality. The actions following from revised measurement of school quality change, and our interpretation of the indicator needs to change if we want to understand what is going on. The key to understanding this process is not the intentions behind it but the self-logic of that process. Regardless of whether these changes are intended or unintended, or invented along the way, they are real social constructions with real consequences.

The more burdens placed on an indicator in organizational, managerial, and political terms, the more questions arise as to the methodological purity of an indicator and the clarity of its interpretation (Shadish, Cook, and Leviton 1991, 141).

For example, if teachers adopt a number of deliberate strategies to influence children's test scores, the meaning of a test score in schools changes over time. In an interesting study of school exclusion rates, Vulliamy and Webb (2001) found that a number of practical strategies aimed at schoolchildren with behavioral problems were or were not counted as formal school exclusion. Because of the seriousness of being excluded from school, a number of softer strategies were adopted. In addition, schools sought to exert influence on the social composition of incoming children, because this would in turn influence the school's subsequent school exclusion rate. Vulliamy and Webb (2001, 361) conclude that the official school exclusion rate is a social construction reflecting the meanings and strategies accorded to them by different groups. Not only would potential effects of an intervention seeking to reduce the school exclusion rate be masked by the constitutive effects of the intervention on the exclusion rates themselves; the very meaning of the term *school exclusion rate* would change because of the second-order change in the indicator. What we conventionally call the *validity* of an indicator is thus a social construction that can change depending on social reactions to the indicator, which in turn create a different reality as the object of measurement. We understand how indicators work only if we grasp how they fit into long social processes (Pollitt 1989).

In some situations, an indicator used as an evaluation criterion influences the credibility of another indicator. Weingart (2005) exemplifies how this goes on. He suggests that bibliometric indicators are increasingly used to control the productivity of the research system. Bibliometric evaluation machines are a result of legitimation pressures and of distrust in scientists' own classical form of evaluation, the peer review. The trust lost by the peer review system is tantamount to loss of autonomy for the scientific community and to greater involvement of political steering mechanisms (121). This shift is based on two mistaken assumptions, namely that bibliometric figures are reliable, and that they are independent of the peer review process. However, most bibliometric indicators that are taken seriously distinguish between publications that are peer-reviewed and those that are not. Imagine a situation where an editor of a publication needs contributions. He or she is tempted to claim that the journal is peer-reviewed in order to attract good authors. The editor may also be tempted to promise authors that the peer review will have no serious effect on the choice to publish the work. Articles may be peer-reviewed and published. The meaning of peer review in this situation changes, however, because most people have believed so far that peer review had an impact on the quality of the contribution, and ultimately on the decision to publish it. Next time the term *peer review* is mentioned, it cannot be trusted to mean the same as before, unless the concept is held in place in other situations by other journals with other editors. But the concept is up for grabs because it obviously means different things. In this manner, using a particular indicator (bibliometrics) has an effect—some would say an undermining effect—on the social construction and meaning of another evaluation mechanism, the peer review.

The implications of these complications for steering through evaluation machines are important. First, it is necessary to be aware of second-order changes in indicators. We can no longer accept a claim that an evaluation criterion is a purely technical matter in a stable world. Second, under complex modern conditions, a project or initiative that includes evaluation should be able to register and reflect on the constitutive effects of its own measuring tools and concepts as well as other measuring tools and concepts affected by its operations. The project should be in a position to understand and respond to the broader social processes triggered by the evaluation itself.

Effects of Qualitative Evaluation over Time

Complex effects of evaluation over time are not confined to quantitative indicator systems only. In some qualitative forms of evaluation, people are asked to compare their workplace with an ideal workplace. Then they are to take some initiatives to make improvements to close the gap between the two. Various creative formats used by qualitative evaluators facilitate such processes. After some time in the business, however, participants may give up their utopian visions. They learn that if they express such far-reaching visions in the morning session, they just have to do so much more work during the afternoon session, because they are the only ones who have the responsibility to close the gap between vision and reality; the evaluation consultant is just the facilitator. Over the years with this form of qualitative evaluation, life becomes easier if visions are reduced. Forms of evaluation help develop how we report about the world.

One philosophically interesting aspect of evaluation machines is that they do not just describe, measure, and influence the world in particular ways. Evaluation machines also directly and indirectly influence the social construction of the indicators we use to derive knowledge about the world. After evaluation machines have intervened, their intervention must be included in our interpretation of the quantitative data that we otherwise believe describe the world for us.

This has not only epistemological and methodological implications but also democratic ones.

The Democratic Aspect of Evaluation Criteria

Evaluators have traditionally disagreed as to how to derive legitimate evaluation criteria. However, there is a tradition of engaging in the discussion. Textbooks suggest that normative criteria should be explicit and justified (Shadish, Cook, and Leviton 1991). As evaluation machines become mandatory, and sometimes legitimized by other evaluation machines, there is an institutional necessity in them, a self-circularity, and an abstraction from the subject matter they describe that reduces their attention to careful selection of evaluation criteria. Some criteria must be set up, even if there are no good criteria available.

For example, the rate of caesarean sections in birth clinics is monitored. It is difficult to identify a desirable standard, since both too many and too few c-sections are problematic. No algorithm is able to deliver the best achievable figure. In practice, an evaluation machine is put into place that measures the rate of caesareans in every clinic compared to the national average. It is then assumed that clinics will initiate a reflection process about why they are above or below the national average, taking the national average as a norm. Whether the national average is something we should use as a standard in our monitoring of social activities, or whether the national average is really a good figure representing what we want, remains unclear. On closer inspection, a deviation from the national average may or may not turn out to be well justified. Monitoring of deviations from an average is, at best, an alarm bell that something may need further attention and investigation. Making sure the bell does not ring, however, is not in principle a democratic goal. Nevertheless, staying near the average may often be constituted as a goal in itself in the eyes of managers of birth clinics.

Publishing a comparison between the national rate and the rate of every clinic may be helpful in stimulating reflection in the clinics about whether their obstetric practices are normal or not. In an extreme situation, they may also help put public shame and blame on clinics having deviant practices for bad reasons. However, a more fundamental democratic problem may be forgotten. If the national rate of caesareans goes up (which has actually occurred in many countries), should we continue to cite individual clinics that deviate from the national aggregate trend, or should we discuss whether the national trend is itself socially desirable? Are we really satisfied as long as all clinics conform to the national average, whatever that may be?

To me, the latter issue may be the more pressing democratic question. Regrettably, the evaluation machine installed to compare individual clinics tends to draw our attention in another direction. Democratically speaking, we have never gathered together to deliberate the question whether the national average was indeed an acceptable standard, regardless of whether this standard rises or falls over the years.

Evaluation machines often help confuse the distinction between what is measured and what is socially desirable. Even if democracies should always seek a balance between legitimacy and effectiveness, evaluation machines ignore the legitimacy issue. Evaluation machines are built on the assumption that if we have a system to identify low scores on some criteria (which may or may not be valid indicators of effectiveness) then the legitimacy of the whole scoring system is not a relevant issue.

Evaluation machine engineers, audit bodies, and evaluation institutes become de facto interpreters of policy (Power 2005, 339), but it is not clear how and to what extent they are democratically accountable. In fact, much performance information is in the hands of managers and evaluation specialists, but there seems to be a missing link regarding its democratic use in the hands of ministers, legislators, and citizens (Pollitt 2006).

The observation that evaluation machines are likely to have constitutive effects on the definition of public services and social interventions only increases the democratic problem related to defining evaluation criteria, if not the whole functioning of evaluation machines. If the concept of constitutive effects is taken seriously, evaluation machines do not just have dysfunctional or unintended consequences. Rather, they help reshape the meanings attached to common activities and interventions in society.

There are serious challenges concerning the democratic handling of evaluation machines. Not only should their first-order criteria be democratically accountable; constitutive effects and second-order changes in indicators should also be objects of democratic debate, to the extent that indicators measure social realities and define them as well.

This idea presents us with a number of obstacles. We do not have long historical experience with how published indicators help constitute social and political realities in society. The processes through which this happens are complex and often not seen or understood by the public. The media tends to report scandals about low scores on this or that indicator; there is a demand for comfort and assurance among politicians, managers, and citizens that makes discussions of these matters complicated. Critics of evaluation machines can often be portrayed as adversaries of quality, since the evaluation machines and the social constructions supporting them claim that quality is exactly what *they* already grasp. Nevertheless, with the increased importance of evaluation machines, their constitutive effects have become a significant democratic problem.

The discussion of the relation between democracy and evaluation machines is a complicated one, however, because although evaluation machines sometimes have a logic of their own apart from democratic ambitions, at other times evaluation machines perhaps help implement and fulfill a particular political will. Consider the following case.

How an Evaluation Machine Works in Practice

This chapter ends with a case study of how an evaluation machine works in practice. The reader is invited to consider the many factors at play, and how good and bad effects interact.

The teaching of Danish as a second language for adults (immigrants and refugees) takes place in special schools. It is financed by social authorities if the students do not have an employer who pays for their courses in Danish. Every student has a right to attend language courses for three years.

Students are assigned among three programs depending on whether they are familiar with the alphabet, and if so, how much schooling they have had. The programs are divided into a handful of modules, each of which is concluded by a test provided by national authorities. Students are expected to move at regular intervals from one module test to another. To achieve Danish citizenry, it is necessary to pass the test on the final module in the program for people with higher education. In a similar vein, a permanent permit to stay in Denmark depends on passing another module test.

It is extremely difficult for some non-Western immigrants to climb through the whole module system and pass the final test within the three-year limit. Students sometimes complain about what they believe to be an unfair system—a viewpoint that several teachers agreed with—and teachers explained that the whole system of testing, in combination with restrictions in immigration policies, was defined not by the school but by the Danish government.

The existence of a school depends on who wins a tender process. Only the winner of the process can sign a contract with authorities for subsequent years. According to such a contract, the school will be paid according to the number of students passing the tests. The financial framework for the school depends exclusively on this income.

Within this institutional arrangement, the system of tests—which is equivalent to what we call an evaluation machine—plays a decisive role for the school and for the practice of teachers.

In interviews, teachers describe an ambiguous attitude toward the testing system. On the one hand, most of them like the idea that the progress of every student can be documented relatively objectively. The same is true for allocation of students to modules, which would otherwise be more chaotic.

On the other hand, teachers believe that tests cover only selected aspects of what immigrants and refugees need when it comes to Danish. For example, grammatical correctness is favored at the expense of practical use of the language in daily-life situations. Teachers believe that knowledge of Danish society and its rules, structure, and culture should be part of teaching in Danish, but these aspects are not tested. In addition, teachers believe that some parts of the tests are in fact school-oriented artificial exercises with little relevance in practice. Summarizing short books, for instance, is really a test of conformity to the rules of going to school rather than of command of the Danish language. For immigrants without previous education, it takes a lot of time simply to explain what a given assignment is all about.

Several teachers explain that the testing system exerts great influence on how they teach, since they must prepare the students for the next test. The pressure to do so is not directly coming from management, or at least not from management alone. Management does not give every teacher performance targets describing how many students should pass; nor is the individual teacher informed about his or her actual "productivity" from management. (Teachers say that the absence of individual measures is good because otherwise teachers would struggle to avoid all the "slow" students. Instead, teachers can volunteer to teach newcomers or advanced students as they prefer.) But management sometimes informs teachers about the whole financial situation of the school; so it is up to teachers to conclude how much general pressure there is on having students pass the test. Students themselves often ask during lessons whether a particular activity will help them pass the next test. Teachers also intuitively sense that their perceived quality depends in part on whether their students successfully pass the tests. In other words, the pressure to have students pass the test is "in the air" of the whole school as a social construction; it is not just a direct command from management. Another indication that this pressure exists in the collective conscience is that when organizational changes are necessary—for example, as a result of the tender process—those teachers who are most "troublesome" are said to be fired before others. In this indirect way, it pays to adopt to the test system as an integrated part of reality in the school.

There are several ways in which tests influence the practice of teaching. Since teachers cannot take tests out of the testing room, they produce home-made versions that allow students to practice the type of exercises known to appear in the official tests. If a student fails to pass a particular test, the teacher will focus precisely on the skills demonstrated to be lacking with the student.

Yet teachers maintain a fairly high degree of professional discretion when it comes to choice of teaching methods. Some use a lot of news in the lessons and facilitate discussion of the news with the students. In this way, students learn about Danish society and improve their language skills. Or teachers may refuse to talk with students about the tests for a couple of months, and then focus on testing only a few weeks before the actual test.

Test performance is evaluated by a special group of independent testers, some of whom are also teachers of other students. One teacher describes himself as a "dove" rather than a hawk when it comes to evaluating the written test results produced by students. He says it is difficult enough to learn a foreign language, and he thinks student should be met with kindness if they make an effort. One teacher has flatly refused to work as a tester because of the tough consequences of tests for some students.

One of the most difficult moments for a teacher is when it is necessary to explain to a student why he or she did not pass a test, especially if the student worked very hard, or if the failed test has severe consequences for the student. Sometimes teachers know that particular students are not likely to pass an upcoming test.

Other stressful moments include a student bringing personal problems to the teacher. A poor female student from Southeast Asia, for instance, explained to the teacher that she wanted to send money home to her even-poorer mother; she asked the teacher if it was a good idea in Denmark to work as a prostitute in order to earn money. Other teachers told similar stories about difficulties among students. Teachers believe, however, that over the years they learn to relate to students in a competent and professional way that does not require too much personal or emotional involvement.

Another stressful factor is that many students move into and out of the program. It is also stressful that many lessons are held in the evening and at other odd (or working) hours, especially stressful for teachers with small children.

In other words, the stress flowing from the testing system (an evaluation machine) is a relatively limited one, all things considered. Although teachers agreed that the effect tests have on teaching was substantial (what we have analytically called constitutive effects), teachers accepted and lived with these effects. The factors making this possible were, for example, that teachers found it sloppy that before the tests students could participate in Danish classes for a long time without any sign of progress; before the test system, teachers had very little definition of goals and little professional structure; despite their limitations, tests describe at least what teachers found to be some relevant aspects of what the students need to learn; teachers maintain discretion concerning the choice of pedagogical method, even if test results are measured strictly; as of now, the schools are in fairly good economic condition because the socioeconomic composition of Danish immigrants changed in a favorable direction (more coming from countries close to Denmark and more with higher education); and last but not least, the test system has become a factual reality, so it makes little sense to discuss things endlessly.

In the big picture, the constitutive effects of the evaluation machine are perhaps so solid because teachers tend to learn to live with them, or have to live with them. In a larger political perspective, tests help define which immigrants are accepted into Denmark and which are not, while their own effort, participation, and performance in tests of course provides official legitimization for the selection. Further, schools are invited to become partners in implementing official Danish immigration policy, because their financing depends on test results, and life is easier for the schools if students come with national and educational backgrounds that are favored in the present immigration policy.

Constitutive effects do not operate in isolation.

Epilogue

Perspectives for Evaluation

There is a crack in everything. That's how the light gets in.

—Leonard Cohen

The purpose of this final chapter is to show how the analysis in this book promotes a kind of thinking about evaluation that is an alternative to the present self-understanding of contemporary evaluation practices. Such alternative thinking is not for evaluators alone. Evaluation so deeply involves professionals, managers, and users of services that it is a broad social responsibility to think cleverly about evaluation and use it intelligently.

The central thesis of this book is that if we want to understand many of the norms, values, and expectations that evaluators and others bring to evaluation (sometimes unknowingly), we should understand how evaluation is demanded, formatted, and shaped by the two great principles of social order in modernity, called *organization* and *society*.

In the organizational part of the book, it was argued that modern evaluation is deeply embedded in organizational logics. We cannot think of modern evaluation apart from modern organization. Furthermore, the thinking of evaluation is formed and shaped according to the dominant organizational model, of which we looked at three, in brief called the rational, the learning, and the institutional models. Although the rational model connotes control and predictability, most evaluators subscribe to the positive vision of the learning organization.

However, it was argued—perhaps provocatively—that learning is not just troublesome and time-consuming; the learning model in its optimism does not quite grasp why evaluation processes in organizations are sometimes inconsistent, disconnected, ritualistic, and hypocritical. The institutional model was offered as an alternative to better grasp these apparently peculiar phenomena. A key theoretical insight learned from the institutional model is that organizations do evaluation—and attend to such components as topics, criteria, designs, and follow-up actions—in ways that reflect norms, values, and expectations in organizational environments regardless of whether there is any consistency in evaluation and its use as such.

The idea of evaluation as a ritual supported by societal norms is thus central to our analysis. The institutional and managerial support for the idea of evaluation is much stronger than the empirical evidence about the instrumental use of actual evaluations. So, evaluations must be carried out for institutional and normative reasons. In our society, the pressure to *do* evaluation is stronger than the pressure to *do good* evaluation.

The full meaning of the idea of evaluation as a ritual mandated by society, however, did not unfold until sociological analysis was carried out, by means of a tripartite distinction among modernity, reflexive modernity, and the audit society. Faith in evaluation has been deep, because it is deeply rooted in fundamental modern beliefs and values. Yet in every epoch of modernity (such as reflexive modernity and the audit society) evaluation is shaped and colored by the dominant myths and values.

Evaluation has been clever in how it has incorporated myths, values, and norms from different epochs through the history of modern societies.

The field of evaluation has never slept. It has constantly come up with new models, approaches, and ways to evaluate to compensate for weakness in earlier approaches. In doing so, it has managed to remain in close contact with dominant ways of thinking characteristic of each sociohistorical phase in society. Evaluation has constantly found new forms, but each has also allowed some myths and values from its corresponding sociohistorical milieu, untouched by evaluation, to have an influence—perhaps exactly because the ideal of an ever-transparent and ever-self-transforming social reality was an unachievable ideal in the first place.

Many value choices in evaluation take place with reference to values taken for granted in a particular era. Many evaluation criteria, indicators, and standards are floating around in a given sociohistorical climate, just waiting to become attached to particular evaluands. Combine this with the general pressure to evaluate, and it becomes less necessary for evaluators and evaluation systems to be always careful, detailed, and mindful with the elaboration of evaluation criteria.

Our history of evaluation in modernity, reflexive modernity, and the audit society is not a story of increasing perfection. Instead, each phase has its own limitations and tensions.

In reflexive modernization, evaluation signals a willingness to listen and reflect on side effects of and reactions to one's practice. Evaluation becomes popular in an unprecedented way. It is now fashionable practice, signifying the appearance of reflexivity as a social norm. In the name of reflexivity, evaluation opens up for contingency and multiple perspectives, not only of various stakeholders but of a number of paradigms and approaches in evaluation itself. On the other hand, evaluation therefore gives way to relativity, contingency, perspectivity, arbitrariness, and unpredictability.

These very problems in evaluation—as well as in the organizations that host them—pave the way for new alliances between evaluation and organization in terms of evaluation culture, capacity building, systems, and policies defining evaluation.

The most radical response, antithetical to the subjectivism, contingency, and apparent arbitrariness of reflexively modern evaluation, is what I call evaluation machines, an ideal type describing the preferred form of evaluation in the audit society.

Steering, control, accountability, and predictability come back on the throne. The purpose of evaluation is no longer to stimulate endless discussions in society, but to prevent them. Instead of human subjectivity, a style of coolness, objectivity, and technocracy becomes the dominant ideal in evaluation.

There is a particular social investment in evaluation machines that can be understood only if we mobilize a combination of theoretical elements: the organizational legitimacy that organizations attain through consistency with broader themes, norms, values, and expectations in society; experiences with faulty, inconsistent, subjectivist, unpredictable, and overly complex evaluation processes in reflexive modernization; a new social imaginary that makes fear and risk management central cultural themes and that celebrates a new rigorism concerning what cannot be up for critique and discussion; and a strong comeback of rational, bureaucratic, management-oriented organization that is believed to guarantee predictability, nonsubjectivism, and order.

Reflexive modernization encouraged reflexivity, which itself encourages multiperspectivity and fragmentation. It left a vacuum with regard to how a perspective on society as a whole can be represented—a vacuum that evaluation machines try to fill on the basis of an imagery of objectivity, rational measurement, and depersonalized procedure.

It is highly debatable, however, whether evaluation machines represent social reality in a way that allows society to handle its complex problems adequately. Evaluation machines tend to lock evaluees into micro-oriented accountability structures. Evaluation machines often overfocus on defensive, reassuring measurement of microquality at the expense of attention to complex macroproblems that call for offensive, experimenting, and future-oriented views of quality.

Among the many problems evaluation machines have are their hidden costs, the rigidity of their control procedures, degradation of the work of professionals, and constitutive effects.

Constitutive effects are complex, relational, and contextual. They emerge through definitions, categorizations, and measurements that enhance some social constructions of reality but not others. Indicators do not merely communicate about an activity; they also meta-communicate about the identities and roles of human beings and their relations. Indicator systems produce socially relevant labels that stick to practices and people, and that help organize social interaction in particular ways. To categorize constitutive effects of evaluation as unintended, negative, pathologic, and dysfunctional is to assume a technical, pure, and unrealistic model of how knowledge can be applied to social realities. There is an open-ended nondeterminism in the concept of constitutive effects. It suggests that the finality of evaluation is not determined by the data as such, nor by intentions behind evaluations, but by complex processes of social construction.

A More Modest Evaluation Industry

One of the things we have learned from the analysis in this book is that although evaluation is formed and shaped by two large forms of social order to which it belongs (organization and society), the evaluation field itself has been active, dynamic, and almost self-transformative in its responses to challenges and problems. One must admire the flexibility and dynamic creativity in the field. On the other hand, forms of evaluation that are meaningful at one time as a response to a particular problem or societal situation may, even if they were conceived with the best of intentions, turn out to create a new set of problems in the next phase of history.

For example, the emphasis that evaluators put on learning may have contributed to an emptying of the concept, to time-consuming and frustrating initiatives seeking to foster eternal personal and organizational development, and to evaluation fatigue. Another example: the fragmentation of perspectives in reflexive modernization may have led to unpredictable evaluation and a loss of common perspective that pave the way for rigid evaluations of a much more controlled and predictable nature. And finally: the closer alliance of evaluation and management and the integration of evaluation systems into organizations may at first sight have been meaningful from a utilization perspective but turn out to be problematic for the democratic debatability of evaluation.

Only if we look at evaluation in a broad historical and sociopolitical perspective can we discover the ambiguities and tensions inherent in what appear to be reasonable innovations in evaluation, if we look at them in specific isolated situations. A more modest evaluation industry would be aware of such ambiguities and tensions.

An important task is to attend to constitutive effects of evaluation machines, such as performance indicator systems in practice. Compared to widespread belief in the value of evaluation machines as political and administrative regimes, relatively little is known about their extrinsic impact on social realities. Although this book, like Modell (2004), suggests that performance measurement does not work according to its own myth, much remains to be known about what else is happening. It would be helpful to know more about the socially constructed nature of the validity of indicators and standards. Evaluation criteria and indicators can be developed with more or less advanced substantial understanding of the relationships among policy, programs, and outcomes in particular fields (Courtney, Needell, and Wulczyn 2004). It would also be informative to map some of the wash-back effects of evaluation machines on larger cultural, organizational, and democratic systems. Of special interest is how knowledge flowing from indicator systems is handled in media discourse in the public arena. Too often, evaluation in general and evaluation machines in particular are introduced on the basis of values and belief in evaluation as a general good, but without any substantial demonstration of the actual effects of evaluation on social realities.

Perhaps evaluators see these processes without seeing them. Perhaps we have reached a point where the design and use of evaluation machines are determined more by the architects and guardians of evaluation machines than by any other sector or agent in society. Perhaps the contemporary philosophy of surveillance serves surveyors, monitors, and auditors more than other groups. Through evaluation systems and evaluation machines, the burden of data collection may decrease, or be streamlined, but only from the viewpoint of an inspector or evaluator.

This does not necessarily mean that evaluation systems are not required to produce enormous amounts of data. The point is that the burden placed on the inspector or evaluator is relieved. This is done by requiring the inspected organization to produce the data necessary for inspection or by raising the level of abstraction to which the inspector or evaluator has to operate. Whether "the system is in place" or not can be turned into an operational question in the eyes of an inspector.

Evaluation machines are based on abstraction and "de-skilling," meaning an operator of a mechanically functioning evaluation machine may have quite limited insight into the practices under evaluation. The operators of evaluation machines may have less insight into the practice under evaluation than designers of evaluation machines do, and designers may know less about the practice under evaluation than practitioners themselves. Evaluation machines in schools may incorporate some knowledge about quality management, but very little about teaching. Through this abstraction—inspection systems inspecting systems—complexity is reduced considerably. Evaluators no longer need substantial insight into what is evaluated; they can rely on broad and fairly vague assumptions about the virtues of particular organizational recipes (Meyer 1994; Røvik 1998). The legitimacy of the evaluation industry depends on the extent to which citizens and other audiences buy into the taken-for-grantedness of these fashionable organizational recipes.

However, in evaluation not too much should be dependent on beliefs. The time has come to compare the enormous costs of operating evaluation machines with the actual social effects of evaluation, negative as well as positive. Some of the self-congratulatory rhetoric of the evaluation industry may be unwarranted. It is time to consider, as this book has argued, whether the marginal utility of evaluation may be decreasing, and whether there are sometimes good reasons for evaluation fatigue.

If the analysis presented in this book is correct, evaluators should make only modest promises. A rhetoric of endless development, learning, and improvement may be too disconnected from reality to be a trustworthy promise on behalf of evaluation. So, too, may a rhetoric of total quality management, control, and predictability. There is no such thing as total quality (Weick 2000). Management is never total, and neither is quality in a complex world. Although many evaluation machines emphasize defensive quality and prospective control, they not only reduce risk but also reallocate risks (and create them anew) because evaluation machines have their own effects on those who are under evaluation, and because many of their wider effects are not predictable or not consistent with the official purposes of evaluation machines.

Evaluators should be more aware of the social imagery they transmit when they make promises about the wonderful benefits of evaluation. Evaluators should also be aware that today they are no longer just working on the fringes of organizations to create reflexivity. Instead, they come in with mandatory evaluation backed up by the full force of institutionalized bureaucratic machinery. They should admit that, and they should behave with care.

One way to make the evaluation industry more realistic would be to break down some of the barriers between evaluation and the practices under evaluation. Evaluation machines may stand in between evaluators and their understanding of the practices they evaluate.

Good professionals have always evaluated their work, at least informally or tacitly. In reflexive modernization, a central idea was to reconnect users and professionals, programs and effects, planning and reflection in order to break with the self-containment found among all of them. Reflexivity should be expanded through feedback loops and dialogue. In the audit society, however, the design of evaluation machines is more and more separated from the doing of work, and evaluation procedures are abstracted and generalized as they move up the organization hierarchy toward the managerial layers. Handbooks, manuals, indicators, and evaluation systems constitute a large and complicated social interface between evaluators and the realities they evaluate. For this reason, evaluators become specialists who are not held accountable for the consequences of their evaluation, and who are not faced with the experience hereof, because there is too much social interface in time and space between evaluation and its consequences. In an era in which we are losing faith in rational knowledge as such, God-like rationality per se cannot guarantee the good social consequences of evaluation. Evaluators must therefore be confronted, in new, socially embedded ways, with the consequences of their products.

Evaluation and Good Work

Evaluators should recognize that they are not performing evaluation on isolated evaluands in an empty world. Before evaluation, there was not a social desert without values, norms, and control mechanisms. There was a complex social world with relational and embedded practices (Schwandt 2002, 2003), with historical traditions and expectations, and sometimes imperfect institutions—but there was not nothing. A teacher without formal external evaluation is not necessarily an isolated, anomic, irresponsible, and nonproductive teacher. However, the benefits of evaluation are easier to see if the benefits of all other values, norms, and social regulations are ignored.

Instead, evaluation must demonstrate new attention to qualities that are hard to demonstrate in quality measurement. Some qualities may be local, situational, historic, embedded, or just unique (Stake 2004). Especially in the era of evaluation machines, evaluation should be more attentive to the value of practices and work. The meaning of work is an important ingredient in the culture of the West, and it is also an important ingredient in well-functioning public organizations. There is in our time practical interest in recruiting well-qualified staff in teaching, health, social work, and research, and in fact in all areas of public organization, and there is sociological and philosophical interest in restoring pride in work and a sense of craftsmanship (Sennett 2008). Following Arendt's distinction between types of human activity, labor is biologically necessary, and work is purely instrumental. Action, however, is where we realize ourselves as human beings in the light of our own aspirations and the recognition of others. Using this distinction, we cannot afford evaluation machines that reduce the meaningfulness of action in what is done by teachers, nurses, policemen, social workers, and all others who carry out important tasks on behalf of society. Evaluation machines in their present form have too many similarities with the industrial surveillance techniques under early industrialization: time-oriented, abstract, dehumanized, and too separated from the meaning of work itself. We already know the consequences of that philosophy for the meaningfulness of industrial work, so there is no need to let contemporary evaluation machines repeat the same mistakes with respect to human services and work in public organizations. It would be counterproductive to undermine responsibility and honor in the name of accountability and effectiveness. Instead, there is a need for a new philosophy in evaluation working together with the values of good craftsmanship, pride in work, and a sense of recognition.

Evaluation and Democracy

In our time of evaluation machines, there is no clear functional distinction among accreditation, auditing, quality assurance, and evaluation. I see no particular need in society to carve out and defend the identity of evaluation and evaluators in a narrow sense. This is—at best—the project just of evaluators.

By choosing evaluation and attending to its changing definitions, I have been able to carve out a particular object of organizational and sociological analysis, but also to show that its boundaries and forms have changed considerably over time. However, one of the main reasons I have precisely maintained the term *evaluation* as this headline is the inherent democratic dimension that has been in evaluation from its beginning. The democratic issue and mandate is both inherent and debatable for all the practices I have dealt with under the headline of evaluation, regardless of whether these practices like to identify themselves as evaluation, audit, accreditation, or quality assurance.

"The political" is a particular opening that appears in societies that have discovered that their destiny lies in their own hands—the discovery of societal autonomy, if you will. The political is where society works on itself (Rosanvallon 2009). The political is the self-constitution of society.

Democracy is an answer to how the political can be handled. Democracy is the way in which society handles its self-appropriation. Evaluation therefore fits into a democracy, that is, a society appropriating itself through deliberate and self-conscious inquiry into the effects of its own actions and initiatives. Whether they like it or not, whether they know it or not, evaluators and others like them are embedded in the terrain where society works with itself, and works on itself. This is what democracies do.

Evaluation is thus inherently political. It aspires to help democracy work. Evaluation is—not the least in its constitutive sense—"societing" (Woolgar 2004, 454), because it helps define social realities, and not only describe them. The political and the democratic concern is an ever-present aspect of evaluation (Karlsson Vestman and Conner 2006). It is not a "dark side of life" that should be "expelled" from the "rational, well-planned and well-intended" noble art of evaluation.

However, as Rosanvallon (2009) shows, democratic ambition is full of tensions and ambiguities. It is thus a problematic solution to the question of the political. The dream of the good society is full of inherent vagueness, and it must be so (Rosanvallon 2009, 19). For this reason—and because of the difficulties of establishing any rational and legitimate authority, of representativeness, and of demarcating "the people" who qualify for political participation—there is instability in the very essence of democracy. This analysis is thus very close to the ambiguities pointed out by Castoriadis regarding the tension between rationality and autonomy as key modern principles. There is a necessary element of fiction in the ideas of "people," "progress," "justice," "equality," etc., which are candidates to be the structuring principles of the democratic constitution. In Rosanvallon's view, there can be no fixed normative determination of these principles; they will remain "contested concepts" (Gallie 1955). It is necessary to clarify them and develop them according to the moment in the history of democratic nations and according to the situation.

Exactly the same is true for key terms in evaluation such as "means," "ends," "effectiveness," "stakeholders," "indicators," "quality," "values," "evaluands," and "use of evaluation"—not to mention evaluation itself! All are ambiguous structuring principles with democratic relevance. However, the meaning of each of these terms is itself a democratic riddle rather than a fixed technological or methodological given. What evaluators do as they work with these terms in practice is therefore also inherently a democratic undertaking, whether they think of it this way or not.

In evaluation is true what is also true in democracy: it is the most fundamental terms that are hardest to define (Rosanvallon 2009, 45). In this sense, an evaluation is something that takes a particular standpoint in relation to a democratic problem; it cannot just be the imposition of an ideal order (Rosanvallon 2009, 39).

If we understand that democracy is a regime instituting itself, time is an active and constructive variable (Rosanvallon 2009, 40). Evaluation must thus be an unstable democratic striving or ambition; it cannot be a nonnegotiable solution. This is because there is no origin of origins that helps keep the standpoint of standpoints fixed. Democracy is an opening that must remain open for questioning. Any evaluation must reflect this.

Yet there are various simultaneous forms of democracy coupled to different temporalities (Rosanvallon 2009, 44). In evaluation, we have some constitutions that are several hundred years old, we have policies and programs and goals that are years old, and we have various claims and demands for legitimacy that are uncoordinated with each other. And there are multiple relevancies in one particular evaluand in a practical context. Evaluation is full of examples of conflicting heritages and legitimacies.

In a democratic light, however, we should not fall for the temptation to install just one principle of legitimacy or authority, and neither should we replace democratic concerns with technocratic evaluation machines. In fact it is the *resonance* between our experiences and our society that should be listened to; it is the *resonance* between evaluation and our concern for democracy that turns evaluation into a truly democratic phenomenon.

Democracy is alive, though, only to the extent that democratic responsibilities are taken up by people. The political depends on the notion of people living together, sharing a sense of common social destiny, and acting on this feeling. Evaluators have a role to play in highlighting the democratic character of public initiatives, showing that there is society in public activities, because what is done by one part in society is never really isolated from the rest of society. Evaluation is societing.

Each of the phases analyzed in this book—modernity, reflexive modernity, and the audit society—poses a particular and specific set of democratic challenges to evaluation. In modernity, strong emphasis on rationality and progress leads to technocratic mentalities that tend to suppress the political element in evaluation. In reflexive modernity, evaluators give voice to a cacophony of perspectives that do not add up to a common agenda. A societal perspective is vanishing.

Evaluators under reflexive modernity should remember to connect local feedback loops with broader societal concerns. They should remember to connect particular voices with an obligation toward a larger democratic picture. They should not escape into entirely local contexts in order to carry out responsive and participatory evaluation, but return to the public arena to enlighten democratic audiences about their results. They should also remember to take part in discussion about policies, and not only their local ramifications.

The audit society and its evaluation machines present another set of complicated democratic problems. Evaluation criteria that are democratically problematic are often used in a robotlike manner. Evaluation machines break accountability down to its most atomized, measurable, and manageable parts, but they cannot motivate different partners in society to work together to solve complex and dynamic problems. They sacrifice macroquality for microquality. They also overemphasize defensive quality at the expense of offensive quality. Because they are mandatory and work repetitively in alliance with powerful institutional structures, evaluation machines transform the whole classical utilization problem in evaluation. The most pressing problem may no longer be nonutilization, but the constitutive effects of evaluation machines on a variety of social and professional practices. How evaluation prestructures the reality it claims to measure is an important and often ignored democratic problem, but even more relevant in the audit society.

As evaluators help build up evaluation capacities, cultures, policies, and machines that regulate evaluation, they should be aware that they are also building institutional structures. In a democratic light, however, institutions support identities (Wildavsky 1987), and democracy presupposes institutional structures that favor identities having a preference for democracy and attention to the democratic perspective on problems in society.

A good thing about democracy, however, is exactly what Rosanvallon calls its historicity, or what Arendt (1950) might call the principle of natality. It is unfinished business, never complete. It never works according to its ideals; it can always be improved. And there are no guarantees.

If we take Rosanvallon's view of democracy as unfinished business seriously, a new skepticism about evaluation systems, machines, capacity, and evaluation policies should be aired. Although advocates of these ways of streamlining and structuring evaluation are correct in pointing out that it may too often be left to chance and to the caprices of subjective individuals (which may be relatively true under reflexive modernization), there are also dangers in too strict planning of evaluation. If it is inherently democratic and political, and democracy constantly renews itself according to the principles of historicity and natality, then evaluation should also sometimes cut across, neglect, or challenge official definitions of what needs to be counted, measured, and controlled. A policy of evaluation that denies such opening of democracy toward itself sounds too much like organizing in advance what can be said in the democratic debates of the future. For this reason, evaluation may serve the political better if it is not tightly described and regulated in an evaluation policy, and not made automatic by an evaluation machine.

Although I have described in this book the many organizational and social forces that help shape evaluation, it is my hope that I have also portrayed all these forces as social constructions, that is, the products of human beings. And as my analysis has suggested that different organizational and social principles sometimes overlap, and that the environment in which evaluation unfolds is often inconsistent, ambiguous, or fragmented, there is often space for evaluators to make an argument. In fact, evaluation and its use has a lot to do with making good arguments (Valovirta 2002).

Perhaps to the surprise of some evaluators, these arguments can best be seen in the context of what some philosophers call weak thinking.

Evaluation and Weak Thinking

Increased awareness of the democratic role of evaluators must, as already mentioned, go hand in hand with a new modesty among evaluators. Evaluators should acknowledge that there is no indebatable anchor in "truth," "method," or "objectivity," nor in any particular normative vision of "learning," "development," "effectiveness," "risk management," or "quality assurance."

Truly, some forms of knowledge are more qualified, elaborate, systematic, and verifiable than others. But the means of controlling, checking, and discussing knowledge are social and contingent rather than God-given. No knowledge is independent of perspective; knowledge is itself contingent and uncertain (Morin 1992). In addition, no knowledge can guarantee its own utilization.

Vattimo (2004) offers a way of talking about these uncertainties. To him, as well as to other philosophers with roots in hermeneutics (Schwandt 2000), interpretation is not a special activity based on a particular algorithm or procedure, but something we do in general as human beings. Our interpretation of the world does not begin with some external objectivity, but with our "thrownness" into particular historical, institutional, cultural, relational, and biographical realities. Our interpretations are bound to our radical historicity (Vattimo 2004, 76). For this reason, there is no absolute list of fundamental categories describing how our being should be understood. The origins of the institution of being turn out to be relative to changing epochs (Vattimo 2004, 13). We must recognize that any interpretive perspective is partial, unstable, and temporary.

Modernity has led to a quite particular social space for the making of experiences. Modernity has led to division of labor, specialization, segmentation of our spheres of values and of existence, fragmentation of our sense of reality, and many discontinuous forms of life. On top of this social order, we have increased pace of social change (Vattimo 2004, 86–87).

If we take modernity seriously, we can see that perspectives are partial; we can see that our interpretations of earlier epochs and of societies other than our own are tied to our own perspectives. If not, we should consult ethnography, anthropology, philosophy, and the sociology of knowledge. In other words, there is in modernity an inherent pluralism and antifoundationalism that is not coincidental. It is in fact the very modernist belief in clarity and transparency that has had this consequence. A mythical belief it turned out to be.

Philosophical hermeneutics, says Vattimo, cannot respond to this situation by insisting on a metaphysical foundation that can be used as a critical platform against modernity. If philosophical hermeneutics will take its own theory about the historicity of interpretations seriously, it must step into modern conditions or, perhaps more precisely, recognize that it is already there and accept the loss of metaphysical absolutes. Postmetaphysical thinking, a thinking without reference to absolutes, must recognize that it has no legitimation outside of its sociohistorical being. It must thus see itself as both a result of and a response to modernity. On the other hand, hermeneutics is exactly a winning position with respect to how it reflects its own historicity, and reflects on the pluralism in modern society.

The departure from the ideals of progress and the continued perfection of human life in fact amount just to recognizing that modernity was not a departure from metaphysics, as it believed itself to be, but really the high point of metaphysics. Even if modernity declared to cancel the relevance of all metaphysical imaginaries for collective social life (Schanz 1990), it in fact inaugurated a grand new metaphysical tale of autonomy, rationality, and progress that was merely the "last great objectivist metaphysics" (Vattimo 2004, 154). The fall of this metaphysics should not be bemoaned, however. It opens up new social opportunities without an imposing master principle or project.

The thinking under these conditions must be without neurosis and remorse. Thinking must be "weak," without insisting on one's own truth. This is why Vattimo's philosophy has been called weak thinking. This type of philosophy has itself democratic propensities, and it does not attempt to fall back onto stronger, more comforting, more authoritarian, and more threatening versions of the real (Vattimo 2004, 20).

Weak thinking is thus thinking against neorigorism. Weak thinking takes away the charms of authoritarian tendencies, be they ethnic, military, social, ideological, or managerial. This is no minor accomplishment. With Vattimo, ethics, politics, law—and, may I add, evaluation!—cannot be legitimized by means of a particular content or procedure. Vattimo does not accept Habermasian rules for a dominance-free discourse (which would lead one to nullify the statements of others if they were made under nondominance-free rules). Following Vattimo, the rules of politics, law, ethics, and evaluation are earthly, pedestrian, context-bound, and historical, much like Rosanvallon's democracy. But they do not embody one particular ideal procedure or content. Nor do they impose their own image of social reality on those realities in violent or authoritarian ways.

Truly, evaluators can help do good things. They can increase the sensitivity of practitioners and decision makers to the effects and side effects in society of what they do. They can question political, organizational, and ideological assumptions and demonstrate how initiatives work in practice. They can increase society's sensitivity to the macroquality of social interventions. They can connect what is otherwise disconnected in hypocritical organizations (such as goals and activities, promises, and deeds). They can remind society of its own ambitions and its mistakes in achieving them.

But all this should take place in the context of weak thinking. What would weak thinking mean for evaluation? It would mean that any approach in a given evaluation is aware that it has no metaphysical anchor and cannot subscribe to one pregiven form of legitimacy only. It is also aware that it embodies one perspective among several possible perspectives. Weak thinking in evaluation also implies modesty about the promises of all good consequences of evaluation. An evaluator knows that results are debatable and that the uses of evaluation are in the hands of an imperfect human collective. A hermeneutically conscious evaluator also knows that evaluation helps shape reality in unforeseen ways, and that the perspectives of others are democratically respectable. Weak thinking also implies respect for those social realities that are difficult to represent within a given evaluation. Furthermore, evaluators with weak thinking would incorporate a healthy dose of hesitation, care, modesty, inconsistency, and lack of total dominance in any evaluation. Responsible evaluators would question the democratic legitimacy and use of evaluation machines as a necessary dimension in the very construction of such machines. They would also lay bare those aspects of evaluation ideologies that are derived from myths inherent in modern societal and organizational ideals.

A good evaluator knows that although under present social conditions the demands for evaluation are increasing, the need for wisdom and modesty in evaluation is greater than ever before.

References

Abma, Tineke A., and Mirko Noordegraf. 2003. "Public Managers Amidst Ambiguity: Towards a Typology of Evaluation Practices in Public Management." *Evaluation* 9(3): 285–330.

Albæk, Erik. 1988. *Fra sandhed til information: Evalueringsforskning i USA–før og nu* [From Truth to Information: Evaluation Research in the U.S.—Then and Now]. Copenhagen: Akademisk Forlag.

————. 1993. "Evalueringsforskning i Norden" [Evaluation Research in the Nordic Countries]. *Politica* 25(1): 6–26.

————. 1998. "Knowledge, Interests and the Many Meanings of Evaluation: A Developmental Perspective." *Scandinavian Journal of Social Welfare* 7: 94–98.

Alkin, Marvin C., and Joan A. Ruskus. 1984. *Reflections on Evaluation Costs: Direct and Indirect.* Los Angeles: Center for the Study of Evaluation, UCLA.

Alkin, Marvin C., Michael Quinn Patton, and Carol H. Weiss. 1990. *Debates on Evaluation.* Newbury Park, CA: Sage.

Andersen, Simon Calmar. 2004. "Hvorfor bliver man ved med at evaluere folkeskolen" [Why Keep on Evaluating the Public Schools]. *Politica* 4: 452–468.

Andersen, Vibeke Normann, and Peter Dahler-Larsen. 2008. "The Framing of Public Evaluation Data: Transparency and Openness in Danish Schools." In *Open to the Public*, eds. R. Boyle, J. D. Breul, and P. Dahler-Larsen, 99–116. New Brunswick, NJ: Transaction.

Appadurai, Arjun. 1990. "Disjuncture and Difference in the Global Cultural Economy." *Theory, Culture and Society* 7(2): 295–310.

Arendt, Hannah. 1950. *The Human Condition.* Chicago: University of Chicago Press.

Argyris, Chris, and Donald A. Schön. 1978. *Organizational Learning: A Theory of Action Perspective.* Reading, MA: Addison-Wesley.

Audit Commission (UK). 2002. *Recruitment and Retention: A Public Service Workforce for the Twenty-First Century.* London: Audit Commission.

Ålvik, Trond. 1996. *School Self-Evaluation: What, Why, How, by Whom, for Whom?* Dundee: Scottish Consultative Council on the Curriculum.

Baier, Vicki E., James G. March, and Harald Sætren. 1986. "Implementation and Ambiguity." *Scandinavian Journal of Management Studies* 2(3/4): 197–212.

Bailey, Kathleen M. 1996. "Working for Washback: A Review of the Washback Concept in Language Testing." *Language Testing 13*(3): 257–279.

Baizerman, Michael, Donald W. Compton, and Stacey H. Stockdill. 2005. "Capacity Building." In *Encyclopedia of Evaluation*, ed. S. Mathison. Thousand Oaks, CA: Sage.

Barthes, Roland. 1972. *Mythologies.* New York: Hill and Wang.

Bateson, Gregory. 1972. *Steps to an Ecology of Mind.* New York: Ballantine.

Bauman, Zygmunt. 1983. "Industrialism, Consumerism and Power." *Theory, Culture and Society 1*(3): 32–43.

———. 1989. *Modernity and the Holocaust.* Oxford: Polity Press.

———. 1995. *Life in Fragments.* Oxford: Blackwell.

———. 2000. *Liquid Modernity.* Cambridge, UK: Polity Press.

———. 2002. *Society Under Siege.* Cambridge, UK: Polity Press.

Beck, Ulrich. 1992. *Risk Society: Towards a New Modernity.* London: Sage.

———. 1994a. "The Reinvention of Politics: Towards a Theory of Reflexive Modernization." In *Reflexive Modernization*, eds. U. Beck, A. Giddens, and S. Lash, 1–55. Palo Alto, CA: Stanford University Press.

———. 1994b. "Replies and Critiques." In *Reflexive Modernization*, eds. U. Beck, A. Giddens, and S. Lash, 198–215. Palo Alto, CA: Stanford University Press.

———. 1997. *The Reinvention of Politics: Rethinking Modernity in the Global Social Order.* Cambridge, UK: Polity Press.

———, Anthony Giddens, and Scott Lash. 1994. *Reflexive Modernization: Politics, Tradition and Aesthetics in the Modern Social Order.* Palo Alto, CA: Stanford University Press.

Bereiter, Carl. 2002. *Education and Mind in the Knowledge Age.* Mahwah, NJ: Erlbaum.

Berger, Peter L. 1964. "Some General Observations on the Problem of Work." In *The Human Shape of Work: Studies in the Sociology of Occupations*, ed. P. L. Berger, 211–241. New York: Macmillan.

———, Brigitte Berger, and Hansfried Kellner. 1973. *The Homeless Mind: Modernization and Consciousness.* New York: Vintage Books.

Berger, Peter L., and Thomas Luckmann. 1966. *The Social Construction of Reality: A Treatise in the Sociology of Knowledge.* New York: Doubleday.

Boltanski, Luc, and Eve Chiapello. 2007. *The New Spirit of Capitalism*. London: Verso.

Bouchet, Dominique. 1989. "Det hellige i sociologisk perspektiv" [The Sacred in Sociological Perspective]. *Paradigma 3*(4): 31–41.

———. 2007. "The Ambiguity of the Modern Conception of Autonomy and the Paradox of Culture." *Thesis Eleven: Critical Theory and Historical Sociology 88*(1): 31–54.

Bouckaert, Geert, and Walter Balk. 1991. "Public Productivity Measurement: Diseases and Cures." *Public Productivity & Management Review 15*(2): 229–235.

Brunsson, Nils. 1986. "Organizing for Inconsistencies: On Organizational Conflict, Depression, and Hypocrisy as Substitutes for Action." *Scandinavian Journal of Management Studies 2*: 165–185.

Campbell, Donald T. 1969. "Reform as Experiments." *American Psychologist 24*: 409–429.

———. 1984. "Hospital and Landsting as Continuously Monitoring Social Polygrams: Advocacy and Warning." In *Evaluation of Mental Health Service Programs*, eds. B. Cronholm and L. von Knorring, 13–39. Stockholm, Sweden: Forskningsraadet Medicinska.

———. 1988. *Methodology and Epistemology for Social Science: Selected Papers*. Chicago: University of Chicago Press.

———. 1991 [1971]. "Methods for the Experimenting Society." *Evaluation Practice 12*(3): 223–260.

Castoriadis, Cornelius. 1982. "The Crisis of Western Societies." *Telos 53*: 17–28.

———. 1987a. *The Imaginary: Creation in the Social-Historical Domain*. Palo Alto, CA: Stanford University Press.

———. 1987b. *The Imaginary Institution of Society*. Cambridge: Polity Press.

———. 1997. *World in Fragments: Writings on Politics, Society, Psychoanalysis, and the Imagination*. Palo Alto, CA: Stanford University Press.

Chelimsky, Eleanor. 2006. "The Purposes of Evaluation in a Democratic Society." In *The Sage Handbook of Evaluation*, eds. I. Shaw, J. C. Greene, and M. M. Mark, 33–55. London: Sage.

Cheney, George, Jill McMillan, and Roy Schwartzman. 1997. "Should We Buy the 'Student-as-Consumer' Metaphor?" *Montana Professor 7*(3): 8–11.

Christensen, Majbritt, Tove Rønne, and Annette H. Christiansen. 1999. "MFR-Vaccination af børn med æggallergi" [MMR Vaccination of Children with Egg Allergy]. *Ugeskrift for Læger 1999*(9): 1270.

Christiansen, John K., and Hanne F. Hansen. 1993. *Forskningsevaluering i teori og praksis* [Research Evaluation in Theory and Practice]. Copenhagen: Samfundslitteratur.

Clemet, Kristin. 2006. Presentation at the Sorø Meeting, arranged by the Danish Minister of Education Bertel Haarder. Sorø, Denmark, August 4.

Compton, Donald W., Michael Baizerman, and Stacey H. Stockdill. 2002. "Editors' Notes." *New Directions for Evaluation 2002*(93): 1–2.

Cooper, Robert, and Gibson Burrell. 1988. "Modernism, Postmodernism and Organizational Analysis: An Introduction." *Organization Studies 9*(1): 91–112.

Coopey, John. 1996. "Crucial Gaps in 'The Learning Organization': Power, Politics and Ideology." In *How Organizations Learn*, ed. K. Starkey, 348–367. London: Thomson Business Press.

Courtney, Mark E., Barbara Needell, and Fred Wulczyn. 2004. "Unintended Consequences of the Push for Accountability: The Case of National Child Welfare Performance Standards." *Children and Youth Services Review 26*: 1141–1154.

Cousins, J. Bradley. 2003. "Utilization Effects of Participatory Evaluation." In *International Handbook of Educational Evaluation. Part One: Perspectives*, eds. T. Kellaghan, D. L. Stufflebeam, and L. A. Wingate, 245–268. Dordrecht: Kluwer Academic.

Cousins, J. Bradley, and Lorna M. Earl. 1992. "The Case for Participatory Evaluation." *Educational Evaluation and Policy Analysis 14*(4): 397–418.

Cousins, J. Bradley, and Lorna M. Earl. 1995. *Participatory Evaluation in Education: Studies in Evaluation Use and Organizational Learning*. London: Routledge-Falmer.

Cronbach, Lee J., and Karen Shapiro. 1982. *Designing Evaluations of Educational and Social Programs*. San Francisco: Jossey-Bass.

Cronbach, Lee J., et al. 1980. *Toward Reform of Program Evaluation: Aims, Methods, and Institutional Arrangements*. San Francisco: Jossey-Bass.

Czarniawska, Barbara, and Guje Sevon. 1996. *Translating Organizational Change*. Berlin: de Gruyter.

Dahlberg, Magnus, and Evert Vedung. 2001. *Demokrati och brukarutvärdering* [Democracy and User Evaluation]. Lund, Sweden: Studentlitteratur.

Dahler-Larsen, Peter. 2000. "Surviving the Routinization of Evaluation: The Administrative Use of Evaluations in Danish Municipalities." *Administration and Society 32*(1): 70–91.

———. 2001. *Den rituelle reflektion. Om evaluering i organisationer* [The Ritual Reflection: On Evaluation in Organizations]. Odense, Denmark: Odense Universitetsforlag.

———. 2006a. "Hvorfor skal skolen evaluere?" [Why Should Schools Evaluate?]. In *Almen Didaktik: Relationer mellem undervisning og læring* [General Didactics: Relations Between Teaching and Learning], eds. B. G. Hansen and A. Tams, 353–368. Værløse: Billesø & Baltzer.

———. 2006b. "Organizing Knowledge: Evidence and the Construction of

Evaluative Information Systems." In *From Studies to Streams*, eds. R. Rist and N. Stame, 65–80. New Brunswick, NJ: Transaction.

———. 2007. "Constitutive Effects of Performance Indicator Systems." In *Dilemmas of Engagement: Evaluation Development Under New Public Management and the New Politics*, ed. S. Kushner, 17–36. New York: Elsevier.

———. 2008. *Kvalitetens beskaffenhed* [The Nature of Quality]. Odense, Denmark: Syddansk Universitetsforlag.

———. 2009. "Learning-Oriented Educational Evaluation in Contemporary Society." In *The Sage Handbook of Educational Evaluation*, eds. K. E. Ryan and J. B. Cousins, 307–322. Los Angeles: Sage.

———, Vibeke Normann Andersen, Kasper Møller Hansen, and Carsten Strømbæk Pedersen. 2003. *Selvevalueringens hvide sejl* [The White Sails of Self-Evaluation]. Odense: Syddansk Universitetsforlag.

Dahler-Larsen, Peter, and Hanne K. Krogstrup. 2001. *Tendenser i evaluering* [Trends in Evaluation]. Odense, Denmark: Odense Universitetsforlag.

———. 2003. *Nye veje i evaluering* [New Ways in Evaluation]. Århus, Denmark: Systime.

de Bruijn, Hans. 2002. *Managing Performance in the Public Sector*. London: Routledge.

de Leon, Peter. 1978. "A Theory of Policy Termination." In *The Policy Cycle*, eds. J. V. May and A. B. Wildawsky, 279–300. Beverly Hills: Sage.

———. 1988. *Advice and Consent: The Development of the Policy Sciences*. New York: Russell Sage.

Doran, Harold C. 2003. "Evaluating the Consequential Aspect of Validity on the Arizona Instrument to Measure Standards." Paper presented at the annual meeting of the American Educational Research Association (AERA): Accountability for Educational Quality—Shared Responsibility. Chicago, Illinois, April 21–25.

Dunsire, Andrew. 1986. "A Cybernetic View of Guidance Control and Evaluation in the Public Sector." In *Guidance, Control and Evaluation in the Public Sector*, eds. F. X. Kaufmann, G. Majone, and V. Ostrom, 327–348. Berlin: de Gruyter.

Durkheim, Emile. 1968. *The Rules of Sociological Method*. New York: Free Press.

Easthope, Gary. 1974. *A History of Social Research Methods*. London: Longman.

Edelman, Murray. 1977. *Political Language. Words That Succeed and Policies That Fail*. New York: Academic Press.

Edwards, Richard. 1997. *Changing Places? Flexibility, Lifelong Learning and a Learning Society*. London: Routledge.

———, and Robin Usher. 2001. "Lifelong Learning: A Postmodern Condition of Education." *Adult Education Quarterly* 51(4): 273–287.

Eisenberg, Eric M. 1984. "Ambiguity as Strategy on Organizational Communication." *Communication Monographs* 51: 227–242.

EPI News. 1997, November 19. *Tilslutning til børnevaccinationsprogrammet 1988–1996* [Consent to the Child Vaccination Programme 1988–1996]. Copenhagen: Statens Serum Institut.

———. 2008, September 3. *MFR-vaccination—tilslutning ultimo 2007* [MMR Vaccination—Consent 2007]. Copenhagen: Statens Serum Institut.

Eriksen, Thomas H. 2008: *Storeulvsyndromet. Jakten på lykken i overflodssamfunnet* [The Big Bad Wolf Syndrome: The Quest for Happiness in the Abundance Society]. Oslo: Aschehoug.

Espeland, Wendy Nelson, and Michael Sauder. 2007. "Rankings and Reactivity: How Public Measures Recreate Social Worlds." *American Journal of Sociology* 113(1): 1–40.

Etzioni, Amitai. 1964. *Modern Organizations*. Englewood Cliffs, NJ: Prentice-Hall.

Falkner, Gerda. 1999. "European Social Policy: Towards Multi-Level and Multi-Actor Governance." In *The Transformation of Governance in the European Union*, eds. B. Kohler-Koch and R. Eising, 83–97. London, New York: Routledge.

Feldman, Martha S., and James G. March. 1981. "Information in Organizations as Signal and Symbol." *Administrative Science Quarterly* 26(2): 171–186.

Fetterman, David M., Shakeh J. Kaftarian, and Abraham Wandersman. 1996. *Empowerment Evaluation: Knowledge and Tools for Self-Assessment and Accountability*. Thousand Oaks, CA: Sage.

Fitzpatrick, Jody L., James R. Sanders, and Blaine R. Worthen. 2004. *Program Evaluation: Alternative Approaches and Practical Guidelines*. Boston: Pearson Education.

Flap, Henk. 2001. "Organizations: Unintended Consequences." In *Encyclopedia of the Social and Behavioral Sciences, Vol. 16*, eds. N. J. Smelser and P. B. Baltes, 10973–10976. Oxford: Elsevier.

Forss, Kim, Claus C. Rebien, and Jerker Carlsson. 2002. "Process Use of Evaluations: Types of Use That Precede Lessons Learned and Feedback." *Evaluation* 8(1): 29–45.

Foucault, Michel. 1980. "Power/Knowledge." In *Selected Interviews and Other Writings 1972–1977 by Michel Foucault*, ed. C. Gordon. New York: Harvester.

———. 1991. "Orders of Discourse Technologies of the Self." In *Post-Structuralist and Post-Modernist Sociology*, eds. S. E. Lash and S. Lash. Aldershot: Elgar.

Fountain, Jane E. 2001. "Paradoxes of Public Sector Customer Service." *Governance* 14(1): 55–73.

FTF (Confederation of Professionals in Denmark). 2007. "Documentation in the Public Sector." Survey conducted in 2007 among 404 public FTF leaders in the educational, health, pedagogical, social, and police fields. Conducted by the Research Bureau Catinét A/S. Copenhagen: FTF.

Furubo, Jan-Eric, Ray C. Rist, and Rolf Sandahl (eds.). 2002. *International Atlas of Evaluation*. New Brunswick, NJ: Transaction.

Gaertner, Gregory H., and S. Ramnarayan. 1983. "Organizational Effectiveness: An Alternative Perspective." *Academy of Management Review 8*(1): 97–107.

Gallie, Walter B. 1955. "Essentially Contested Concepts." *Proceedings of the Aristotelian Society 56*: 157–198.

Geppert, Mike. 1996. "Paths of Managerial Learning in the East German Context." *Organization Studies 17*(2): 249–268.

Gibbons, Michael, Camille Limoges, Helga Nowotny, Simon Schwartzman, Peter Scott, and Martin Trow. 1994. *The New Production of Knowledge: The Dynamics of Science and Research in Contemporary Societies*. London: Sage.

Giddens, Anthony. 1990. *The Consequences of Modernity*. Cambridge, MA: Polity Press.

Giddens, Anthony. 1994. "Reflexivity and Its Doubles." In *Reflexive Modernization*, eds. U. Beck, A. Giddens, and S. Lash, 56–109. Stanford: Stanford University Press.

Gordon, Colin. 1980. "Afterword." In *M. Foucault, Power/Knowledge: Selected Interviews and Other Writings 1972–77*, ed. C. Gordon. New York: Pantheon.

Gordon, Ian, Janet Lewis, and Ken Young. 1993. "Perspectives on Policy Analysis." In *The Policy Process: A Reader*, ed. M. Hill, 5–9. Hertfordshire: Wheatsheaf Harvester.

Greene, Jennifer C. 1994. "Qualitative Program Evaluation." In *Handbook of Qualitative Research*, eds. N. K. Denzin and Y. S. Lincoln, 530–544. Thousand Oaks, CA: Sage.

———. 1997. *Participatory Evaluation*. London: JAI Press.

Greenwald, Anthony G., Brian A. Nosek, and N. Sriram. 2006. "Consequential Validity of the Implicit Association Test: Comment on Blanton and Jaccard." *American Psychology 61*(1): 27–41.

Guba, Egon G., and Yvonna S. Lincoln. 1989. *Fourth Generation Evaluation*. Newbury Park, CA: Sage.

Hammerlin, Joakim. 2009. *Terrorindustrien* [The Terror Industry]. Oslo: Manifest.

Hansen, Hanne F. 2003. *Evaluering i staten: Kontrol, læring eller forandring?* [Evaluation in the State: Control, Learning or Change?]. Copenhagen: Samfundslitteratur.

———. 2005. "Kvalitet i evalueringspraksis" [Quality in Evaluation Practice]. *Nordisk Administrativ Tidsskrift 86*(1): 27–42.

Harmon, Michael, and Richard Mayer. 1986. *Organization Theory for Public Administration*. Glenview: Scott, Foresman.

Harris, Henriette. 2007, July 25. "Klogere end lægerne" [Smarter Than the Doctors]. *Information*.

Hasenfeld, Yeheskel. 1983. *Human Service Organizations.* Upper Saddle River, NJ: Prentice-Hall.

Hastrup, Kirsten. 1993. "Self-Defining Worlds: The Anthropological Notion of Reality." *Danish Yearbook of Philosophy 28*: 61–79.

Hedberg, Bo. 1981. "How Organizations Learn and Unlearn." In *Handbook of Organizational Design, Vol. 1,* eds. P. Nystrom and W. Starbuck, 3–27. Oxford: Oxford University Press.

Hellstern, Gerd-Michael. 1986. "Assessing Evaluation Research." In *Guidance, Control and Evaluation in the Public Sector,* eds. F. X. Kaufmann, G. Majone, and V. Ostrom, 279–313. Berlin: de Gruyter.

Hochschild, Arlie. 2004. "Gennem sprækker i tidsfælden" [Through Cracks in the Time Bind]. In *Arbejdssamfundet* [The Labour Society], eds. M. Hviid, and J. Tonbo, 109–131. Copenhagen: Hans Reitzels Forlag.

Hood, Christopher. 2002. "The Risk Game and the Blame Game." *Government and Opposition 37*(1): 15–37.

———. 2007. "Public Service Management by Numbers: Why Does It Vary? Where Has It Come From? What Are the Gaps and the Puzzles?" *Public Money and Management 27*(2): 95–102.

House, Ernest R. 2008. "Blowback: Consequences of Evaluation for Evaluation." *American Journal of Evaluation 29*(4): 416–426.

———, and Kenneth R. Howe. 2000. "Deliberative Democratic Evaluation." In *New Directions for Evaluation,* eds. K. E. Ryan and L. DeStefano, 3–12. San Francisco: Jossey-Bass.

Howlett, Michael. 1991. "Policy Instruments, Policy Styles and Policy Implementation: National Approaches to Theories of Instrument Choice." *Policy Studies Journal 19*(2): 1–21.

Højlund, Holger, and Anders la Cour. 2001. "Standardiseret omsorg og lovbestemt fleksibilitet Organisationsændringer på et kerneområde i velfærdsstaten" [Standardized Care and Statutory Flexibility: Organizational Changes of a Core Field in the Welfare State]. *Nordiske Organisasjonsstudier 2*(3): 91–117.

Jasinsky, Frank J. 1956. "Use and Misuse of Efficiency Controls." *Harvard Business Review 34*: 105–112.

Jennings, Jack, and Diane S. Rentner. 2006. *Ten Big Effects of the No Child Left Behind Act on Public Schools.* Bloomington, IN: Phi Delta Kappa Educational Foundation.

Jepperson, Ronald L., and John W. Meyer. 1991. "The Public Order and the Construction of Formal Organizations." In *The New Institutionalism in Organizational Analysis,* eds. W. Powell and P. DiMaggio, 204–231. Chicago: University of Chicago Press.

Jones, Lyle V., and Ingram Olkin (eds.). 2004. *The Nation's Report Card: Evolu-*

tion and Perspectives. Bloomington, IN: Phi Delta Kappa Educational Foundation.

Jørgensen, Torben Beck, and Preben Melander. (1992). *Livet i offentlige organisationer. Institutionsdrift i spændingsfeltet mellem stat, profession og marked* [Life in Public Organizations: Managing of Institutions in the Tension Field Between State, Profession, and Market]. Charlottenlund: Jurist- og Økonomforbundets Forlag.

Karlsson Vestman, Ove, and Ross F. Conner. 2006. "The Relationship Between Evaluation and Politics." In *The Sage Handbook of Evaluation*, eds. I. Shaw, J. Greene, and M. M. Mark, 225–242. New York: Sage.

Kehlmann, Daniel. 2006. *Measuring the World*. New York: Pantheon.

Kelman, Steven, and John N. Friedman. 2009. "Performance Improvement and Performance Dysfunction: An Empirical Examination of Distortionary Impacts of the Emergency Room Wait-Time Target in the English National Health Service." *Journal of Public Administration Research and Theory 19*(4): 917–946.

Kirkhart, Karen E. 2000. "Reconceptualizing Evaluation Use: An Integrated Theory of Influence." *New Directions for Evaluation 88*: 5–24.

Klein, Jacob. 1977. *Plato's Trilogy: Theaetetus, the Sophist, and the Statesman*. Chicago: University of Chicago Press.

Klein, Naomi. 2008. *The Shock Doctrine*. New York: Metropolitan.

Klouzal, Linda, Julia D. Shayne, and John Foran. 2003. "Visions 4." In *Feminist Futures: Re-Imagining Women, Culture and Development*, eds. K.-K. Bhavnani, J. Foran, and A. P. Kurian, 256–275. London, New York: Zed.

Knorr-Cetina, Karin D. 1981. *The Manufacture of Knowledge*. Oxford: Pergamon Press.

Koselleck, Reinhart. 2007. "Begreber, tid og erfaring. En tekstsamling [Concepts, Time, and Experience: An Anthology]." Copenhagen: Hans Reitzels Forlag. Collection of chapters originally published in R. Koselleck, *Zeitschichten: Studien zur Historik* (Frankfurt am Main: Suhrkamp Verlag, 2000.)

Kreiner, Kristian. 1989. "Organisationsteoriens postmoderne epoke" [The Postmodern Epoch of Organization Theory]. In *Kalejdoskopiske fortællinger fra en videnskabelig verden* [Kaleidoscopic Tales from a Scientific World], ed. J. Molin, 41–56. Copenhagen: Akademisk Forlag.

Krogstrup, Hanne K. 1998. "Brugerinddragelse i evaluering: Hvorfor og hvordan" [User Involvement in Evaluation: Why and How]. *Social Kritik 1998*(56): 28–36.

Lane, Jan-Erik. 1993. *The Public Sector*. London: Sage.

Langer, Susanne K. 1979. *Philosophy in a New Key: A Study in the Symbolism of Reason, Rite, and Art*. 3rd ed. Cambridge: Harvard University Press.

Lascoumes, Pierre, and Patrick Le Gales. 2007. "Introduction: Understanding

Public Policy Through Its Instruments: From Nature of Instruments to the Sociology of Public Policy Instrumentation." *Governance 20*(1): 1–21.

Latour, Bruno. 1987. *Science in Action: How to Follow Scientists and Engineers Through Society.* Stony Stratford, UK: Open University Press.

Lawn, M. 2007. "The Platinum Metre: Standardizing a European Education Policy Space." Paper presented at the European Evaluation Society (EES) Conference: Evaluation in the Knowledge Society. Odense, Denmark, October 18–19.

Leeuv, Frans L., and Jan-Eric Furubo. 2008. "Evaluation Systems: What Are They and Why Study Them?" *Evaluation 14*(2): 157–169.

Levin-Rozalis, Miri, and Barbara Rosenstein. 2005. "The Changing Role of the Evaluator in the Process of Organizational Learning." *Canadian Journal of Program Evaluation 20*(1): 81–104.

Levitt, Barbara, and James G. March. 1988. "Organizational Learning." *Annual Review of Sociology 14*: 319–336.

Lindblom, Charles E. 1959. "The Science of Muddling Through." *Public Administration Review 19*(2): 79–88.

Lindeberg, Tobias. 2007. *Evaluative Technologies: Quality and the Multiplicity of Performance.* Copenhagen: Copenhagen Business School.

Lipsky, Michael. 1980. *Street Level Bureaucracy.* New York: Russell Sage Foundation.

Longino, Helen E. 2002. *The Fate of Knowledge.* Princeton, NJ: Princeton University Press.

Luhmann, Niklas. 1989. *Ecological Communication.* Chicago: University of Chicago Press.

Lyotard, Jean-Francois. 1984. *The Postmodern Condition: A Report on Knowledge.* Minneapolis: University of Minnesota Press.

Manovich, Lev. 2001. *The Language of New Media.* Cambridge, MA: MIT Press.

March, James G., and Johan P. Olsen. 1976. *Ambiguity and Choice in Organizations.* Bergen, Norway: Universitetsforlaget.

———. 1984. "The New Institutionalism: Organizational Factors in Political Life." *American Political Science Review 78*(3): 734–749.

———. 1989. *Rediscovering Institutions: The Organizational Basis of Politics.* New York: Free Press.

———. 1995. *Democratic Governance.* New York: Free Press.

Mark, Melvin M. 2008. "Building a Better Evidence Base for Evaluation Theory: Beyond General Calls to a Framework of Types of Research on Evaluation." In *Fundamental Issues in Evaluation*, eds. N. L. Smith and P. R. Brandon, 111–134. New York: Guilford Press.

———, and Gary Henry. 2002. "The Multiple Methods and Pathways Through Which Evaluation Can Influence Attitudes and Action." Paper presented at the Fifth European Evaluation Society (EES) Biennial Conference: Learning, Theory and Evidence. Seville, Spain, October 10.

———. 2004. The Mechanisms and Outcomes of Evaluation Influence. *Evaluation* 10(1): 35–57.

———, and George Julnes. 2000. *Evaluation: An Integrated Framework for Understanding, Guiding, and Improving Public and Non-profit Policies and Programs.* San Francisco: Jossey-Bass.

Mathison, Sandra. 1991. "Role Conflicts for Internal Evaluators." *Evaluation and Program Planning 14*(3): 173–179.

———, ed. 2005. *Encyclopedia of Evaluation.* Thousand Oaks, CA: Sage.

McBriarty, Mark A. 1988. "Performance Appraisal: Some Unintended Consequences." *Public Personnel Management 17*(4): 421–434.

McNeil, Linda. 2000. *Contradictions of School Reform: Educational Costs of Standardized Testing.* New York: Routledge Falmer.

Messick, Samuel. 1989. "Validity." In *Educational Measurement*, ed. R. L. Linn, 13–103. New York: Macmillan.

Meyer, John W. 1994. "Rationalized Environments." In *Institutional Environments and Organizations*, eds. W. R. Scott and J. Meyer, 28–54. Thousand Oaks, CA: Sage.

———, John Boli, and George M. Thomas. 1994. "Ontology and Rationalization in the Western Cultural Account." In *Institutional Environments and Organizations*, eds. W. R. Scott and J. W. Meyer, 9–27. Thousand Oaks, CA: Sage.

———., and V. Gupta. 1994. "The Performance Paradox." *Research in Organizational Behavior 16*: 309–369.

———., and Brian Rowan. 1977. "Institutionalized Organizations: Formal Structure as Myth and Ceremony." *American Journal of Sociology 83*(2): 340–363.

Milgram, Stanley. 1974. *Obedience to Authority.* London: Tavistock.

Modell, Sven. 2004. "Performance Measurement Myths in the Public Sector: A Research Note." *Financial Accountability & Management 20*(1): 39–55.

Mongin, Olivier. 1982. "La Démocratie à Corps Perdu." *Esprit 2*: 206–214.

Monsen, Lars. 2003. "School-Based Evaluation in Norway: Why Is It So Difficult to Convince Teachers of Its Usefulness?" In *School-Based Evaluation: An International Perspective*, ed. D. Nevo, 73–88. Oxford: Elsevier Science.

Morgan, Gareth. 1986. *Images of Organization.* Thousand Oaks, CA: Sage.

Morin, Edgar. 1992. *La Méthode 3. La Connaissance de la Connaissance. Anthropologie de la Connaissance.* Paris: Editions du Seuil.

Munro, Eileen. 2004. "The Impact of Audit on Social Work Practice." *British Journal of Social Work 34*(8): 1075–1095.

Nevo, David. 2002. "Dialogue Evaluation: Combining Internal and External

Evaluation." In *School-Based Evaluation: An International Perspective*, ed. D. Nevo, 3–16. Oxford: Elsevier.

———. 2006. "Evaluation in Education." In *Handbook of Evaluation*, eds. I. F. Shaw, J. C. Greene, and M. M. Mark, 441–460. Thousand Oaks, CA: Sage.

Nisbet, Robert. 1966. *The Sociological Tradition.* London: Heinemann.

———. 1980. *History of the Idea of Progress.* New York: Basic Books.

———, and Robert Perrin. 1977. *The Social Bond.* New York: Knopf.

Nonaka, Ikujiro. 1994. "A Dynamic Theory of Organizational Knowledge Creation." *Organization Science* 5(1): 14–37.

Novoa, Antonio, and Tali Yariv-Mashal. 2003. "Comparative Research in Education: A Mode of Governance or a Historical Journey?" *Comparative Education* 39(4): 423–438.

Nystrom, Paul C., and William H. Starbuck. 1984. "To Avoid Organizational Crises, Unlearn." *Organizational Dynamics* 12: 53–65.

Nørretranders, Tor. 2005. *Menneskeføde: Vejviser ud af en overvægtig verden* [Human Food: Guide out of an Obese World]. Copenhagen: Tiderne skifter.

Osterloh, Margit, and Bruno S. Frey. 2010. "Academic Rankings Between the 'Republic of Science' and 'New Public Management.'" Working paper. Zurich: CREMA (Center for Research in Management, Economics and the Arts).

Patton, Michael Quinn. 1986. *Utilization-Focused Evaluation.* London: Sage.

———. 1997. *Utilization-Focused Evaluation: The New Century Text.* Thousand Oaks, CA: Sage.

———. 1998. "Discovering Process Use." *Evaluation* 4(2): 225–233.

Pawson, Ray, and Nick Tilley. 1997. *Realistic Evaluation.* London: Sage.

Pedersen, Carsten Strømbæk, and Peter Dahler-Larsen. 2009. "Has Quality Assurance and Evaluation Made It Less Attractive to Be a Teacher? A Survey in Five National Contexts." Paper presented at the American Evaluation Association (AEA) Conference: Context and Evaluation. Orlando, Florida, November 9–14.

Perrin, Burt. 1998. "Effective Use and Misuse of Performance Measurement." *American Journal of Evaluation* 19(3): 367–379.

Perrow, Charles. 1977. "Three Types of Effectiveness Studies." In *New Perspectives on Organizational Effectiveness*, eds. P. S. Goodman and J. M. Pennings, 96–105. San Francisco: Jossey-Bass.

Pollitt, Christopher. 1989. "Performance Indicators in the Longer Term." *Public Money and Management* 9(3): 51–55.

———. 1995. "Justification by Works or by Faith? Evaluating the New Public Management." *Evaluation* 1(2): 133–154.

———. 2006. "Performance Information for Democracy. The Missing Link?" *Evaluation* 12(1): 38–55.

Popper, Karl R. 1969. *The Open Society and Its Enemies.* London: Routledge.

Powell, Walter W., and Paul J. DiMaggio, eds. 1991. *The New Institutionalism in Organizational Analysis*. Chicago: University of Chicago Press.

Power, Michael. 1996. "Making Things Auditable." *Accounting, Organizations and Society 21*(2/3): 289–315.

———. 1997a. *The Audit Society: Rituals of Verification*. Oxford: Oxford University Press.

———. 1997b. "From Risk Society to Audit Society." *Soziale Systeme 3*(1): 3–21.

———. 2004. *The Risk Management of Everything*. London: Demos.

———. 2005. "The Theory of the Audit Explosion." In *The Oxford Handbook of Public Management*, eds. E. Ferlie, L. E. Lynn, and C. Pollitt, 327–344. New York: Oxford University Press.

Premfors, Rune. 1989. *Policyanalys. Kunskap, praktik och etik i offentlig verksamhet* [Policy Analysis: Knowledge, Practice and Ethics in Public Management]. Lund, Sweden: Studenterlitteratur.

Preskill, Hallie. 1994. "Evaluation's Role in Enhancing Organizational Learning." *Evaluation and Program Planning 17*(3): 291–297.

———, and Rosalie T. Torres. 1999. *Evaluative Inquiry for Learning in Organizations*. Thousand Oaks, CA: Sage.

Rabo, Annika. 1994. "Utvärderinger som moderna ritualer: Ett antropologiskt perspektiv" [Evaluations as Modern Rituals: An Anthropological Perspective]. Paper presented at the SCORE conference Utvärdering som styrmedel [Evaluation as Means of Control]. Stockholm, Sweden, September 13–14.

Ridgway, Van F. 1956. "Dysfunctional Consequences of Performance Measurements." *Administrative Science Quarterly 1*(2): 240–247.

Rigsrevisionen [Danish National Audit Office]. 2005. *Beretning til statsrevisorerne om statens anvendelse af evalueringer* [Report to the National Auditors on the State's Application of Evaluations]. Copenhagen: Rigsrevisionen.

———. 2009. *Beretning til statsrevisorerne om mål- og resultatstyring i staten med fokus på effekt* [Report to the National Auditors on Objectives-Based and Results-Based Management in the State Focusing on Effect]. Copenhagen: Rigsrevisionen.

Rist, Ray C. 1994. "Influencing the Policy Process with Qualitative Research." In *Handbook of Qualitative Research*, eds. N. Denzin and Y. Lincoln, 545–558. Thousand Oaks, CA: Sage.

———, and N. Stame, eds. 2006. *From Studies to Streams*. New Brunswick, NJ: Transaction.

Ritzer, George. 1996. *Sociological Theory*. Singapore: McGraw-Hill.

Rosanvallon, Pierre. 2009. *Demokratin som problem* [Democracy as the Problem: "Inaugural Lecture at Collège de France" and "Towards a Conceptual History of Politics"]. Hägersten, Sweden: Tankekraft Förlag.

Rose, Nikolas. 2003. "At regere friheden: En analyse af politisk magt i avanceret liberale demokratier" [To Govern Freedom: An Analysis of Political Power in Advanced Liberal Democracies]. In *Perspektiv, magt og styring: Luhmann og Foucault til diskussion* [Perspective, Power and Management: A Discussion of Luhmann and Foucault], eds. C. Borch and L. T. Larsen, 180–199. Copenhagen: Hans Reitzels Forlag.

Rossi, Peter H., and Howard E. Freeman. 1985. *Evaluation: A Systematic Approach.* 3rd ed. Beverly Hills: Sage.

———, and Mark W. Lipsey. 2004. *Evaluation: A Systematic Approach.* Thousand Oaks, CA: Sage.

Rothstein, Henry, Michael Huber, and George Gaskell. 2006. "A Theory of Risk Colonization: The Spiralling Regulatory Logics of Societal and Institutional Risk." *Economy and Society 35*(1): 91–112.

Rowe, Ken J. 2000. "Assessment, League Tables and School Effectiveness: Consider the Issues and 'Let's Get Real'." *Journal of Educational Inquiry 1*(1): 73–98.

Ryan, Katherine E., Merrill Chandler, and Maurice Samuels. 2007. "What Should School-Based Evaluation Look Like?" *Studies in Educational Evaluation 33*(3/4): 197–212.

Ryan, Katherine E., and Bradley J. Cousins, eds. 2009. *The Sage International Handbook of Educational Evaluation.* Thousand Oaks, CA: Sage.

Røvik, Kjell A. 1992. "Institusjonaliserte standarder og multistandardorganisasjoner" [Institutionalized Standards and Multi-Standard Organizations]. *Norsk Statsvitenskapelig tidsskrift 8*(4): 261–284.

———. 1998. *Moderne organisasjoner. Trender i organisasjonstenkningen ved tusenårsskiftet* [Modern Organizations: Trends in Organizational Thinking at the Millennium]. Bergen-Sandviken, Norway: Fagbokforlaget.

Sabatier, Paul A. 1985. "What Can We Learn from Implementation Research?" In *Guidance, Control and Evaluation in the Public Sector,* eds. F. X. Kaufmann, G. Majone, and V. Ostrom, 313–326. Berlin: de Gruyter.

Sahlin-Andersson, Kerstin. 1996. "Imitating by Editing Success: The Construction of Organizational Fields." In *Translating Organizational Change,* eds. B. Czarniawska and G. Sevon, 69–92. Berlin: de Gruyter.

———. 2004. "Utvärdering i det transnationella samhället" [Evaluation in the Transnational Society]. Paper presented at the Swedish Evaluation Society (SES) Conference: Utvärdering i Sverige—Makt, kunskap och lärande [Evaluation in Sweden—Power, Knowledge and Learning]. Stockholm, April 22–23.

Sahlins, Marshall. 1976. *Culture and Practical Reason.* Chicago: Aldine.

Sanders, James R. 2002. "Presidential Address: On Mainstreaming Evaluation." *American Journal of Evaluation 23*(3): 253–259.

Schanz, Hans-Jørgen. 1990. *Forandring og balance. Refleksioner over metafysik og modernitet* [Change and Balance: Reflections on Metaphysics and Modernity]. Århus, Denmark: Modtryk.

Schmidt, Vivien A. 2010. "Taking Ideas and Discourse Seriously: Explaining Change Through Discursive Institutionalism as the Fourth 'New Institutionalism'." *European Political Science Review 2*(1): 1–25.

Schutz, Alfred. 1973. *Collected Papers. Vol. 1: The Problem of Social Reality.* Ed. M. A. Natanson. The Hague: M. Nijhoff.

Schwandt, Thomas A. 2000. "Three Epistemological Stances for Qualitative Inquiry: Interpretivism, Hermeneutics, and Social Constructivism." In *Handbook of Qualitative Research*, eds. N. K. Denzin and Y. S. Lincoln, 189–214. Thousand Oaks, CA: Sage.

———. 2002. *Evaluation Practice Reconsidered.* New York: Peter Lang.

———. 2003. "Back to the Rough Ground! Beyond Theory to Practice in Evaluation." *Evaluation 9*(3): 353–364.

———. 2006. "Opposition Redirected." *International Journal of Qualitative Studies in Education 19*(6): 803–810.

———. 2009. "Globalization Influences on the Western Evaluation Imaginary." In *The Sage International Handbook of Educational Evaluation*, eds. K. E. Ryan and B. J. Cousins, 19–36. Thousand Oaks, CA: Sage.

———, and Peter Dahler-Larsen. 2006. "When Evaluation Meets the 'Rough Ground' in Communities." *Evaluation 12*(4): 496–505.

Scott, W. Richard. 1987. "The Adolescence of Institutional Theory." *Administrative Science Quarterly 32*(4): 493–511.

———. 1992. *Organizations: Rational, Natural and Open Systems.* 3rd ed. Englewood Cliffs, NJ: Prentice-Hall.

———. 1995. *Institutions and Organizations.* Thousand Oaks, CA: Sage.

Scriven, Michael. 1991. *Evaluation Thesaurus.* Newbury Park, CA: Sage.

Sechrest, Lee. 1992. "Roots: Back to Our First Generations." *Evaluation Practice 13*(1): 1–7.

Sennett, Richard. 2002. *The Corrosion of Character: The Personal Consequences of Work in the New Capitalism.* New York: Norton.

———. 2008. *The Craftsman.* London: Penguin.

Seo, Myeong-Gu, and W. E. Douglas Creed. 2002. "Institutional Contradictions, Praxis, and Institutional Change: A Dialectical Perspective." *Academy of Management Review 27*(2): 222–247.

Sevon, Guje. 1996. "Organizational Imitation in Identity Transformation." In *Translating Organizational Change*, eds. G. Sevon and B. Czarniawska, 49–67. Berlin: de Gruyter.

Shadish, William R., Thomas D. Cook, and Laura C. Leviton. 1991. *Foundations of Program Evaluation: Theories of Practice.* Newbury Park, CA: Sage.

Shaw, Ian, Jennifer C. Greene, and Melvin M. Mark. 2006. *Handbook of Evaluation: Publications, Policies, Programs and Practices.* London: Sage.

Shulha, Lyn M., and J. Bradley Cousins. 1997. "Evaluation Use: Theory, Research and Practice Since 1986." *Evaluation Practice 18*(3): 195–208.

Silverman, David. 1970. *The Theory of Organizations.* London: Heinemann.

Smith, M. F. 2005. "Article on Evaluability Assessment." In *Encyclopedia of Evaluation*, ed. S. Mathison, 136–139. Thousand Oaks, CA: Sage.

Smith, Peter. 1995. "On the Unintended Consequences of Publishing Performance Data in the Public Sector." *International Journal of Public Administration 18*(2/3): 277–310.

Spencer, L. D., and A. Dale. 1979. "Integration and Regulation in Organizations: A Contextual Approach." *Sociological Review 27*(4): 679–702.

Stake, Robert E. 1997. "The Fleeting Discernment of Quality." In *Advances in Program Evaluation: Evaluation and the Postmodern Dilemma, Vol. 3*, ed. L. Mabry, 41–59. Greenwich, CT: JAI Press.

———. 2004. *Standard-Based and Responsive Evaluation.* Thousand Oaks, CA: Sage.

Stehr, Nico. 1994. *Knowledge Societies.* London: Sage.

———. 2001. *The Fragility of Modern Societies: Knowledge and Risk in the Information Age.* London: Sage.

Strang, David, and John W. Meyer. 1994. "Institutional Conditions for Diffusion." In *Institutional Environments and Organizations*, eds. W. R. Scott and J. Meyer, 100–112. Thousand Oaks, CA: Sage.

Suen, Hoi K. 2003. "Some Very Long-Term and Some Chronic Effects: The Invisible Dimension of the Consequential Basis of Validity." Paper presented at the International Symposium on Issues in the Development of High-Stakes Testing, Korean Institute of Curriculum and Evaluation, Seoul, Korea, July.

Taylor, C. 1987. "Overcoming Epistemology." In *After Philosophy: End or Transformation?* eds. K. Baynes, J. Bohman, and T. McCarthy, 464–488. Cambridge: Cambridge University Press.

Thompson, John. 1995. *The Media and Modernity: A Social Theory of the Media.* Cambridge, UK: Polity Press.

Tilbury, Clare. 2004. "The Influence of Performance Measurement on Child Welfare: Policy and Practice." *British Journal of Social Work 34*(2): 225–241.

Tompkins, Philip K. 1987. "Translating Organizational Theory: Symbolism over Substance." In *Handbook of Organizational Communication: An Interdisciplinary Perspective*, eds. F. M. Jablin, L. L. Putnam, K. H. Roberts, and L. W. Porter, 70–96. Newbury Park, CA: Sage.

Valovirta, Ville. 2002. "Evaluation Utilization as Argumentation." *Evaluation 8*(1): 60–80.

van Maanen, J., and S. Barley. 1984. "Occupational Communities: Culture and Control in Organizations." In *Research in Organizational Behavior, Vol. 6*, ed. L. L. S. Cummings, 265–287. Greenwich, CT: JAI Press.

van Thiel, Sandra, and Frans L. Leeuw. 2002. "The Performance Paradox in the Public Sector." *Public Performance and Management Review 25*(3): 267–281.

Vattimo, Gianni. 1992. *The Transparent Society*. Cambridge: Polity Press.

———. 2004. *Nihilism and Emancipation. Ethics, Politics, and Law*. New York: Columbia University Press.

Vedung, Evert. 1997. *Public Policy and Program Evaluation*. New Brunswick, NJ: Transaction.

Virillo, Paul. 2005. *City of Panic*. New York: Berg.

Vulliamy, G., and R. Webb. 2001. "The Social Construction of School Exclusion Rates: Implications for Evaluation Methodology." *Educational Studies 27*(3): 357–370.

Wagner, Peter. 1994. *A Sociology of Modernity: Liberty and Discipline*. London: Routledge.

———. 2001. *A History and Theory of the Social Sciences*. London: Sage.

Weber, Max. 1978. *Economy and Society*. Berkeley: University of California Press.

Weick, Karl E. 1976. "Educational Organization as Loosely Coupled System." *Administrative Science Quarterly 21*(1): 1–19.

———. 1979. *The Social Psychology of Organizing*. Reading, MA: Addison-Wesley.

———. 1991. "The Vulnerable System: An Analysis of the Tenerife Air Disaster." *Journal of Management 16*(3): 571–593.

———. 1995. *Sensemaking in Organizations*. Thousand Oaks, CA: Sage.

———. 2000. "Quality Improvement: A Sensemaking Perspective." In *The Quality Movement and Organization Theory*, eds. R. E. Cole and W. R. Scott, 155–172. Thousand Oaks, CA: Sage.

———. 2009. "The Reduction of Medical Errors Through Mindful Interdependence." In *Medical Errors: What Do We Know? What Do We Do?* eds. M. M. Rosenthal and K. M. Sutcliffe, 177–199. San Francisco: Jossey-Bass.

———, and Karlene H. Roberts. 1993. "Collective Mind in Organizations: Heedful Interrelating on Flight Decks." *Administrative Science Quarterly 38*(3): 357–381.

Weick, Karl E., and Kathleen M. Sutcliffe. 2006. "Mindfulness and the Quality of Organizational Attention." *Organization Science 17*(4): 514–524.

Weingart, Peter. 2005. "Impact of Bibliometrics upon the Science System: Inadvertent Consequences?" *Scientometrics 62*(1): 117–131.

Weiss, Carol H. 1972. "Evaluating Educational and Social Action Programs: A Treeful of Owls." In *Evaluating Action Programs: Readings in Social Action and Education*, ed. C. Weiss, 3–27. Boston: Allyn and Bacon.

———. 1977. "Research for Policy's Sake: The Enlightenment Function of Social Research." *Policy Analysis 3*: 531–547.

———. 1983. "Evaluation Research in the Political Context." In *Handbook of Evaluation Research*, eds. E. L. Struering and M. B. Brewer, 31–45. Beverly Hills: Sage.

———. 1984. "Increasing the Likelihood of Influencing Decisions." In *Evaluation Research Methods: A Basic Guide*, ed. L. Rutman, 159–190. Beverly Hills, CA: Sage.

———. 1990. "If Program Decision Hinged only on Information." In *Debates on Evaluation*, eds. M. C. Alkin, M. Q. Patton, and C. H. Weiss, 208–222. Newbury Park, CA: Sage.

———. 1998. *Evaluation: Methods for Studying Programs and Policies.* 2nd ed. Upper Saddle River, NJ: Prentice-Hall.

———, and Michael J. Bucuvalas. 1980. *Social Science Research and Decision-Making.* New York: Columbia University Press.

———., Erin Murphy-Graham, and Sarah Birkeland. 2005. "An Alternative Route to Policy Influence." *American Journal of Evaluation 26*(1): 12–30.

Wildavsky, Aaron. 1979. *Speaking Truth to Power: The Art and Craft of Policy Analysis.* Boston: Little, Brown.

———. 1987. "Choosing Preferences by Constructing Institutions: A Cultural Theory of Preference Formation." *American Political Science Review 81*(1): 3–21.

Willinsky, John. 2009. "Test ødelægger elevers forståelse af intellektuel ejendom" [Tests Destroy Pupils' Understanding of Intellectual Property]. *Asterisk— Danmarks Pædagogiske Universitetsskole 48*: 24–25.

Winter, Søren. 1994. *Implementering og effektivitet* [Implementation and Efficiency]. Herning, Denmark: Systime.

Woolgar, Steve. 2004. "Marketing Ideas." *Economy and Society 33*(4): 448–462.

Ziehe, Thomas. 2004. *Øer af intensitet i et hav af rutine: Nye tekster om ungdom, skole og kultur* [Islands of Intensity in a Sea of Routine: New Texts on Youth, School and Culture]. Copenhagen: Forlaget Politisk Revy.

Index

Abma, Tineke A., 18
Accreditation, 11–12, 79, 167, 178–179
Alkin, Marvin C., 185
Anomie, 156, 158
Appadurai, Arjun, 130
Arendt, Hannah, 194, 233, 237
Audit society, 27, 100, 169–170, 175–176, 227–228, 232, 236–237. *See also* Power, Michael
Auditing, 11–12, 27, 167, 179, 197
Authority, 126–127, 143, 147, 152, 183

Balk, Walter, 200
Bauman, Zygmunt, 36, 104, 142
Beck, Ulrich, 120–121, 141
Berger, Brigitte, 39, 105
Berger, Peter L., 22, 39, 105
Bildung, 211
Birkeland, Sarah, 92
Boltanski, Luc, 16, 28, 58, 158
Bouckaert, Geert, 200
Bureaucracy, 38, 39–42, 181, 194

Campbell, Donald T., 106–108
Castoriadis, Cornelius, 27, 142, 235
Chiapello, Eve, 16, 28, 58, 158
Clemet, Kristin, 161
Cognitive pillars of institutions, 22, 58–59, 62, 68, 92, 197

Colonization, 90–91
Competence trap, 50–52
Complexity, 113, 114, 125, 131–132, 137, 141, 147, 161–162, 180, 186
Consequential validity, 80, 82
Constitutive effects, 39, 80, 198–218, 221, 225, 229–230, 237
Consultants, the role of, 61, 75
Context: organizational, 34–35, 53, 68, 94, 112, 134, 167, 175; social, 8–11, 22–26, 68, 103, 113–116, 151, 154, 163, 167, 201
Contingency, 10, 118, 128–132, 133, 144, 149–150, 153, 155, 159
Control, 191–198
Cook, Thomas D., 118
Costs of evaluation, 184–187
Cousins, J. Bradley, 53, 54
Craftsmanship, 195, 233, 234
Cronbach, Lee J., 113

Danish charter schools, 70
Danish Folk High Schools, 69
Decoupling, 90–91
Definitions of evaluation, 5–17; combinatory, 8–17; conceptual-analytical, 6–7; purpose-oriented, 7
Degradation of work, 191– 195, 229

Democracy, 9, 113, 117, 159, 182, 219–221, 234–237
Diffusion, 60–63
DiMaggio, Paul J., 62
Documentation, 107, 175, 178, 180, 183, 185, 191–192, 198, 214
Double-loop learning, 49–52, 55; example of, 50–52
Drekkingarhylur, the drowning hole, 23
Durkheim, Emile, 57–59, 158

Earl, Lorna M., 54
Edelman, Murray, 48
Emergency room waiting time, 199, 210
Empowerment evaluation, 149, 154, 157
Evaluability assessment, 109–110, 148, 153, 166, 167, 182, 186–187, 196, 198
Evaluand, 6, 10, 13, 35, 68–70, 76, 78, 101, 105, 157; complexity of, 113–115
Evaluation: capacity, 163–164, 166, 167, 177, 196, 197; criteria, 19, 34, 41, 43, 70–83, 87, 114, 116, 117, 160, 193, 194, 205–207, 219–221, 227, 230, 236; culture, 146, 164–165, 167, 177, 197, 228; design, 83–86; fatigue, 152, 158, 168, 230, 231; imaginary, 27, 99–119, 174, 187, 196, 215; machine, 170, 176–182, 183–225; policy, 165, 174, 177, 197, 237; system, 68, 79–82, 165, 167, 168, 174, 176, 186–188, 197–198, 231, 237; topic, 68–70
Experimental society, 102, 106–108, 115
External: evaluation, 159–160, 179; evaluator, 54, 163

Feedback, 44, 103, 160, 189; loops, 1, 16, 39, 137, 145, 161, 232, 236
Foucault, Michel, 209
Fragile social order, 24, 128, 131
Freeman, Howard E., 7–8, 39
Friedman, John N., 215–216
Furubo, Jan-Eric, 176

Garbage can model, 47
Generalization, 6, 114, 156, 175

Giddens, Anthony, 6
Globalization, 125, 169, 173
Goals, 25–26, 43, 72–73; sequential attention to, 72
Governance, 133–137, 153
Greene, Jennifer C., 112
Guba, Egon G., 117
Gupta, V., 76

Hellstern, Gerd Michael, 2
Henry, Gary, 159
Hermeneutics, 115, 238–240
Højlund, Holger, 211
Holzer, M., 18–19
Hood, Christopher, 187
House, Ernest R., 117, 159
Howe, Kenneth R., 117, 159

Implementation, 35, 106, 134–136, 173, 177, 192
Imposed use, 92, 196
Indicator: performance, 179, 181, 193, 201, 207, 211, 212–213, 230, second-order construction of, 216–219
Individualism, 21, 22, 50, 71
Industrialism, 138–139, 195
Institutional theory, 26, 56–59, 63, 66, 85, 87–88, 91–94, 145, 151; neo-, 26, 91
Institutionalized organization, 39, 56–64; critique of, 93–94; evaluation in, 65–95
Instrumental use of evaluation, 20–21, 41, 95, 111, 113, 146, 153, 200, 227
Internal: evaluation, 159, 160, 179, 180; evaluator, 70, 91, 154
Interpretive frames, 205
Iraq, invasion of, 73
Isomorphism, 60, 62, 71, 197

Jørgensen, Torben B., 19–20
Julnes, George, 159

Kellner, Hansfried, 39, 105
Kelman, Steven, 215–216

Knorr-Cetina, Karin D., 23
Knowledge, 44–45, 55, 66, 94, 107,
115–116, 132, 148, 155, 205–206, 213,
238, 239; social construction of,
22–25

La Cour, Anders, 211
Latour, Bruno, 23
Learning cycle, 44–52, 65–67, 73, 90,
91, 163
Learning organization, 39, 43–56, 74,
226; evaluation in, 52–55; critique of,
55–56
Learning-oriented evaluation, 53–54, 56,
150, 154, 159, 163
Leeuw, Frans L., 176, 202
Legitimacy, 7, 39, 60, 64, 66, 67, 71, 74,
85, 91, 95, 152, 153, 175, 176, 220, 228,
231, 236, 240
Leviton, Laura C., 118
Liminal states, 14–15, 17
Lincoln, Yvonna S., 117
Lindblom, Charles E., 43, 113
Lindeberg, Tobias, 8, 180
Linearity, 21, 22, 201
Lipsey, Mark W., 8
Lise: evaluation wave, 1–2; fatigue, 152
Logic of appropriateness, 59, 144, 150
Longino, Helen E., 24
Loose coupling, 39, 63–65, 79, 87, 92,
153, 192
Luckmann, Thomas, 22

Maginot Line, the, 68
Manovich, Lev, 128
March, James G., 3, 47, 59
Mark, Melvin M., 159
Measurability, 18, 74, 215
Measure fixation, 203–204, 207, 215–
216; advanced, 203, 207, 216; trivial,
203–204, 207, 216
Measurement optimism, 18
Melander, Preben, 19–20
Messick, Samuel, 80, 82
Meta-communication, 83–84

Meyer, John W., 60, 76, 92
Model, organizational, 36–38
Modell, Sven, 230
Modernity, 100–105
Moral integrity, 56
Murphy-Graham, Erin, 92
Myth, 43, 57–58, 60, 61, 102, 150–151,
196, 227

Neorigorism, 169–173, 239
Nevo, David, 159–160
New Public Management, 3, 69, 92, 131,
146, 148, 177, 187, 192, 194, 214
Noordegraf, Mirko, 18
Normative pillars of institutions, 22,
58–59, 62–63, 68, 92, 197
Nørretranders, Tor, 129

Olsen, Johan P., 47, 59
Organizational memory, 46
Organizational recipe, 39, 60–64, 65,
89–91, 145–146, 231; evaluation as,
67–68, 153
Organizationalization of evaluation,
35–36

Participatory evaluation, 53, 111–112, 115,
116, 155, 157, 158, 163, 174, 236
Patton, Michael Quinn, 7, 39, 53, 111
Performativity, 55
PISA studies, 145, 173
Planned social intervention, 105
Pluralism, 154, 156, 239
Pollitt, Christopher, 69, 187
Popper, Karl, 108, 113
Powell, Walter W., 62
Power, Michael, 4, 27–28, 166, 169, 175,
187, 188, 197
Predictability, 38, 40, 155–156, 170, 174,
176, 180–181, 226, 228
Preskill, Hallie, 53
Program: termination, 88; initiation,
89–90
Progress, 15–16, 102–108, 111, 117, 120–
121, 123, 141–143, 148, 152, 236, 239

Public sector, 8–9, 20, 75, 77, 161, 174, 215

Qualitative evaluation methods, 84, 114–116, 200, 218–219
Quality, 138–141, 167, 175, 179; defensive, 187–191, 232, 239
Quality assurance, 11, 139, 167, 175; systems, 187
Quantitative evaluation methods, 84–85, 115–116, 161, 162, 200, 209, 218–219
QWERTY, 51–52

Rabo, Annika, 4, 14
Ranking, 178, 188, 203, 205, 209
Rational organization, 38–43, 74, 170, 181; critique of, 41–44; evaluation in, 40–41
Rationality, formal, 40–43
Reflexive modernity, 120–143; evaluation in, 144–168
Reflexivity, 24, 93, 105, 114, 116, 137, 140, 156, 185, 204, 228, 232
Regulatory pillars of institutions, 22, 58–59, 63, 92, 177, 197–198
Rejection, 90
Research, 132–133
Resistance to evaluation, 4, 87, 164
Responsive evaluation, 114, 115, 157, 236
Risk, 67–68, 121, 125–126, 232; consciousness, 126–127; and disaster, 170–171; management, 171, 176, 182, 187–191, 228, 238; society, 125
Ritual, 57–58, 65, 67, 93, 143, 144, 147, 150, 153, 196–197, 227
Ritzer, George, 180
Rosanvallon, Pierre, 235–237
Rose, Nikolas, 137
Rossi, Peter H., 7–8, 39
Routine, 88–91, 146, 177
Røvik, Kjell A., 61, 64, 75
Rowan, Brian, 92
Ruskus, Joan A., 185

Schutz, Alfred, 39
Schwandt, Thomas, 13, 28, 99, 117, 159, 205
Scriven, Michael, 6–7
Self-evaluation, 3, 14, 86. *See also* Internal evaluation
Sense making, 13–17, 34, 53, 77, 81, 116, 204
Shadish, William R., 118
Shapiro, Karen, 113
Side effects, 113, 114, 115, 121–125, 127–128, 131–132, 141, 147, 153, 163, 185, 215–216, 228
Single-loop learning, 45–52, 55
Social construction, 85, 124, 129, 149, 171, 203, 213, 217–218, 221, 223, 229, 237; of indicators, 217, 219; of knowledge, 22; of quality, 208; of reality, 229; of risk, 125–126
Social engineering, 102–103
Social science methods, 105
Social-historical differences in evaluation, 4, 5, 11, 12, 100
Sociohistorical, 5, 11, 17, 26, 36, 56, 95, 99, 165, 167, 227, 231
Sociological constant, 17
Stake, Robert E., 114
Steering vs. rowing metaphor, 195
Stehr, Nico, 24
Strang, David, 60

Taken-for-granted social reality, 22, 64, 93, 95
Taming, 90–91
Torres, Rosalie T., 53
Transparence, 119

Unintended consequences, 26, 80, 115, 134, 201–203, 221, 229
Unlearning, 48
Unpredictable evaluation, 154–156, 165, 174, 176, 228, 230
Utilization, 18, 108–113, 146, 160, 237; lack of, 153–154, 162–163; problem

of, 21, 85, 113, 196–198. *See also* Instrumental use of evaluation
Utilization-focused evaluation, 7, 157

Vaccination program, 135–137
Validity, 22, 23, 80–82, 116, 160, 207–208, 230; consequential, 80, 82; of indicators, 217
Value, 116–119, 158; catalogue, 71–72, 74, 76–77, 87; pluralism, 154, 156
van Thiel, Sandra, 202
Vattimo, Gianni, 103, 119, 143, 238–240
Vedung, Evert, 8, 117

Vietnam War, 80
Virus effect, 64, 91, 93
Vulliamy, G., 217

Wagner, Peter, 134
Weak thinking, 238–240
Webb, R., 217
Weber, Max, 38, 40–42, 181
Weick, Karl E., 77
Weingart, Peter, 217
Weiss, Carol H., 92, 111
World's first evaluation, 3–4

Ziehe, Thomas, 5, 143

The authorized representative in the EU for product safety and compliance is:
Mare Nostrum Group
B.V Doelen 72
4831 GR Breda
The Netherlands

www.ingramcontent.com/pod-product-compliance
Lightning Source LLC
Chambersburg PA
CBHW030645270326
41929CB00007B/207